# THE WORLD NEWS PRISM

## Global Information in a Satellite Age

### William A. Hachten and James F. Scotton

## Seventh Edition

**Blackwell**
Publishing

© 2007 by William A. Hachten and James F. Scotton

BLACKWELL PUBLISHING
350 Main Street, Malden, MA 02148-5020, USA
9600 Garsington Road, Oxford OX4 2DQ, UK
550 Swanston Street, Carlton, Victoria 3053, Australia

The right of William A. Hachten and James F. Scotton to be identified as the
Authors of this Work has been asserted in accordance with the UK Copyright,
Designs, and Patents Act 1988.

First published 1981 by Iowa State University Press
Subsequent editions published in 1987, 1992, 1996, 1999, 2002 by Iowa State
University Press
Seventh edition published 2007 by Blackwell Publishing Ltd

1    2007

*Library of Congress Cataloging-in-Publication Data*

Hachten, William A.
  The world news prism : global information in a satellite age / William A.
Hachten and James F. Scotton.—7th ed.
      p. cm.
  Includes bibliographical references and index.
  ISBN-13: 978-1-4051-5057-6 (pbk. : alk. paper)
  ISBN-10: 1-4051-5057-2 (pbk. : alk. paper) 1. Foreign news. 2.
Communication, International. 3. Journalism—Political aspects. I. Scotton, James
Francis, 1932– II. Title.

  PN4784.F6H3 2007
  070.4′332—dc22

                                                                    2006016594

A catalogue record for this title is available from the British Library.

Set in 10.5/12.5pt Bembo
by Graphicraft Limited, Hong Kong
Printed and bound in Singapore
by COS Printers Pte Ltd

The publisher's policy is to use permanent paper from mills that operate a
sustainable forestry policy, and which has been manufactured from pulp processed
using acid-free and elementary chlorine-free practices. Furthermore, the publisher
ensures that the text paper and cover board used have met acceptable
environmental accreditation standards.

For further information on
Blackwell Publishing, visit our website:
www.blackwellpublishing.com

To the many journalists around the world who have been killed, kidnapped, or jailed for reporting the news.

# Contents

# Preface to the Seventh Edition

No matter where people live in the world, most "news" or public information is local. People care about what happens in their community, their country, their region. Yet in today's interconnected and globalized world, people everywhere easily learn about and are affected by news—about wars, civil strife, terrorist attacks, economic upheavals, and great catastrophes, even tsunamis, that occur far from home. More than ever before in history, more people almost everywhere now have opinions—whether about globalization, the United Nations, nuclear proliferation, or world leaders, including President George W. Bush.

On September 11, 2001, an ominous global upheaval—the terrorist attacks on New York's World Trade Center and on the Pentagon in Washington, D.C.—abruptly altered the lives of Americans and sharply impacted on international news communication. With the collapse of those two skyscrapers and about 3,000 lives lost, Americans (and many others) no longer felt secure and personally safe from the perils of a dangerous world. Terrorist hijackings and bombings were not new—from 1983 to 2001, ten attacks had claimed the lives of 100 or more Americans. But the 9/11 attacks were the largest violent taking of life on U.S. soil since the Civil War. Most of us agreed that the nation was at war with terrorism—the first war of the twenty-first century.

A resounding echo of those attacks was heard on the morning of July 7, 2005, when bombs exploded in three subways and another blew up a double decker bus in Central London. Some fifty-two were killed and 700 injured in "7/7," as it was soon called. The collapsing twin towers had a far greater visual impact than the London bombings or the attacks in Madrid on March 11, 2004, when ten bombs exploded on four parked morning commuter trains, killing 191 people and leaving at least 191 people injured. Two weeks after the London attacks, three explosions ripped through Egypt's popular Red Sea resort of Sharm el-Sheikh, killing at least eighty-three and wounding 200 more.

So, after years of looking inward and ignoring news about the outside world, frightened and insecure citizens suddenly began taking a serious interest in world affairs again—trying to comprehend the threat of terrorism and the complex politics of the Middle East and Central Asia. For a time, Osama bin Laden became a subject of intense public interest.

On 9/11 (and later on 7/7 in London), the news media responded quickly, professionally, and at times magnificently. Global television—up-to-the minute and nonstop, with vivid color video and without commercial interruptions—reported the horrifying details of the tragedy to every corner of the world. The horrific but awesome video of the two airliners crashing into the twin towers of the World Trade Center was etched into the minds of millions. Supplemented by radio, the Internet, and print, much of the world saw the same video and reports as Americans and Britons. This elicited unprecedented responses of sympathy and empathetic support from many other nations. Yet in some places of the Muslim world, there was elation and celebration.

The subsequent and evolving events—war against the Taliban in Afghanistan, and the quick military defeat of Saddam Hussein's army followed by the long insurgent conflict in Iraq—were followed with great interest and thoroughness. The *reporting* of the horrific events and the world's *response* were reminders of how much we have become a global society. Not just in trade and economic affairs but in social and political ways, we are increasingly coming together. But such acts of terrorism also were grim reminders that deep divisions between rich and poor countries remain. Democratic societies, with their open borders and individual freedoms, were vulnerable to stealth attacks. Radical terrorism was termed the dark underside of globalization.

In this revised edition, we will show how the news media have responded to great crises. Journalists from everywhere flocked to the Middle East even as armed forces mobilized. But within months, media coverage and public interest in Iraq had markedly diminished.

Only subsequent events and time will determine how significant the events since 2001 will become in modern history. But there is no doubt that the year 1989 was historic. Then, the world watched on television in dazzled amazement as Communist regimes were toppled in Poland,

East Germany, Hungary, Czechoslovakia, Bulgaria, and Romania. Two years later, the Soviet Union itself, after a right-wing coup failed, went through a convulsive revolution of its own, outlawing the Communist Party and its media as well as dismantling the Soviet Union itself. These historic events also heralded the end of the Cold War, and the demise of the propaganda or "information wars" that had enlivened international communication for forty-five years. However, new propaganda wars, now focused on terrorism and the relations of Muslim nations with the West, have gained momentum in recent years.

The post Cold War world of the 1990s proved to be a harsh and forbidding place. The forces of intense nationalism and unleashed ethnic animosities have led to civil wars, genocide, terrorism, political instability, and economic and social chaos starkly evident in the prolonged and agonizing strife engaging the Bosnian and Kosovo Muslims, Croatians, and Serbs of the former Yugoslavia. Elsewhere, various experiments in democracy and market economies sputtered and foundered.

The decade of the 1990s was also one of great global economic expansion. In China and throughout East and South Asia, economies grew at spectacular rates and world trade expanded as a new phenomenon, *globalization*, was recognized and elaborated. Globalization is an inexact expression for a wide array of worldwide changes in politics, communications, business and trade, life styles, and culture. But, despite great expansion of world trade, many of the economies of Asian nations have had problems: trade disputes, plummeting currencies, and stock markets in free fall have sent shock waves around the world. Even Japan's economy has had severe problems. In our new post Cold War world with its increasingly globalized economy, economic concerns have sometimes taken precedence over political concerns.

Elsewhere, over 120,000 innocent civilians have died in an irrational six-year civil war in Algeria, a half dozen nations have fought a nasty and prolonged regional war over the Congo, genocide has flared up again in Rwanda and Burundi, and in Israel bitter violence continued with the Palestinians; and North Korea's erratic and starving Communist regime, with its potential nuclear threat, has worried the West. Other global concerns: India and Pakistan have both tested nuclear devices but have moved toward reconciliation. In the horrendous earthquake in Pakistan in October 2005, Indian soldiers joined Pakistani troops in relief efforts after 86,000 died. Peace and stability were tantalizingly near, but not realized, in Northern Ireland.

Currently, as the world has worried over potential nuclear bomb threats in Iran and North Korea at the same time genocide has appeared in Sudan and has challenged the United Nations to intervene in the Darfur conflict, which has claimed over 180,000 lives and made two million people homeless refugees.

Before the terror attacks of 2001, there were clear indications that most people had much less interest in what was happening beyond their borders, and the news media themselves responded by reporting a good deal less foreign news and much more trivia. With a diminished nuclear threat and little fear of global warfare, polls showed that people here and abroad were for a time comfortable with the post Cold War era. But as much of twentieth-century history reminds us, the world can change very quickly—and often for the worse.

International communication in general has been affected by world events as it has continued to expand its reach. International broadcasting has become less propagandistic and more informative and entertainment-minded. In most countries, journalists have enjoyed greater access to news. New independent and outspoken publications and broadcast outlets have sprouted like mushrooms in spring. Communication satellites transmitting news and pop culture have proliferated, and media audiences have greatly expanded, especially in China and India.

Further, personalized media—videos, VCRs and DVDs, audiocassettes, personal computers, cellphones, and fax machines—have continued their rapid global penetration, as did cablevision and the Internet. Western Europe has been going through its own regional communication revolution, with transnational competition between commercial cable and satellite systems, as it moves haltingly toward economic integration.

The ongoing rush of technological innovations in foreign reporting has accelerated. Direct broadcasting from portable transmitters to satellites and then back to dish antennas—bypassing complicated, expensive ground installations—has become commonplace. Small portable earth terminals, for example, have enabled broadcast journalists reporting remote news events to send their video reports directly to satellites and thus to the whole world. The cellphone and the videophone have played unexpected roles in news dissemination. A report in Afghanistan or, for that matter, in almost any faraway troubled area, can instantly become a global news event. In just a few years, the Internet has become a player of great and ominous potential in international communication for both journalism and as a device that lets people share ideas freely on a global network.

Bloggers have joined the fray as controversial conveyors of news and comment that critique and challenges traditional news media.

In this age of information, communications systems are at the leading edge of social, economic, and political change. With the unprecedented growth in global telecommunications, an informed public has developed a more immediate concern with both world news and the symbiotic relationship between events and those who report them. For this seventh edition, the text has been thoroughly revised, with new material added to every chapter. A new chapter on China draws on Professor Scotton's recent experiences as a Fulbright scholar in Shanghai. More attention has been given to significant media developments in developing nations—some of which have producing many more media users who respond in different ways to the world news prism.

—W.A.H. & J.F.S.

# Introduction

*After years of global fretfulness about the brute effectiveness of modern armaments, it turned out during one of the most pervasively revolutionary years of the 20th century, if not of all recorded history, that the most potent single weapon in nearly every conflict was the video camera. In nation after nation, vastly superior military forces were stood off and frequently compelled to retreat before the symbolic and testimonial power of televised images.*

—William A. Henry III

As the tragic and war-stained twentieth century (and the old millennium) came to an end, we were reminded both of the changes as well as continuities that have marked journalism and international communications in our times. In 1900, all the elements were in place in Western nations— great metropolitan newspapers, rotary presses and linotypes, the typewriter, the telegraph and the underseas cable, the Associated Press, Reuters, and other cooperative news gathering—as building blocks for the changes to come. News was recognized as a valued and useful commodity in itself and as an essential means of comprehending and coping with a strange and distant world. At the same time, sensationalism and trivia had long been standard fare in the press.

But no one could have foreseen the political and social changes to come in our tumultuous times as a result, in part, of the greatly enhanced speed, volume, and reach of international news and public knowledge. Journalists and broadcasters jetting about the globe with camcorders, Comsat phones, and laptop computers reported great events instantly via satellite and Internet networks and, in so doing, often became participants and catalysts in global news stories. Sometimes they became celebrities themselves.

For over a century, the press has reported news from abroad, but it has been only in the past three decades that we have seen how great events abroad vividly illustrate the technotronic age, the melding of technology and electronics, that planet Earth has entered. It is a new era of information whose potential we but dimly perceive; whose complicated gadgetry only few of us totally grasp; whose social, political, and economic consequences are accelerating change and cleavages among the nations of the world.

For the world we live in today is changing rapidly, in no small part because worldwide television, communication satellites, high-speed transmission of news and data, and other computer and electronic hardware and software (including the Internet) have transformed the ways that nations and peoples communicate with one another. The fact that a news event can be transmitted almost instantaneously to newsrooms and onto television and computer screens (and into cellphones) around the world can be as important as the event itself. Long-distance mass communication has become a rudimentary central nervous system for our fragile, shrinking, and increasingly interdependent, yet fractious, world.

Yet there can be disconcerting side effects. The accelerating speed and efficiency of news media transmission have often created severe strains on the standards and ethics of responsible journalism. The same system can and does report much trivia, sensation, and misinformation. The news eruptions that followed the auto-crash death of Princess Diana or the Michael Jackson trial illustrated how news now breaks twenty-four hours a day, around the clock, instead of at the more leisurely pace that prevailed before the rise of twenty-four hour cable television news and interactive news on the Internet. As fierce competitors such as MSNBC, the Fox Channel, and CNN with their talk shows have proliferated on cable and online, some news organizations have relaxed their rules on checking and verifying sources. There is a growing sense that getting it first is more important than getting it right. One result is journalism that is sometimes shaky, inaccurate, or worse, and with it has come a serious loss of public trust in news media.

High among the various factors contributing to the collapse of communist regimes (and their press) was certainly the global impact of Western communications in all their diversity and seductive appeal. For throughout the 1980s, two great groundswells rolled through the seas of international communication. On an incoming tide, the methods of organizing and distributing news and mass culture developed in Western democracies have washed inexorably over the globe, driven by innovations in media technology and expanding audiences, along with a resurgence of market economies on a global scale.

On an outgoing tide, the theory and practices of communist or Marxist/Leninist public communication have become widely discredited by the many millions living under communist regimes, as well as their own journalists and rulers. The resounding rejection was directly related, of course, to the worldwide failures of socialist political economies and, particularly, the rejection of communist political rule in Eastern Europe. The crowds that protested communist regimes in Warsaw, Beijing, East Berlin, Prague, Budapest, Sofia, and Moscow in 1989 were also calling for more open and free media systems—the kind they knew about from images and sounds from the West. Expanding waves from these astonishing events radiated to the former Third World. Even African countries felt pressures for multiparty democracy.

So far, such high hopes have generally not been realized. Africa—beset by economic stagnation; drought and famine; political unrest and corruption; and brutal civil wars in Sudan, Somalia, Liberia, Congo, and Rwanda—has in fact retrogressed. Hopes for meaningful democracy in Kenya, Zimbabwe, and Congo have all been dashed recently. It is no coincidence that, with the exception of South Africa, these troubled nations have inadequate media systems and cannot participate fully in a globalized world.

Today's unipolar world, with the United States as its uncertain and often unpopular leader, is challenged not only by terrorism but other related problems, such as resurgent nationalism, poverty, racism, and religious fundamentalism. To these can be added the ups and downs of a sometimes faltering global economy.

This book analyzes the changing role of transnational news media in our evolving globalization and its impact on rapidly changing news events. In the ongoing concern about terrorism, global news media have played a major role both in informing the world and in organizing and facilitating responses to terrorism. (The media are also an unwilling accomplice of terrorism by publicizing the atrocities and carrying the e-mail messages of terrorists.) Throughout this book, the emphasis is often on the role of U.S. news organizations, yet we acknowledge that news media of many other nations—East and West—contribute to this cooperative activity of reporting the world to itself. And as the world modernizes, journalists of more and more nations are contributing to the flow of international news and popular culture.

News has increasingly become a powerful political and diplomatic force. For example, when U.S. television shows stark pictures of starving Somali mothers and children, American public opinion becomes concerned, and the White House watches, hesitates, and then sends in the military to help feed the starving and keep the peace. A few months later, a dozen American soldiers are killed in an ambush, and the U.S. public is outraged at seeing on television the body of an American soldier dragged through the streets of Mogadishu. Soon, the White House announces that troops will be withdrawn.

In late 1995, after unrelenting media coverage of Bosnia's bitter civil war, the United States and its NATO allies finally intervened with a bombing campaign that led to a tenuous peace accord. With American troops involved in enforcing the peace, the public's perceptions on how well or how badly things were going in Bosnia has been influenced by news coverage. During NATO's air war with Yugoslavia in 1999, vivid television reports of the brutal treatment of Kosovo refugees created widespread sympathy for the victims and gained support for NATO's aerial bombing of Serbia.

News, instantaneous and vivid, speeds up history as it directly influences diplomacy and government policy. At the same time, in this age of satellites, the Internet, and shortwave radio, tyrants find it impossible to keep unflattering news about their regimes from reaching their own people. (Yet terrorists use the Internet to inform their followers and coordinate acts of terror.) On the one hand are the technological and operational changes taking place in the international news media, with their enhanced capability for global communication that is reshaping "spaceship Earth." Wider communication often seems to exacerbate political and cultural conflicts between the West and Islam, between rich and poor nations. Also, there are the frictions and the problems these changes have wrought, including conflicts over transnational news gathering and the impact of television programming, motion pictures, videos, radio broadcasting, and other aspects of mass culture, most of it coming out of the United States and Europe.

Another source of concern is that, when no crisis intrudes, serious international news seems often to be shunted aside for more profitable content. "Infotainment"—scandal, sensation, celebrities—has become more and more the staple of news media in many countries.

Before 9/11, network television news programs, from which most people get their news, had sharply cut back on the amount of foreign news on the major networks. Similar trends were seen among the news magazines. This reflects (or explains) why Americans and others have been showing a declining interest in news from abroad. The terrorism crisis of 2001 reversed this trend, but only for a few months. This book deals with various facets of the changing media and their impact on transnational journalism and mass communication. It is intended to provide some insights into how and why international news communication is evolving. Few of us can appreciate, much less fully understand, the meaning of the global information revolution we are living through. The major components of this quiet revolution are the computer and telecommunications, principally the communication satellite plus other sophisticated electronic devices that have become as much a part of our lives as the electric light.

We may not be aware of how our perceptions of the world are being changed by the transformed news system, but we quickly learn to take that system for granted. If there is another terror attack on a major city such as Madrid, or another civil war in Africa, we expect to see live television reports the same day or on a twenty-four hour news channel, such as BBC World or CNN, within the hour via satellite. We are fascinated but not surprised to see detailed, computer-refined pictures of the exploration of planet Mars or the dramatic saga of the space shuttle as well as the grim daily stories from Baghdad.

In a broader context, the fact that information of all kinds, including urgent news, can now be communicated almost instantly to almost any-where has profound implications for international organization and inter-action. News of Iraq's invasion of Kuwait, for example, had an almost immediate impact on the price of gas at the pump and initiated an international diplomatic reaction resulting in mass deployment of U.S. military forces. And the world's subsequent perceptions of the crisis and war were certainly shaped and, at times, distorted by the flickering images on television screens. Instant information is often not the whole truth or a complete picture and, on occasion, does sharply distort images that people receive.

Still, global news has many uses. The global financial media's day-to-day reporting of financial crises in Asian stock markets and currencies, and their effects on the financial markets and economies of Japan, Europe, and America, illustrates how many millions around the world, including small stockholders, rely on fast, accurate information in their daily lives.

The global economy simply could not function without the flow of fast and reliable information provided by the growing global business media—both print and electronic.

A new global society of sorts is emerging rapidly and inexorably, though experts disagree about its extent and nature. (Many nations, especially in the Middle East and Africa, do not feel a part of it.) The media of mass communication, along with global telecommunications, air transportation, and growing interdependence of national economies, are providing the essential linkages that make interaction and cooperation—and stealth terrorist attacks—possible.

Full understanding of the nature of this new society requires that today's students of international communication be conversant with world politics and economics, including recent history, and be quick to recognize significant trends as they occur. Further, they must understand national and cultural differences and keep up with technological innovations in communication media, such as the Internet, and with changing journalistic practices.

Communication satellites are just one example of the truly revolutionary impact that communication technology has had on the modern world. The earlier role of transistor radios in the Third World was another; today, the small hand-held video camcorder is having news effects undreamed of. As we will see, the Internet is beginning to be perceived as yet another technological marvel that may dramatically alter international communication. FM radio, cellphones, and cable television are each having unexpected impacts in developing nations.

The interplay of these elements makes the study of international communication fascinating and important. The major emphasis throughout this book is on the journalistic aspects of international communication—the new challenges and perils of reporting the news, the important but imperfect and controversial ways that journalists and mass communicators keep the world informed. Further, the cultural and entertainment facets of media are often significant as well.

Several chapters concern the changing media—the ways that international journalism is adapting to altered global conditions, changing concepts of news, and utilizing the new hardware of our information age.

Currently, for the first time in history, all nations, however remote, have stepped onto the stage of the modern world. What happens in Rwanda or Indonesia, or Afghanistan, can have global significance and often sends repercussions around the world, in part because events happening there are reported. More importantly, a much greater degree of interdependence among all peoples and nations has developed.

The world has been evolving an international news system that moves information and mass culture ever faster and in greater volume to any place on Earth where an antenna can be put on a shortwave radio receiver, where dish antennas can receive television programs from a communication satellite, or, increasingly, where there is a personal computer with a modem hooked onto the Internet. Although politics, economic disparities, cultural and linguistic differences, and ideology keep us apart on many issues, the international news system has on occasion made us one community, if only briefly—as when Neil Armstrong took that "one giant leap for mankind" in 1969. An estimated 600 million people throughout the world watched that first walk on the moon, and they sat before their television sets not as Chinese, French, Africans, or Japanese, but as earthlings watching in awe as one of their kind first stepped onto another planet.

Actually, the reportage of Armstrong's walk has further relevance for this book, because the new information age is partly an outgrowth of the exploration of space. The communication satellite, high-speed data transmission, and miniaturized computer technology are by-products of space technology, and all are playing integral roles in the transformation of international communication and transnational journalism.

The modern practices of globally collecting and distributing news are only about 100 years old and were initiated by news agencies of Britain, the United States, and France. Today, the world agencies—the Associated Press (United States), Reuters (Britain), and Agence France-Presse (France)—are still the principal, but far from only, conduits of transnational news, although they and other media have been transformed by space-age technology. Change has been coming so quickly that it is often difficult to stay current with the ways in which news is being moved. And to understand the future potential of say, the Internet, is like trying to perceive in 1905 what the absurd horseless carriage or the telephone would do in time to the cities and life styles of the twentieth century.

Furthermore, technology and global reach are modifying some of the institutions of transnational communication. Subtly and almost imperceptibly, various media, including the news agencies, are evolving from national to increasingly international, or better, to supranational institutions of mass communication. The successful *International Herald Tribune* reaches a sophisticated non-American readership from Paris to Hong

Kong; *Time* and *Newsweek* publish special editions that are truly international in outlook; *The Asian Wall Street Journal* is widely read by Asian business people; and CNN and BBC World are viewed in almost every country. Britain's *Financial Times* and *The Economist* are read by business elites in many nations. Some may deplore this trend, but there is no doubt that it is a response to the informational needs of a shrinking world and a growing global economy served by a growing business press. Concomitantly, English is clearly the world's leading media language.

Modern media, especially shortwave radio, are utilized by many nations for purposes of "international political communication"—a polite term for propaganda. The international radio broadcasters—the BBC World Service, the Voice of America, Radio Moscow, Deutsche Welle, Radio Cairo, and many others, including small national services in developing nations—use the airwaves to report their version of world news and their views on events such as the war in Iraq. Propagandistic or not, shortwave radio conveys news and information to untold millions, especially in the poorer nations. Today, the Internet increasingly complements shortwave radio.

The international news media, furthermore, are unevenly distributed among nations, creating serious frictions between the haves and have-nots in mass communication. The explosion of communication technology has coincided with the post World War II decolonization of the Third World, and the penetration of Western news and mass culture into the newly independent nations, as well as into the former communist bloc. This has been perceived by some as a new attempt to reassert the domination of the former colonial powers. Certainly, the Western media—and the nations behind them—are much resented in many of what are now referred to as "failed nations."

Part of this book focuses on the differences that frustrate and at times inhibit the flow of international news and divide journalists and mass communicators: political and ideological differences, economic disparities, geographic and ethnic divisions. The media of all nations, it can be argued, reveal biases imposed by the constraints of nationalism and parochialism. When U.S. soldiers are engaged in a military clash in Baghdad, the subsequent news report on NBC television will differ from that carried on Al Jazeera, the Arabic broadcaster. There is no "true" news report of any event, only a variety of conflicting views out of which hopefully a consensus of sorts can be reached about what exactly happened.

The conflicts and frictions in international communication arise in part from divergent concepts of mass communication. In the concept of the press that has evolved in Western democratic nations, journalists are relatively independent of government, free to report directly to the public that uses the information to understand the world and to assess its governors. This view is unacceptable to authoritarian nations, which control and manipulate their media to serve better the goals of the state and their often unelected leaders. In numerous, mostly impoverished nations, a similar theory—the developmental concept—has emerged, which holds that mass media must be mobilized to serve the goals of nation building and economic development.

The deep differences between the media-rich and media-poor nations reflect closely other differences between rich and poor nations. Despite the impressive gains in the technical ability to communicate more widely and quickly, the disturbing evidence is that in some ways the world may be growing further apart rather than closer together. Most of the benefits of the communication and information revolution have accrued to the industrialized nations of the West, and to Japan and the Pacific Rim nations. For an individual to benefit fully from the news media, he or she ideally should be literate, educated, and affluent enough to have access to a variety of news sources. Unfortunately, in our unfair world, the largest share of such individuals are found, for now, in the few industrialized democracies. Yet the world's two most populous nations, China and India, have greatly increased the audiences and readership of their media.

The world's system of distributing news can be likened to a crystal prism. What in one place is considered the straight white light of truth travels through the prism and is refracted and bent into a variety of colors and shades. One person's truth becomes, to another, biased reporting or propaganda—depending on where the light strikes the prism and where it emerges. As we understand the optics of a prism for measuring the spectrum of light, so must we understand and accept the transecting planes of different cultural and political traditions that refract divergent perceptions of our world. Obviously, Islamic terrorists have a radically different view of the world than most Europeans have.

We must acknowledge how the light refracts for us. In considering the problems of international communication, we have tried to be sympathetic to the views and frustrations of people in non-Western nations and the enormous difficulties they face. Journalism is a highly subjective pursuit, tempered and shaped by the political conditions and cultural traditions of the particular society where it is practiced; the news and the world do look different from Shanghai, Lagos, or Baghdad than they do from Chicago.

As products of the Western press tradition, we believe journalists in their pursuit of the news should be suspicious of, and disagree at times with, other political leaders and other journalists as well as the owners of the media. For the essence of journalism is diversity of ideas and the freedom to express them. We agree with Albert Camus, who wrote:

> A free press can of course be good or bad, but certainly without free-dom, it will never be anything but bad. . . . Freedom is nothing else but a chance to be better, whereas enslavement is a certainty of the worst.

And in the dangerous, strife-ridden world of the twenty-first century, we believe that the billions of people inhabiting this planet deserve to know more about the events and trends that affect their lives and well-being. Only journalists who are free and independent of authoritarian controls and other constraints can begin the difficult task of reporting the news and information we all have a right and need to know.

# Chapter 1

# News Communication for a New Global System

*Globalization is not simply a trend or a fad but is, rather, an international system. It is the system that has now replaced the old Cold War system, and like that Cold War system, globalization has its own rules and logic that today directly or indirectly influence the politics, environment, geopolitics and economics of virtually every country in the world.*

—Thomas L. Friedman, *The Lexus and the Olive Tree*

The rapid integration of the world's economy, loosely called globalization, has been facilitated by an information revolution driven by communication technologies that provide a nervous system for our world today. Globalization is a broad and inexact term for a wide array of worldwide changes in politics, economics, trade, finance, life styles, and cultures. To its critics, globalization is trendy and controversial; they see the world becoming a consumer colony of the U.S., led by Coke, McDonald's, Nike, and the vast pop-culture output of Hollywood. How people feel about globalization often depends a lot on where they live and what they do.

With just a visit to a mall, one is struck by the plethora of products and services from many distant lands. In the past twenty years, much of the world's economy has become increasingly integrated; direct foreign investment has grown three times as fast as total domestic investment. From 1980 to 1999, the value of world trade rose sharply, with the total value of world exports estimated at U.S. $5.47 trillion, up from U.S. $2 trillion in 1980. But globalization is more than buying and selling; some see it as a profound interchange of cultures—a communication revolution that is dissolving our sense of boundaries, our national identities, and how we perceive the world.

Deregulation of telecommunications systems and computerization have been called the parents of globalization. Three technologies in particular—computers, satellites, and digitalization—have converged to produce a global communications network that covers the Earth as completely as the atmosphere. Today's era of globalization is characterized by falling telecommunications costs, thanks to microchips, satellites, fiber optics, and the Internet.

The popular culture of the West—movies, television shows, music CDs, video- and audiocassettes, books, magazines, newspapers—has been increasingly flowing about the world. It can be argued that the world is beginning to share a popular culture, based only in part on that of the West. Critics differ about what happens when cultures meet.

Rather than fight, cultures often blend. Frederick Tipson noted, "More like a thin but sticky coating than a powerful acid, this cosmopolitan culture of communication networks and the information media seems to overlay rather than supplant the cultures it interacts with."[1] When cultures receive outside influences, it is said, they ignore some and adopt others, and soon begin to transform them. An example can be something called *bhangra pop* in India—music that sounds like Jamaican reggae but is played on Indian instruments and then amplified.

Critics of this global media market castigate globalization for several reasons: the centralization of media power; and heavy commercialism, which is linked to declines in public broadcasting and public service standards for media performance. Media are seen as a threat to democracy because of lessened public participation and concern with public affairs. Press critics have other concerns about these corporate giants. The news media, they argue, risk becoming submerged and neglected inside vast entertainment conglomerates that are primarily concerned with entertainment profits.

Most of these criticisms are leveled at Western media, and these critics neglect to consider how globalization has spurred the development of media and the audiences in the developing non-Western nations.

Others see globalization in more positive terms. It is argued that many millions more people than ever before now have access to news and information, especially in such countries as China and India and much of Southeast Asia. Globalization means that multitudes now have many newfound choices: how they will spend their leisure time; what they will watch or read; what to buy with newly acquired personal income from rapidly rising standards of living. Anthropologist James Watson wrote, "The lives of Chinese villagers I know are infinitely better off now than they were 30 years ago. China has become more open because of the demands of ordinary people. They *want* to become part of the world—I would say that globalism is the major force for democracy in China. People want refrigerators, stereos, CD players."[2]

Journalist Thomas Friedman wrote that globalization is essentially about change, which is a reality and not a choice: "Thanks to the combination of computers and cheap telecommunications, people can now offer and trade services globally—from medical advice to software writing to data processing—services that could never be traded before. And why not? A three-minute call (in 1996 dollars) between New York and London cost $300 in 1930. Today it is almost free through the Internet."[3]

The primacy of the issue of globalization reminds us of the extent to which most of us now think and act globally—as a matter of course. In his 2005 book, *The World is Flat: A Brief History of the 21st Century*, Friedman expands his earlier views and sees dramatic changes in the forces for global leveling from the fall of the Berlin Wall, which eliminated the ideological divide in the world, to the rise of the Internet and technological changes that have led to new economic models of production and collaboration, including outsourcing and offshore manufacturing. Now nations such as China and India, as well as others in South Asia, have prospered in dramatic ways. The integration of some three billion people into the global economy is of major importance. Just one facet of this global flattening is that the media of communications have become increasingly pervasive in these rapidly modernizing places. Literally many millions are now, through the Internet, cellphones, satellite television, and publications, "in touch" with the greater world. But while the new technologies are closing gaps between parts of India and China and the advanced industrial nations, the gaps between those countries and Africa have been widened. The world's nations may not have a level playing field, but the world is changing in critical ways. And for many millions in those nations considered to be "developing," their standards of living have improved rapidly.

## A Big, Cloudy, Blue, Agate Marble

Perhaps one of the most significant photographs of modern times was taken during the Apollo 11 mission to the moon. The astronauts photographed the earthrise as seen from the moon, and there was our planet, like a big, cloudy, blue, agate marble. The widely reprinted picture illuminated the fragility and cosmic insignificance of our spaceship Earth.

That stunning image coincided with the worldwide concern about ecology and global pollution; even more, it made it easy to grasp why many scientists already treated that cloudy, blue marble as a complete biological system, in which change in one part will inevitably affect other parts.

Certainly in the years since, concerned persons around the world have become more aware of our global interdependence. Although some experts disagree, an important trend of our times is that the world is becoming a single, rudimentary community. Today's world must grapple with an agenda of urgent and complex problems, most of them interrelated: overpopulation; poverty; famine; depletion of natural resources (especially energy); pollution of the biosphere; regional political disputes; continuing arms buildup, including the nuclear threat; and the widening gap between rich and poor nations, which seems exacerbated by economic integration. Recent events, especially in London and Madrid, have pushed terrorism high on the agenda. Terrorist acts are somber reminders of how much hate and anger divide our diverse societies.

These and other global crises ebb and flow on the world's news agendas, but they are truly international in scope; the amelioration—much less solution—of any of them requires cooperation and goodwill among nations. To achieve that, there first must be information and understanding of these challenges, for these are crises of interdependence. No one nation or even combination of nations can deal effectively with such global concerns as international monetary crises, pollution of the air and oceans, population control, terrorism, regional warfare, and widespread famine and food shortages, yet the blinders of nationalism and modern tribalism continue to influence political leaders everywhere to react to international problems with narrow and parochial responses. The news media in all nations will reflect the national views and prejudices of their own societies on these pressing global concerns. It's not necessary that all nations agree on how to respond—and here is where the news media come in—but there should be general agreement about what the problems are.

Lester Brown, an authority on global needs, described the problems of our times as "unique in their scale." Previous catastrophes—famines, floods, earthquakes, volcanic eruptions—were local and temporary. But now, the world's more pressing concerns can be solved only through multinational or global cooperation, yet the institutions to cope with them are largely national. And because each technological innovation seems to create new problems but not the political will capable of resolving them, Brown sees global conditions worsening in the years immediately ahead. Brown's view of world problems, although shared by many, is still not truly understood by great numbers of people. Americans, for example, periodically turn inward and become self-absorbed, failing to comprehend how domestic problems have roots in events that may occur thousands of miles away.[4]

Westerners and some leaders of developing countries are becoming aware that population growth is putting intolerable pressures on the Earth's land, water, and energy resources as well as its economies.

## Pressures of Population

The world's population in 2005 passed 6,446,131,400, according to the U.S. Census Bureau. (In 1950, the world had 2.5 billion people.) At least seventy-four countries, including Nigeria, Iran, Ethiopia, Iraq, and Guatemala, will probably double their populations in thirty years; and in addition, thirty-three countries, twenty of them in Africa, still have a fertility rate of six children per woman.

However, recently, population trends have changed markedly. The problem now is more regional than global, explosive only in a few places such as India and Pakistan. Birth rates in developed countries from Italy to Korea have dropped below levels needed for populations to replace themselves. Since 1968, when the United Nations had predicted that the population would grow to at least 12 billion by 2050, estimates have regularly been revised downward. Global population is now predicted to plateau at nine billions.[5] In places where the world has modernized and average incomes have risen, women have fewer children and populations level off—one more plus for globalization.

The world's political structures, many believe, must be reshaped to enable us to cope with these global challenges: hence the great importance, despite their shortcomings, of international organizations such as the United Nations and its attendant agencies. Recently, there have been frequent calls for reform of the United Nations.

Public opinion polls have long shown that many people are uninformed about international affairs. For example, one Gallup Poll found that half of all Americans did not know that the United States had to import petroleum to meet its needs.

As important as formal education is, its influence sometimes does not change attitudes or improve understanding until a generation or two later. In immediate terms, the media flow of information and news throughout the globe can have a greater impact than education on the world's ability to understand its problems and dangers. Since World War II, an intricate and worldwide network of international news media has evolved, providing an expanded capability for information flows. This relationship between the capacity and the need to communicate rapidly has resulted from the interaction of two long-term historical processes: the evolution toward a single global society and the movement of civilization beyond four great benchmarks of human communication—speech, writing, printing, and electronic communications (telephone and radio)—into a fifth era of long-distance instant communication based on telecommunications and computer technology. The latter are key components of globalization.

Harold Lasswell believed that the mass-media revolution has accelerated the tempo and direction of world history. What would have happened later has happened sooner, and changes in timing may have modified substantive developments.[6]

The toppling of President Ferdinand Marcos from power in the Philippines provided a cogent example of the power of international news media to influence international politics. From the assassination of opposition leader Benigno Aquino through the election campaign, the foreign news media took a close interest in Marcos's affairs, reporting extensively on his "hidden wealth," including New York City real estate, as well as his dubious war record. This scrutiny helped the cause of candidate Corazon Aquino and galvanized U.S. public opinion and the Congress. The Reagan White House in turn was pushed to urge Marcos to step down after full media glare showed his election victory to be a fraud. As Thomas Griffith of *Time* wrote, "The visuals on American TV did Marcos in. It wasn't Dan Rather or George Will. It was the pictures—the nuns, and the crowds wearing a touch of yellow, blocking the path of the armored cars. It was the sight of ballot boxes being dumped. In a few precarious days, it was the total collapse of Marcos' American support that sped the end. TV proved its awesome power."[7]

Commenting on the episode, Walter B. Wriston observed "This is a brand new situation in the world. The global electronic network that has evolved in the last decade is forcing us to redefine our ideas of sovereignty. The rapid transmission of information has become a radical force for change, encouraging the growth of political and economic freedom. Marcos's demise is not an isolated instance."[8] The revolutionary year of 1989 provided further examples of the power of modern communications in the uprisings from Berlin and Prague to Tiananmen Square (see Chapter 5, "The Impact of Great News Events"). Intense global media attention to Indonesia in May 1998 probably contributed to the bloodless coup that toppled President Suharto.

Paradoxically, even with this greatly enhanced capability of involvement in world affairs, comparatively few people are well informed or even care much about what happens beyond their borders. Many who follow the news on television have only a superficial knowledge of events such as a cancellation of an election in Nigeria or a stock-market crash in Indonesia. But for those comparative few who do follow public affairs closely (and they are found in every nation), perceptions of the world are being formed and reshaped by this revolution in long-distance instant communications.

Our ability, or lack of it, to use the fruits of this technological revolution is directly related to our success or failure to act decisively and in concert as a world community. International experts worry whether the world can organize itself and deal effectively with what have been called the seven major interrelated world problems: mass poverty, population, food, pollution, energy, military expenditure, and the world monetary system. To organize, though, we must communicate, since communication is the neural system of any organization. The extent of its ability to communicate determines the boundaries of any community—be it a primitive tribe in Papua New Guinea or a global society—and only expanded and more effective communication can make possible a viable global community.

The technology to circulate that information exists, but the barriers of illiteracy, parochialism and nationalism, poverty, and political constraints keep too many people in the world from receiving it.

The illiteracy situation is particularly vexing. Here are the basic facts and figures:

- There are about one billion nonliterate adults (persons fifteen years and above).
- Ninety-eight per cent of all nonliterate adults are in developing nations.
- Two-thirds of all nonliterates are women.

- One half of all nonliterates are in China and India.
- It has been estimated that 30 to 50 million people are added each year to the numbers of nonliterates due to population increases.
- So, worldwide the percentage of adult illiteracy is declining, but the absolute number of nonliterates is increasing.

Over the long run, worldwide illiteracy dropped from 38.5 percent in 1970 to about 22 percent in 2000. Yet there is much room for improvement: currently about 670 million school-age children are not in school.

Literacy is the key skill for modernization, education, and use of mass media and computers. Illiteracy is widespread in Africa, so it is no wonder that there are only about 125 daily newspapers in all of Africa, compared with more than 1,770 dailies in the United States. In any country, therefore, the proportion of people able to receive news and information will vary greatly according to the availability of news media and the ability of people to use them. Those living in such "information societies" as Japan, Western Europe, or the United States are overwhelmed with information and news, whereas throughout the many poor nations only a tiny fraction of persons is able to participate in the international news flow. Regardless of where they live, however, too few people take advantage of opportunities to acquire and use information about the solution of urgent transnational problems.

## The Importance of Foreign News

Much of the essential information we need for our personal lives comes from the news media. Our economy, our society, and our government would have difficulty functioning without the flow of reliable news and information. An open, democratic society without independent news media is impossible to imagine.

Foreign news is a special genre of news. It's not just from afar but also news of widespread significance. The earthquake/tsunami of late 2004 was major news everywhere. Serious journalists and editors have long held that important information from overseas should be reported capably and thoroughly, even though most people are primarily concerned about what happens in their own communities or to themselves personally. Yet foreign news is perceived through the distorting prisms of culture and personal predilection.

Throughout our turbulent times, events beyond our borders have directly affected, and disrupted, many lives: two world wars, a worldwide depression, the rise of Hitler and Stalin, decolonization of great empires, the Cold War, and, more recently, the rise of an interdependent global economy. In an open, democratic society, the public must know what is happening in the outside world in order to judge how well their government and leaders respond to challenges from abroad. The history of independent journalism clearly shows that the best and most responsible news media have always given high priority to foreign news. This is still true today, especially for a handful of great daily newspapers.

Yet for many in recent years, foreign news did not seem as important and relevant as it was before the Cold War ended. Who is to blame: the press, our political leaders, or the public? Perhaps all three. Without a crisis demanding our attention—a famine and civil war in Sudan, genocide in Rwanda, civil war and aerial bombing in Bosnia and Kosovo—the average daily paper carries usually only about six short items from abroad—unless American soldiers are involved, as in Somalia, Bosnia, Afghanistan, or Iraq.

Most people rely on television for their news, yet anyone regularly watching network news is aware that foreign news has been typically reduced to several short items ("And now the news from abroad . . .") unless some video with violent footage is available (50 percent of television's foreign coverage does portray violence). Critics say that serious foreign news on television has been pushed aside in favor of scandal, celebrity, or the so-called "you news"—self-help and advice stories.

The public apparently does not mind. A recent survey of the U.S. public by the Pew Research Center found that among regular users of the news media, the topics of most interest were, in this order, crime, local news about people and events, and health news. International news ranked ninth, well behind sports, local government, science, religion, and political news. Another 2001 poll (before 9/11), by Andrew Kohut, found that fewer than one in five Americans was strongly interested in serious news programs and publications—international, financial, government, and politics. Gender, generation, and education are keys: college-educated men over forty years of age and older have the most interest; lesser-educated, younger women have decidedly the least.[9]

Other surveys conducted by the Pew Research Center in 1997 found that the percentage of people following foreign news dropped from 80 percent in the 1980s to 20 percent in 1990. The decline was most precipitous among young people, who were turned off by such traditional categories as international politics, security, war, and peace. The relatively few serious news stories that attract the attention of adult Americans are those that deal with national calamities or the use of American military force. The obverse is that readers in the affluent West show little interest in tragic and harsh news stories coming out of developing nations. The admirable group, Doctors Without Borders, who aid destitute people abroad, annually lists what it considers the "Most Under-Reported Humanitarian Stories." Their list for 2004 was expressed in vivid headlines:

1. "Intense Grief and Fear in Northern Uganda" (an eighteen-year conflict has displaced nearly 1.6 million people).
2. "No End in Sight in Devastating Conflict in Congo."
3. "Civilians Caught in Colombia's Cross-fire."
4. "Tuberculosis Spiraling out of Control."
5. "Somalia Shattered by Anarchy and Chaos."
6. "Trauma of Ongoing War in Chechnya."
7. "User Fee System Excludes Burundi's Poorest from Basic Health Care."
8. "North Koreans Endure Massive Deprivation and Repression."
9. "Constant Threat of Hunger and Disease in Ethiopia."
10. "War is Over but Liberians Still Live in Crisis."

We agree with Stephen Hess of the Brookings Institution, who argued that we have become a nation with a two-media system, especially in regard to foreign news. Hess wrote, "Our society is awash in specialized information (including foreign news) available to those who have the time, interest, money, and education to take advantage of it. The other society encompasses the vast majority of Americans, who devote limited attention to subjects far removed from their necessary concerns (again, foreign news). They are content to turn to the top stories of television networks' evening news programs and their community's daily news-papers for the information."[10] We would argue that this happens in other affluent nations as well.

Yet perhaps this diminished interest in international events is not as significant as it would seem. Recent polls show that although the public is turned off by some foreign news, the public does crave engagement in the world's crises, but not in ways defined by government, academics, and the media. For example, a University of Maryland poll found that 74 percent of people wanted a sharing of power internationally, whereas only 13 percent wanted the United States to assert itself as the only superpower. Also, although Congress held up $1.5 billion in overdue assessments for the United Nations, a Pew Center survey found that Americans hold the organization in high regard. The Pew survey found broad support for cooperative action to halt global warming, even if it meant applying fuel consumption standards leading to higher U.S. gasoline prices.

In short, the publics everywhere seem highly concerned about issues they see as directly affecting their own lives. The British clearly felt their lives threatened by the July 7, 2005 attacks. They are also concerned about immigration and trade negotiations that could have an impact on their jobs and taxes, as well as environmental issues such as global warming, resource depletion, health threats, drug trafficking, and other cross-border crime.[11]

## Moving Together or Apart?

Whether the problem is pollution of the seas or proliferation of nuclear weapons, the fact remains that international society is marked by the absence of effective collective procedures, by competition rather than cooperation, and by the lack of a commitment to a common goal. The world is ruled by nation-states, not by an effective international organization, and each state will usually act according to its own interests and needs. In several African nations, such as Somalia, Liberia, and Sierra Leone, an even more discouraging trend has emerged: the complete breakdown of a nation into warring camps without a coherent central government. Some academics argue that the apparent thrust toward global unity and globalization is actually misleading. Political scientist Steven Krasner of Stanford believes that the idea that the world has fundamentally changed lacks historical perspective. The international transfer of ideas, trade, and capital has been going on for four or five centuries, he says. Others agree that the idea of global integration has been overblown and that we are not yet up to the late-nineteenth-century standard of integration. They argue that the current globalization is a return to a process interrupted by two world wars.[12] From the mid-1880s to the Great Depression, the world experienced a similar age of globalization. The volumes of trade and capital flows across borders and the flow of labor across borders, relative to populations, in the pre World War I era of globalization was similar to what we are living through today. But today, powerful communications, including the media, drive our current globalization.

Others feel that the world is both converging and diverging at the same time. In 1993, *The New York Times* listed forty-eight nations where long-suppressed ethnic, religious, and sectional conflicts had surfaced. Policy makers say the ethnic conflicts are actually the third wave of this century, with the first having taken place after World War I and the second with the explosion of anticolonial movements in Africa and Asia after World War II. Most of these nations' ancient rivalries and bigotry have remained largely unaffected by communication technology. The rise of international terrorism to the top of the world's agenda is further strong evidence of global divisiveness. Also, the sharp opposition of many Western nations to the U.S. invasion of Iraq certainly indicated a shattering of political consensus.

On the other hand, powerful technotronic forces are binding the world together—circulating news, ideas, and information faster and in greater volume than ever before. These technologies are transforming many economic enterprises into truly global businesses. Further, countless more individuals are, through education and media participation, joining the modern world. So, although global integration may seem both real and illusory, there may be encouragement in the futuristic views that science fiction writer Arthur C. Clarke expressed more than twenty-five years ago regarding the communication satellite:

> What we are now doing—whether we like it or not—indeed, whether we wish it or not—is laying the foundation of the first global society. Whether the final planetary authority will be an analogue of the federal systems now existing in the United States or the USSR I do not know. I suspect that, without any deliberate planning, such organizations as the world meteorological and earth resources satellite system and the world communications satellite system (of which INTELSAT is the precursor) will eventually transcend their individual components. At some time during the next century they will discover, to their great surprise, that they are really running the world.
>
> There are many who will regard these possibilities with alarm or distaste and may even attempt to prevent their fulfillment. I would

remind them of the story of the wise English king, Canute, who had his throne set upon the seashore so he could demonstrate to his foolish courtiers that even the king could not command the incoming tide. The wave of the future is now rising before us. Gentlemen, do not attempt to hold it back. Wisdom lies in recognizing the inevitable—and cooperating with it. In the world that is coming, the great powers are not great enough.[13]

Some signs of this trend are visible; a slow but perceptible movement toward internationalization of the world's news media is taking place. The world's news agencies, a few newspapers and magazines, and both radio and television broadcasting (CNN and BBC World in particular) are transcending the national states from which they arose and are serving international audiences. With this has come, from the West, a pervasive popular culture. Such a transition will be welcomed by some as a contribution to better world understanding or resented by others as efforts by some nations to impose their models of mass communication and pop culture on everyone.

The technological capability for worldwide communication has never been greater, but then never have truly global problems and challenges seemed more urgent. Not enough people anywhere understand these problems or are in a position to cooperate with others in resolving them. Serious questions can be posed about the quality and adequacy of today's system of global news communication, but little doubt exists about the importance to the world of the newspapers, news agencies, and broadcasters that report the world's news to itself.

## Notes

1. Erla Zwingle, "Goods Move. People Move. Ideas Move. And Cultures Change," *National Geographic*, August 1999, 12.
2. Ibid., 13.
3. Thomas Friedman, *The Lexus and the Olive Tree* (New York: Anchor Books, 2000), xviii.
4. Lester R. Brown, *World Without Borders* (New York: Vintage Books, 1973), 10–12.
5. Donald McNeil, "Demographic Bomb May Only Go Pop," *The New York Times*, August 29, 2004, 4.

6.  Harold Lasswell, "The Future of World Communication; Quality and Style of Life", Papers of the East–West Communication Institute, Honolulu, no. 4 (September 1972), 3.
7.  Thomas Griffith, "Newswatch," *Time*, March 17, 1986, 72.
8.  Walter B. Wriston, "Economic Freedom Receives a Boost," *The New York Times*, April 15, 1986, 31.
9.  Andrew Kohut, "Balancing News Interests," *Columbia Journalism Review*, July/August 2001, 58.
10. Stephen Hess, *International News & Foreign Correspondents* (Washington, D.C.: Brookings Institution, 1996), 8.
11. Barbara Crossette, "U.S. Likes Its Foreign Affairs in Non-Traditional Terms, Polls Say", *The New York Times*, December 28, 1997, 8.
12. Susan Wels, "Global Integration: The Apparent and the Real," *Stanford Magazine*, September 1990, 46.
13. Arthur C. Clarke, "Beyond Babel: The Century of the Communication Satellite," in *Process and Effects of Mass Communication*, W. Schramm and D. Roberts, eds. (Urbana: University of Illinois Press, 1971), 963.

# Chapter 2

# Changing Ideologies of Press Control

*A journalist is a grumbler, a censurer, a giver of advice, a regent of sovereigns, a tutor of nations. Four hostile newspapers are more to be feared than a thousand bayonets.*

—Napoleon

*Abuses of the freedom of speech ought to be repressed, but to whom dare we commit the power of doing it?*

—Benjamin Franklin

The impressive technological improvements in international news exchanges cannot give editors and broadcasters any real control over how news will be perceived as it emerges from the global news prism, whose planes and surfaces have been cut and polished by diverse and frequently antagonistic political and social systems. As the news passes through the prism, what one journalist considers to be truthful, objective reporting can bend into what another journalist elsewhere in the world considers to be distortion or propaganda.

Despite our impressive technological expertise, political and regional differences and cultural conflicts prevent the international news process from working smoothly and harmoniously. More and faster news communication across national borders does not automatically lead to better understanding; often, it results in enmity and distrust, because the cultural and social differences that characterize the world community preclude even agreement on what is legitimate news. As mentioned, one person's truth is another person's propaganda, and vice versa.

As a result, international journalism has often been the subject of rancor and mutual suspicion. Mass communication's powerful ability to publicize, to expose, to glorify, to criticize, to sensationalize, to denigrate, and to mislead or propagandize is universally recognized and often feared. At one time or another, government leaders in every land become unhappy or dismayed with the press. In the West, a president or prime minister may complain bitterly that his or her programs are unfairly reported by press opponents and try to bring pressure to bear on the offending publication.

In an African country, an offending foreign correspondent may be thrown into jail or expelled from the country. In Iraq under Saddam Hussein, Farzad Bazoft, an Iranian-born journalist with a British newspaper and carrying a British passport, was executed after he investigated an explosion at a secret chemical plant. Under duress and perhaps torture, Bazoft confessed to spying for Israel. The incident illustrated the often narrow line between espionage and journalism in Iraq, as elsewhere. Throughout the world today, journalists have become the victims of violence from those who do not want some particular information reported.

The differing perceptions about the nature and role of journalism and mass communication are rooted in divergent political systems and historical and cultural traditions, and are broadly reflected in five political concepts of the press found in the world today: (1) Authoritarian, (2) Western, (3) Communist, (4) Revolutionary, and (5) Developmental.[1] These are normative concepts that reflect how the media ideally should perform under certain political conditions and social values. We believe that an understanding of these contrasting approaches to the role and function of transnational journalism can help to clarify some of the issues that divide the world's press.

Authoritarianism is the oldest and most pervasive concept and has spawned two twentieth-century modifications: the Communist and Developmental concepts. The Western concept, under which the press in Western democracies with market economies generally functions, represents a fundamental alternative to the Authoritarian concept and contains elements of both eighteenth-century political liberalism and twentieth-century views of Social Responsibility. The Revolutionary concept has one trait in common with the Western: they both try to operate outside of governmental controls. The Developmental concept is an emerging pattern associated with the developing nations, most of which still lack adequate media resources, as well as effective political and economic institutions.

Newspapers, television, and other mass media, always and everywhere, function within some kinds of governmental, societal, and economic constraints. Even the "freest" or most independent press system must deal with varying degrees of regulation by political authority. In the relationship between government and mass communication, the basic question is not whether government controls the press but the nature and extent of those controls. All press systems exist somewhere along a continuum, from complete controls (absolute authoritarianism) at one end to no controls (pure libertarianism) at the other. Absolute freedom of expression is a myth. Beyond that, controls on the press are so varied and complex that it is difficult, if not impossible, to compare press freedom in one nation with that in another. In one country, newspapers may be under harsh, arbitrary political restraints; in another, they may be under more subtle, yet real, economic and corporate restrictions. As Hallin pointed out, "news media around the world vary in their styles, structures, and social and political roles. The differences are less dramatic in 2004 than they were a generation ago. 'Globalization' resulted in a considerable degree of homogenization of media systems, as a similar, mainly commercial structure and a common culture of journalism have increasingly spread around the world. However, the differences among the media systems continue to be striking."[2]

A basic tenet of the following analysis is that all press systems reflect the values of the political and economic systems of the nations within which they operate. The trend toward globalization notwithstanding, print and broadcast systems are still controlled and regulated by their own national governments. And in this era of increasing transnational communication, journalists from an open society often must work and collect news abroad in a closed or autocratic society, thereby increasing opportunities for friction between divergent concepts.

## Authoritarian Concept

Authoritarian political systems were the norm at the time the printing press was invented by Gutenberg in the mid-fifteenth century and, in the years since, more people have lived under an authoritarian press concept than under any other. The basic principle of authoritarianism is simple: The press is always subject to direct or implied control by the state or sovereign. A printing press (or, later, a broadcasting facility) cannot be used to challenge, criticize, or in any way undermine the sovereign. The press functions from the top down: The king or ruler decides what will be published because truth (and information) is essentially a monopoly of those in authority.

To the authoritarian, diversity of views is wasteful and irresponsible, dissent is an annoying nuisance and often subversive, and consensus and standardization are logical and sensible goals for mass communication. There is a certain compelling logic behind this.

Under traditional authoritarianism, the press operates outside government and is permitted to gather and publish news, but it must function for the "good of the state." The government usually leaves the press alone as long as it does not criticize authority or challenge the leadership in any way. If the press does attack authority, then the political authority intervenes, imposing censorship or even closing down publications and jailing editors. Under the Authoritarian concept, the constraint of potential censorship, if not actual prior restraint itself, always exists. Editors and reporters exercise a good deal of self-censorship, but never know for sure just how far they can go without triggering official disfavor and intervention. They must support the status quo and neither advocate change, criticize the nation's leadership, nor give offense to the dominant moral or political values.

So wherever governments arbitrarily intervene and suppress independent newspapers and broadcasters, the Authoritarian concept flourishes. For example, the Suharto government barred from Indonesia a *New York Times* correspondent, Steven Erlanger, for a published story about the business interests of Suharto's children and their success in winning government contracts. The *International Herald Tribune*, which carried the story in Asia, was barred from circulating in Indonesia.[3]

The Authoritarian concept is alive and well today in other South Asian nations, especially Singapore and Malaysia. Singapore, despite its prosperity and economic ties to the West, has been unusually hostile to foreign publications, having restricted or banned distribution of *The Asian Wall Street Journal*, *Time*, *Asiaweek*, and *Far Eastern Economic Review* at various times.

Authoritarianism is widespread today, especially if, as some scholars aver, the Communist and Developmental concepts are understood to be variations of traditional authoritarianism. In 2005, Freedom House reported that other nations recently under Authoritarian press controls include Kenya, Pakistan, Burma, Cuba, Libya, North Korea, Turkmenistan, Belarus, Equatorial Guinea, Eritrea, Uzbekistan, and Zimbabwe. Many apparently democratic nations, with political parties and elected presidents, are not in fact very democratic because rulers often act arbitrarily, dissidents and minorities lack legal rights, and local journalists operate under strict controls, including harassment, torture, and imprisonment.

Moreover, authoritarian practices cannot always be clearly delimited. Democracies in time of war or crisis (Britain during World War II, for example) sometimes adopt authoritarian controls on the press for the duration. Democratic France, under Charles de Gaulle and several of his successors, suffered under heavy-handed authoritarian control of its television system. In many nations, especially in Latin America, the media have moved back and forth between freedom and controls as the governments have changed from military to democratic regimes and back again.

Foreign correspondents pose a special challenge to authoritarian regimes, and Western journalists often encounter a variety of difficulties: Entry visas are denied; stories are censored; telephone and Comsat facilities are refused; and sometimes reporters are harassed, mistreated, jailed, or expelled.

## Western Concept

The Western concept represents a distinct deviation from the traditional authoritarian controls and evolved during the rise of democracies in Europe and North America. During the long constitutional struggle in England among the crown, the courts, and the Commons and, later, in the United States, a press relatively free of arbitrary government controls slowly evolved. In fact, one definition of freedom of the press is the right of the press to report on, comment on, and criticize its own government without retaliation or threat of retaliation from the government. This has been called "the right to talk politics." Historically, seditious libel meant criticism of government, laws, or officials. The absence of seditious libel as a crime has been considered the true pragmatic test of a country's freedom of expression, because politically relevant speech is what press freedom is mostly about. By this demanding test the Western concept—the right to talk politics—is comparatively rare.

Although many authoritarian governments give it lip service, a free or independent press is usually found in only a dozen or more Western nations that share these characteristics: (1) a system of law that provides meaningful protection to individual civil liberties and property rights (here, common-law nations, such as the United States and Britain, seem to do better than nations, such as France or Italy, with civil law traditions); (2) high average levels of per capita income, education, and literacy; (3) governance by constitutional parliamentary democracy, or at least with legitimate political oppositions; (4) sufficient capital or private enterprise to support media of news communication—that is, market economies; and (5) an established tradition of independent journalism.

Among Western media, Hallin and Mancini identify three models: the liberal model found in the United States, Britain, Canada, Ireland, Australia, and New Zealand; the "polarized model" found in Italy, Spain, and France, to an extent; and the "democratic corporatist" model found in Scandinavia and Central European states.[4] Any list of other nations meeting these criteria for a Western press today would certainly include the Netherlands, Belgium, Austria, Iceland, Israel, and Switzerland. In addition to these Western nations, highly developed and westernized Japan surely should be added. And India, the world's largest democracy, has enjoyed a remarkably free press despite its diverse problems.

Journalists in many other nations support and practice the Western concept but, because of political instability, their media over the years have swung back and forth between freedom and control.

By and large, the Western nations that meet the criteria include those that do most of the world's news gathering from other nations and whose correspondents most often come in conflict with authoritarian regimes. This is because the Western concept holds strongly that a government—any government, here or abroad—should not interfere in the process of collecting and disseminating news. The press, in theory, must be independent of authority and, of course, exist outside government and be well protected by law and custom from arbitrary government interference. And so an independent press usually means one situated in a democratic, market economy and enjoying the same autonomy as other private business enterprises. As globalization spreads, more and more nations are evolving in this direction.

The ideals of Western libertarian journalism are, to a large extent, a by-product of the Enlightenment and the liberal political tradition reflected in the writings of John Milton, John Locke, Thomas Jefferson, and John Stuart Mill. Primarily, there must be a diversity of views and news sources available, a "marketplace of ideas" from which the public can choose what it wishes to read and believe, for no one person or no authority, spiritual or temporal, has a monopoly on truth. United States Judge Learned Hand expressed it well:

> That [newspaper] industry serves one of the most vital of all general interests: the dissemination of news from as many different sources, and with as many different facets as is possible. . . . It presupposes that right conclusions are more likely to be gathered out of a multitude of tongues than through any kind of authoritarian selection. To many this is, and always will be, folly; but we have staked upon it our all.[5]

Underlying this diversity of views is the faith that citizens will somehow make the right choices about what to believe if enough voices are heard and government keeps its hands off. In American Constitutional theory, this libertarian view is based upon certain values deemed inherent in a free press: (1) by gathering public information and scrutinizing government, the press makes self-government and democracy possible; (2) an unfettered press ensures that a diversity of views and news will be read and heard; (3) a system of free expression provides autonomy for individuals to lead free and productive lives; and (4) it enables an independent press to serve as a check on abuses of power by government.[6]

Carried over to the international context, the Western concept argues that there must be a free flow of information, unimpeded by any intervention by any nation. ("Free flow," it is argued, does not necessarily mean a balanced or two-way flow of news, as desirable as that may be.) No government anywhere should obstruct the gathering and dissemination of legitimate news. Only news media free of official restraints will be credible to readers and viewers here and abroad. Advocates say that the Western concept serves the cause of global news flow in several important ways. It makes possible the gathering and dissemination of reliable and accurate news. In a global economy, the business press plays an essential role of providing fast and reliable news of global business and finance.

A free press, operating on a global scale, provides news and important information to peoples living in authoritarian regimes that censor their own media. International shortwave radio broadcasters—the BBC, VOA, and others—relay news and information from Western news gatherers, as do the interactive news media on the Internet.

Western news media, of course, are not without their shortcomings. Critics charge that too many news media have become submerged into giant, entertainment-oriented conglomerates, all primarily concerned with turning a profit. In so doing, Western media are accused of slighting serious news in favor of sensation, scandal, and celebrity. Furthermore, Western media certainly are not immune to pressures from their own governments. Political freedom does not preclude economic and corporate interference with journalistic practices. A privately owned media system will, in varying degrees, reflect the interests and concerns of its owners. Yet to stay independent of external controls, including government, the publishers and broadcasters must be financially strong and profitable. Journalistic excellence and profitability are not identical goals, although some of the best news media are also very profitable; for some owners, however, making money is the primary purpose of journalism, and independence and public service mean little. Then, too, diversity at both national and international levels appears to be in decline, and the marked increase of media conglomerates and ownership concentration has reduced the number of independent voices heard in the marketplace. Further, Western news media have suffered loss of both credibility and audiences due in part to the rising and increasingly harsh political rhetoric within democratic societies.

In some democracies, such as Norway and Sweden, the government maintains diversity of political views by providing subsidies to the newspapers of various political parties, a practice not without potential danger to press independence.

Some modifications of the Western concept fall under the rubric of Social Responsibility. This view holds that the media have clear obligations of public service that transcend moneymaking. Public service implies professional standards for journalists as well as reliable and objective reporting. The media are obligated, in addition, to ensure that all voices and views in the community are heard. Further, government is granted a limited role in intervening in media operations and in regulating conditions if public interests are not being adequately served. Government regulation of broadcasting in its earliest years in the United States, for example, represented an example of the Social Responsibility position.

Two other related modifications are the Democratic Socialist concept and the Democratic Participant concept, suggested by Robert Picard. Expressing fears concerning the abuses of private ownership, the

Democratic Socialist theory says that state action is needed to institute new forms of ownership and management and to intervene in the economics of the media.[7] Similarly, Democratic Participant theory reflects a reaction against commercialization and monopolization of the privately owned media, as well as against the centralism and bureaucratization of public broadcasting. Denis McQuail summarized several of its principles: (1) media should exist primarily for their audiences, and not for media organizations, professionals, or clients of media; (2) individual citizens and minority groups have rights of access to media (rights to communicate) and rights to be served by media according to the peoples' own determination of need; (3) the organization and content of the media should not be subject to centralized political or state bureaucratic control; and, finally, (4) small-scale, interactive, and participative media forms are better than large-scale, professionalized media.[8]

These evolving views, which represent some disillusionment with mass-media performance, are found throughout Western democracies, but especially in Northern Europe. Their major disadvantage is that such decentralized, small-scale media are less able to check the abuses of government and corporate power, whether at home or abroad. Yet this debate illustrates a built-in advantage of the Western concept: It enjoys the freedom to criticize and reform its own media system through democratic processes, something that is lacking in the other concepts.

Finally, the Western press concept, with its emphasis on the individual's rights to send and receive information, is well suited as a conceptual framework for the new "personalized media"—computers with modems, faxes, interactive television, and bloggers on the Internet— that are now playing a growing role in international communication (see Chapter 4, "The Internet, Comsats, and Bloggers").

## The Rise and Fall of the Communist Concept

For more than seventy years, the Western concept of the press had been under direct challenge by advocates of the Communist press theory, just as capitalism itself was under assault by Marxist/Leninist economic doctrines. Lenin had written that " 'freedom of the press' of a bourgeois society consists in freedom of the rich systematically, unceasingly, and daily in the millions of copies to deceive, corrupt, and fool the exploited and oppressed mass of the people, the poor."[9]

Many intellectuals and writers were convinced that the Western liberal democracies and their press were outdated and doomed and that the U.S.S.R.'s communism and its party-controlled media were the wave of the future. Even among its critics, the Leninist theory was seen as something new and different—certainly more positive and meaningful than the traditional Authoritarian concept.

Mass media controlled and directed by the Communist Party, Lenin argued, can concentrate on the serious task of nation-building by publishing news relating to the entire society's policies and goals as determined by the top party leadership. To Lenin, the press was an integral part of the Communist Party, which was itself seen as a teacher to instruct the masses and lead the proletariat. The basic postulates of the theory deriving from Marx and Engels with rules of application of Lenin were summarized by McQuail:

> Media should serve the interests of, and be in control of, the working class and should not be privately owned. Media should serve positive functions for society by socialization to desired norms, education, information, motivation, and mobilization. Within their overall task for society, the media should respond to wishes and needs of their audiences. Society has a right to use censorship and other legal measures to prevent, or punish after the event, anti-societal publication. Media should provide a complete and objective view of society and the world according to Marxist–Leninist principles. Media should support progressive movements at home and abroad.[10]

Aside from normative theory, the characteristics of the Soviet press concept that set it apart from Western journalism were these: It was, first, a planned and completely government- and party-controlled system that permitted no competing private media. As Lenin said, there is no freedom for the enemies of socialism; his concept would avoid the abuses of the capitalist press. Second, this one-party press enjoyed a monopoly on news, both coming in and going out. Information was controlled by the state; the Party version of events was all that mattered. This condition lasted through the Stalin years, when foreign broadcasts were jammed and foreign publication barred at the borders. Third, news itself was defined as "positive" information that furthered the goals of the Party, not information of direct interest or relevance to the lives of the Soviet people themselves. A plane crash or a nuclear accident was not news; a government farm report or a new tractor factory was.

Finally, the press, in concert with the Communist Party and secret police, was used to control the people as well as to promote government policies and prepare the public for future policy changes.

The Communist media faithfully served the Party's ruling elite, but their fatal flaw was that they did not serve the interests of the people themselves. As the peoples under communist regimes in Central and Eastern Europe, deprived of political freedoms, saw their economies crumble and fall behind those of the West, they became increasingly disillusioned with their own mass media, which spoke only for authority and failed to criticize or report weaknesses in the ruling communist elites. In the U.S.S.R., much of the same disillusionment existed, but it can be argued that some impetus for reform came from above as Mikhail Gorbachev's *glasnost* policies led to media changes beginning in 1985, well before the upheaval of 1991.

The Communist press theory unraveled over a number of years. First came loss of faith in Leninist ideology: the slogans and buzzwords became increasingly empty. From the 1970s onward, Marxist press advocates no longer extolled the superiority of communist theory and focused instead on criticizing Western media. The practices of communist mass communication, especially as a means of controlling and leading public opinion, continued with some modifications into the 1980s, but without the old ideological fervor. In the Soviet Union's final stages, the communist media were reduced to playing a role similar to that of the secret police: another means of controlling the people.

Concurrently, Western mass communication kept intruding on the closed societies of Eastern Europe and appears to have facilitated the demise of communist regimes. The Soviet media's monopoly on news began to crack early in the Cold War. The BBC World Service, the Voice of America, Radio Free Europe, and other Western broadcasters were widely heard. East Germans watched Western television beamed from West Berlin and the Federal Republic of Germany. Alternative and unofficial forms of publication flourished in the U.S.S.R., and the West learned a new word, *samizdat* ("self-publishing" in Russian).

Despite efforts to keep them out, Western rock music and videocassettes found their way into communist cultures and became hugely successful.

The nuclear accident at Chernobyl in April 1986 signaled a change in the Soviet media's handling of a major "bad news" story. At first, the Soviet government made an extraordinary effort to deny that any catastrophe had occurred, and restricted information even while airborne radiation was detected in Scandinavia and Poland. This reflexive retreat into secrecy illustrated the Kremlin's traditional unwillingness to concede any failings before its people and the world. But abroad, the Kremlin was harshly criticized for failing to provide prompt information about the radioactivity spreading across Europe and for neglecting to warn its own citizens. Gradually, Soviet media were forced, by Western media coverage, to report details even though they were released weeks after the event.

The news void on Chernobyl was filled in part by Radio Free Europe and Radio Liberty, which provided breaking news to communist bloc listeners. In such emergencies, Eastern Europeans were likely to turn to Western radio for information unavailable elsewhere. To obtain information by radio, Voice of America officials reported, people traveled out of the cities to rural areas where jamming was ineffective. Finally, four years later, in April 1990, the Soviet Union finally acknowledged that the medical, environmental, and political consequences of the Chernobyl disaster had been much greater than the Kremlin had ever frankly discussed.

As the Chernobyl disaster showed, the communist media could not deal with foreign competition, something unforeseen in Lenin's closed-system press theory. With Mikhail Gorbachev's proclamation of *glasnost* and *perestroika* in the mid-1980s, changes in media theory and practice accelerated. A Soviet weekly, *Argumenti i Fakti*, with a circulation of more than 20 million, published in 1989 the most detailed account of Stalin's victims yet presented to a Soviet mass audience, indicating that about 20 million Soviet citizens died in labor camps, forced collectivization, famine, and executions. The same year in Warsaw, the first independently published daily newspaper in the Eastern bloc appeared: *Gazeta* supported the newly legalized Solidarity trade union. And, in East Germany, the communist media turned on their former masters and behaved like Western investigative reporters. *Neues Deutschland*, the main communist paper, *Berliner Zeitung*, and *Junge Welt* all published accusations of corruption and profiteering by high Communist Party officials under Erich Honecker. East German television, a week earlier a subservient tool of the Honecker regime, ran a series of sixteen reports depicting the high living of the top Party members. These revelations scandalized the public and reinforced the outcry that forced the Honecker regime from power. From East Berlin to Warsaw to

Prague to Budapest to Moscow, the Communist theory of the press has been left in shambles—in effect, tossed into the much-utilized dustbin of history.

In recent years, as Roger Cohen reported, "Journalism has been reinvented in Eastern Europe as a craft involving independence and objectivity, but politicians remain uneasy and sometimes ruthless about the new press freedom. Through satellite dishes, cable systems and a wide range of publications, the people of the former East Bloc have access to a range of information and entertainment unthinkable under Communism."[11] This is not to say that authoritarian or even totalitarian controls will not return from time to time to some of the news media of Eastern Europe. In Prague, there are fifteen dailies, not all of which may survive. Although media diversity has been established, various problems remain because of economic collapse, legislative confusion, and nationalist awakening. Much concern exists over the future of television, as always a powerful political instrument. Despite efforts to end state television monopolies and open the way for private networks, governments hesitate to act.

Russia's media have increasingly been endangered since Vladimir Putin became president and began presiding over an alarming assault on press freedom. The Kremlin has imposed censorship on news about the lingering civil war in Chechnya, orchestrated legal harassment against private media outlets, and granted sweeping powers of surveillance to security forces. During 2000–2001, numerous violent attacks on journalists were carried out with impunity across Russia. In April 2001, the Kremlin-controlled Gazprom corporation took over NTV, the country's only independent national TV network. Within days, the Gazprom coup had shut down a prominent Moscow daily and ousted leading journalists from the country's most prestigious newsweekly. Despite Gazprom's insistence that these changes were strictly business, the Committee to Protect Journalists reported that the main beneficiary was Putin himself, whose primary critics have now been silenced. Many of NTV's best journalists joined TV-6, which was Moscow's only independent television outlet and had a smaller, but still loyal audience. But then, in December 2001, a Russian court also shut down TV-6. The station's managers and most outside analysts called it a Kremlin plot to force it off the air. Authoritarian may be the best adjective to describe Russia's news media today. By 2004, press freedom and free speech had become so restricted in Russia that Freedom House downgraded the country to "Not Free"—the only country to be so downgraded that year. Putin was said to have adopted the Chinese press model: overly controlled and often intimidated. Russia had become a nation where, it was said, you could kill a journalist and get away with it. Putin's government had failed to solve the murders of eleven important journalists. The national television media were working almost completely under the Kremlin's fist. Newspaper and magazine journalists now show independence at their own peril. Russia extended its press hostility to ABC Television News when it barred all journalists working for the U.S. network on August 30, 2005. The crackdown came in retaliation for ABC's *Nightline* broadcast interview with a Chechen rebel leader who had carried out terrorist attacks in Russia.

Russia provided a harsh example for its fifteen former republics, all of which but the three Baltic states had seen a decline of press freedom. In Turkmenistan, Belarus, and Ukraine (under its former leader Kuchma) ways were found to thwart, control, or even kill journalists. Authoritarian was the best way to describe the news media in that part of the world.

## Revolutionary Concept

Lenin provided both some of the ideology and rationale for another and more ephemeral view: the Revolutionary. Simply stated, this is a concept of illegal and subversive communication, using the press and broadcasting to overthrow a government or wrest control from alien or otherwise rejected rulers.

Lenin in his famous work *What Is to be Done?* (written in exile before the 1917 Revolution) proposed that the revolutionaries establish a nationwide, legal newspaper inside czarist Russia. Such a paper could obviously not advocate revolutionary goals, but its distribution system could be an excellent mechanism for a political machine. The newspaper, Lenin postulated, would be a cover for a far-flung revolutionary organization. The early *Pravda*, although it was not a legal newspaper (and was edited by Stalin at one time), was published outside czarist Russia, and smuggled copies were widely distributed—a fine example of the Revolutionary concept.

The revolutionary press is a press of people who believe strongly that the government they live under does not serve their interests and should be overthrown. They believe they owe such a government no loyalty whatsoever. Pure examples are difficult to find, but one surely was the underground press in Nazi-occupied France during World War II. The editors and journalists of the clandestine press literally risked their lives to put out their papers and pamphlets. Other examples of the Revolutionary concept were the *samizdat*, the secretly typed and mimeographed copies of books, political tracts, and the like that were passed at great risk from hand to hand among dissidents inside the Soviet Union. The history of anticolonialist movements in the former Third World is replete with examples. Throughout the British Empire, especially in West Africa, political dissidents published small newspapers, often handwritten, that first expressed grievances against the British rulers, then encouraged nationalism, and finally advocated political independence. Aspiring political leaders such as Azikiwe, Awolowo, Nkrumah, Kaunda, and Kenyatta were all editors of these small political newspapers that informed and helped organize the budding political parties and nationalist movements. The British authorities were surprisingly tolerant, even though they disapproved of and sometimes acted against the publications and their editors.

Much in the Anglo-American political tradition supported these newspapers, and the editors claimed the rights of British journalists. Had not Thomas Paine used political pamphlets to help run the British out of the American Colonies? Had not Thomas Jefferson said that the people have a right to revolution, including the right to subsequent revolutions if that proved necessary?

In the post-independence years, radio broadcasting has become a valuable tool of revolutionary groups seeking to overthrow the fragile governments of developing nations. Black Africa has been plagued with numerous coups d'etat, and during times of acute political crisis, radio broadcasting has often played a significant role as the primary medium of communication in most nations. So rebels have recognized the importance of controlling information at the political center of power. Hence, insurgents have often seized the radio station before heading for the presidential palace. Military struggles during a coup attempt frequently occur outside the broadcast station, because if rebels can announce over the nation's only radio station that a coup has been accomplished (even while the issue is still in doubt), it helps achieve the desired end.

In Iran, two other communication devices—the photocopying machine and the audiocassette—have proved useful in revolutionary efforts.

The revolution of the Ayatollah Khomeini has been called the first cassette revolution. Thousands of cassette recordings of the Ayatollah's speeches propagating his revolutionary ideas were played in the mosques, which were not kept under surveillance by the Shah's secret police. These small, portable instruments were able to reach millions while circumventing the government-controlled press, radio, and television. At the same time, when revolutionary "night letters" and pamphlets arrived mysteriously at offices in Tehran, sympathetic secretaries made many photocopies, quickly and more secretly than possible with a printing press.

Anthony Sampson said that "the period of television and radio monopolies may prove a passing phase, as we find ourselves in a much more open field of communications, with cassettes and copied documents taking the place of the books and pamphlets that undermined 18th century governments." He suggested an epitaph for the Shah's regime: "He forgot the cassette."[12]

Personalized media, with their interactive capabilities, all present challenges to centralized autocracies trying to control news and information. The continuing struggle of Chinese dissidents for civil rights is an example of the Revolutionary concept. That struggle goes on with dissidents now using the Internet and cellphones to advocate democratic change in China.

## Developmental Concept

By its very nature, the Revolutionary concept is a short-term affair: The successful subversive use of communication to topple a despised regime is self-limiting. After goals are achieved, the gains must be consolidated and then another concept takes over. In recent decades, a variation on the Authoritarian concept—the Developmental concept— has emerged in the wake of political independence in impoverished nations throughout the developing world.

The Developmental concept is an amorphous and curious mixture of ideas, rhetoric, influences, and grievances. As yet, the concept is not clearly defined. Some aspects are taken straight from Lenin and the Communist concept of the press. Perhaps of greater importance are the influences of Western social scientists who have posited a major role for mass communication in the process of nation-building in newly independent countries. American academics such as Wilbur Schramm, Daniel Lerner, and others, all democrats at heart, have argued that the communication process is central to the achievement of national integration and economic development. In so doing, they may have unintentionally provided a rationale for autocratic press controls.

Other more radical academics, mostly Europeans, have echoed Marxist views and added a touch of anti-Americanism to the concept, for the concept is to some extent a critique of and reaction against the West and its transnational media. It also reflects the frustrations and anger of poor and media-deficient nations.

The Developmental concept is an approach to mass communication in nations that are clearly lacking in newspapers, broadcasting, and video facilities—the world's "have-nots" in media resources.

In general, the concept holds that:

• All the instruments of mass communication—newspapers, radio, television, motion pictures, national news services—must be mobilized by the central government to aid in the great tasks of nation building: fighting illiteracy and poverty, building a political consciousness, assisting in economic development. Implicit here is the Social Responsibility view that the government must step in and provide adequate media service when the private sector is unable to do so, as is the case in many poor nations.

• The media therefore should support authority, not challenge it. Dissent or criticism has no place, in part because the alternative to the ruling government would be chaos, it is argued. Freedom of the press, then, can be restricted according to the development needs of the society.

• Information (or truth) thus becomes the property of the state: the flow of power (and truth) between the governors and the governed works from the top down, as in traditional authoritarianism. Information or news is a scarce national resource; it must be utilized to further the national goals.

• Implied, but not often articulated, is the view that individual rights of expression and other civil liberties are somewhat irrelevant in the face of the overwhelming problems of poverty, disease, illiteracy, and ethnicity that face a majority of these nations. (Critics argue that the concept provides a palatable rationale for old-fashioned authoritarianism.)

- This concept of a guided press further implies that in international news each nation has a sovereign right to control both foreign journalists and the flow of news back and forth across its borders. Good examples of this concept are Ghana under Kwame Nkrumah, Tanzania under Julius Nyerere, and Zimbabwe under Robert Mugabe.

Some critics argue that central to the Developmental concept is a rejection of the Western view. As British journalist Rosemary Righter has written, there is a growing feeling that the Western model of the press is undesirable in itself. Instead of backing diversity and free flow, the mass media must adopt a didactic, even ideological, role of explaining to the people their part in forging a new social order.[13]

Western news media are attacked on several scores. To begin with, some critics say that the Western international media are too monopolistic and powerful; they penetrate too widely and effectively. The world news organizations—the AP (the Associated Press), CNN, Reuters, the BBC, and AFP (Agence France-Presse)—are particular targets, charged with creating a clear imbalance, a one-way flow, and a near monopoly of news that favors the affluent North. Furthermore, Western media represent an alien viewpoint, which they impose on nations trying to build independent modern identities. Traditional cultures, it is charged, have been threatened by the inundation of news and mass culture—television programs, pop music, movies, videocassettes, and audiocassettes—principally from the U.S. and Britain. Such domination, it is argued, amounts to cultural aggression. But nonetheless, in recent years, the Western approach has been gaining wider acceptance.

Finally, a few proponents of the Developmental concept have long charged that the Western media are part of an international conspiracy by which the economic and political interests of the capitalist nations are using global mass communication to dominate, even subjugate, the developing nations. Some advocates of this concept argue that the world needs a "new international information order" to redress these imbalances.

The Developmental concept is a view of mass communication from the many nations of the former Third World, where most citizens are people of color, poor, ill-nourished, and illiterate, and it reflects resentments against the West, where people are mainly Caucasians, affluent, and literate. The concept is related as well to what some feel is the major problem facing the world today: the widening gap between the rich and the poor, debt-ridden, "failed" nations. The same nations that decry the trade and GNP (gross national product) imbalances between North and South also excoriate the Western news media. Echoes of the Developmental concept are being heard in current protests and demonstrations against globalization.

By the mid-1990s, the Developmental concept appeared to be losing momentum among developing nations. The current global trends toward more democracy and market economies appear to have boosted the Western press concept, but the odds that many of the new democracies will succeed are not good. At the same time, the Communist press concept appears to have disappeared as a viable press theory. Communist regimes persist in North Korea, Cuba, and the People's Republic of China, but the ideological fervor and justification seems to have waned—only police states remain.

China has jettisoned Marxist economic theory while holding onto centralized, totalitarian controls over its people. The resulting mix has been called "market socialism," and has produced a rapidly growing economy that seems to have something in common with the corporate capitalism or neo-authoritarianism of its Asian neighbors, South Korea, Singapore, and Malaysia. The Chinese people have been prospering economically, but enjoy little freedom of expression as China has emerged as a major economic force in the world (for more on China, see Chapter 7).

The controversies engendered by these conflicting concepts of mass communication have long been marked by rancor, but this, too, has shown some signs of abating. Currently, ideological conflict between press systems seems to have clearly subsided, if only temporarily. Some would argue that in today's world only two concepts of the press are viable: the Authoritarian approach, which insists on its right to control news and information and restrict its circulation; and the Western concept with its variations, which argues that news and information, like knowledge itself, belong to all people and that journalists have the right to pursue and report news wherever it can be found.

Yet there remain valid arguments on all sides of these political and cultural confrontations, each reflecting differing social and political traditions that are difficult to reconcile. But as the international news system becomes more integrated and interdependent, the conflicts over how news and information are to be controlled may diminish. Although few if any nations fit neatly into any of these five normative concepts of the press, the concepts are still useful in illustrating some of the divergent perceptions of the nature of news and how it should be disseminated.

Despite the variety of news and views refracted through the world news prism, the great bulk of foreign news is still gathered and disseminated by Western news media. In recent years, two clear trends have emerged: the triumph of the Western or liberal concept of the press and the reality that many more millions of people, mostly in the Eurasian landmass, have joined the vast world audience of international communication. Both trends are integral aspects of the globalization of the media.

## Notes

1. For this analysis, the authors owe a debt to the classic book by Fred Siebert, Theodore Peterson, and Wilbur Schramm, *Four Theories of the Press* (Urbana: University of Illinois Press, 1956). In 2004, another important book, *Comparing Media Systems: Three Models of Media and Politics*, by Daniel Hallin and Paolo Mancini (Cambridge University Press, 2004) has added new insights to the interaction between media and political structures.
2. Daniel Hallin and Robert Giles, "Presses and Democracy," in *The Press*, G. Overholzer and K. H. Jamieson, eds. (New York: Oxford University Press, 2005), 4.
3. "Indonesian Government Bans Correspondent for the Times," *The New York Times*, November 27, 1990, sec. A, 7.
4. Hallin and Giles, "Presses and Democracy," 5.
5. *Associated Press v. United States*, 52 F.Supp.362, 372 (1943).
6. See Vincent Blasi, "The Checking Value in First Amendment Theory," *ABA Research Journal*, no. 3, Summer 1977, 521–649.
7. Robert Picard, "Revisions of Four Theories of the Press," *Mass Comm Review*, Winter/Spring 1982–3, 27.
8. Denis McQuail, *Mass Communication Theory: An Introduction* (Beverly Hills: Sage, 1983), 96–7.
9. Mark Hopkins, *Mass Media in the Soviet Union* (New York: Pegasus, 1970), 55.
10. McQuail, *Mass Communication Theory*, 93–4.
11. Roger Cohen, "Propaganda to Journalism: Europe's Latest Revolution," *The New York Times*, December 27, 1992, sec. A, 15.
12. Anthony Sampson, "Rebel Poli-Techs," *The New York Times*, May 5, 1970, 15.
13. Rosemary Righter, *Whose News: Politics, the Press, and the Third World* (New York: Times Books, 1978), 14–15.

# Chapter 3

# The International News System

*What we are building now is the nervous system of mankind, which will link together the whole human race, for better or worse, in a unity which no earlier age could have imagined.*

—Arthur C. Clarke

When an unexpected global calamity occurs, such as the earthquake and tsunami on December 26, 2004 that reverberated throughout the Indian Ocean, news media immediately begin gathering all available details about the horrendous events (for unusual aspects of reporting the tsunami stories, see Chapter 5).

The tsunami story, like most major news stories, was essentially reported by journalists working for the news organizations of Western nations. To their clients, news has—like electricity, water, and gas—become an essential service that is taken for granted. By merely turning on a radio or television set or picking up a newspaper at the door, or logging on to the Internet, people expect to find the latest news, whether it be from the Middle East, Europe, Africa, or wherever. (Such is not the case, however, among the rural poor of developing nations.)

Indeed, most people in the industrialized world cannot remember when important breaking news was not available immediately (like any other public utility) at the flick of a switch; the technicalities of news delivery are of little public concern and only dimly understood at best. The fact is, however, that global news communication is of fairly recent origin. The far-flung apparatus or "system" through which news flows around the world has evolved and expanded greatly since World

War II, along with our modern information society. We learned, for example, about the important battles of World War II many hours or often several days after they began—and then only through radio or newspapers. About thirty years later, the daily clashes in Vietnam were delivered in full color on our home television screens at dinner time, sometimes on the same day they occurred.

Naturally, the public's perceptions of warfare have always been colored by the way journalists have reported them, but color television pictures of modern wars, including U.S. dead and wounded, had an unusually strong impact on public attitudes. And today, with the ongoing war in Iraq, the public follows many dramatic news events in real time. Hence, the impact is greatly enhanced.

In our time, and particularly since 1945, an intricate web of international communications has been spun about the planet, greatly expanding the capability for news and political interaction at a time when the need for information has become so much more urgent. This rapid growth of what Colin Cherry termed an "explosion" in mass communication around the world has had widespread significance: for international relations and world politics; for the flow of news and information; for the cultural impact abroad of motion pictures, television, and video from the West; and for the institutions of international communication, including news agencies, broadcast networks, international newspapers, magazines, and the now ubiquitous Internet. Today, the world reacts politically and socially much more quickly, and perhaps emotionally, to events than ever before.

As we become, in various ways, a more interdependent world community with common problems and dangers, if not common values and goals, the world's ability to communicate effectively with all its parts has been greatly expanded. We now have an expanding global economy, and we are trying to develop institutions to deal with it. Reliable news and adequate communications are of prime importance in today's world.

This communication explosion has three broad dimensions: geographically, vast areas of Africa, South and East Asia, and Latin America have been drawn into the global communication network for the first time; the amount of traffic and the number of messages carried in the system have multiplied geometrically; and the technical complexity of both the new hardware and the skills and specialized knowledge needed to maintain and run the network has become increasingly sophisticated.

"For two thousand years and more the means of distant communications were various postal services, derived from the Roman cursus publicus, working at the speed of the horse (up to and including the Pony Express); and then the explosion hit us, not immediately upon the invention of the telegraph, but nearly a century later," Cherry wrote. "It is the sheer suddenness of the explosion which is of such profound social importance, principally following the Second World War."[1]

Advancing from crystal sets in 1920 to a television service in 1937 took, as Cherry pointed out, only seventeen years. The first transistor appeared in 1948, and electronic memory chips, the silicon brains of microcomputers, came soon after that. The first Sputnik went up in 1957, and only eight years later Early Bird, the first generation of the global INTELSAT system of communication satellites, went into operation in 1965 and brought television pictures from Europe. Just twenty-five years later, INTELSAT VI was in the heavens and, compared with Early Bird, had fifty-five times more power and a total communications capacity that had increased 170 times. Comparing the communications capacity of Early Bird INTELSAT I to INTELSAT VI, a major carrier of international news, is like comparing the height of a toolshed with a skyscraper in New York City.[2] Today, the Internet with its rambunctious progeny—interactive newspapers, online broadcast media, and many bloggers—has added additional dimensions to international news, including gossip, advocacy, and misinformation.

## The International News Tradition

The expanded international news system is largely an outgrowth of Western news media, especially those of Britain, the United States, and, to a lesser degree, France and Germany. A world news system exists today because the peoples of Western democracies wanted world news, and the great independent newspapers, news magazines, news agencies, and, later, broadcast organizations have cooperated and competed to satisfy those wants and needs. Editors and correspondents, working for independent (that is to say, nongovernmental) and profit-making news organizations, have developed the traditions and patterns of providing the almost instantaneous world news upon which people everywhere have come to rely. The credibility and legitimacy that such news generally enjoys rests on its usually unofficial and independently gathered nature as well as its informational or generally objective content. The enduring ethic of Western journalism was summed up more than 100 years ago by an editor of *The Times* of London:

The first duty of the press is to obtain the earliest and most correct intelligence of the events of the time, and instantly, by disclosing them, to make them the common property of the nation. The duty of the journalist is to present to his readers not such things as statecraft would wish them to know but the truth as near as he can attain it.

That nineteenth-century statement represents a journalistic ideal; actual practice is often much different. Some transnational media have close, compromising ties to their governments, and all independent media are subject to varying kinds of controls and influences from the corporate interests that own them. Nonetheless, the news media of Western nations have more freedom and independence to report world news, and hence more credibility, than media of other nations. And because of greater financial resources and technology, Western media have a greater capability to report world news. Although the press in different nations will differ sharply about the facts and importance of particular news stories, the process is essentially one of international cooperation.

Some press and broadcasting organizations use their own correspondents to report foreign news, but the global workhorses and the linchpins of the world news system have long been the so-called world news services: the AP, UPI (United Press International), Reuters, AFP, and TASS, which are in effect "newspapers for newspapers." It is no coincidence that they come from the United States, Britain, France, and the former Soviet Union. (With the breakup of the U.S.S.R., TASS, now Information Telegraph Agency of Russia, or ITAR-TASS, has slipped considerably in importance.) In a general sense, great powers have been great news powers. Today, however, the continued importance of France and Britain in world news may owe more to relationships developed during their imperial pasts than their geopolitical importance today.

What made these five organizations world agencies was their capability to report news from almost anywhere to almost anywhere else. Although they are sometimes perceived as dominating world news flow, the Western agencies are definitely not in an economic class with such powerful multinational corporations as Mitsubishi, Exxon, or Shell. UPI, for example, has been in a shaky financial condition for more than two decades and has been teetering on the edge of collapse, its operations drastically cut back. AFP has been losing money for years and depends on subsidies from the French government. Reuters is a major news service, yet is only a part of a successful larger organization that specializes in business and financial information.

In 2005, the Associated Press, with 242 bureaus, a total staff of 3,700, and more than 6,000 subscribers, processed 20 million words and 1,000 photos daily and had an annual revenue of about $630 million. Yet, as a cooperative mainly owned by U.S. newspapers, the AP is the dominant institution in the world news system.

News organizations in two great economic powers, Deutsche Press Agentur (dpa) in Germany and Kyodo News Service in Japan, are approaching world-agency status. Other second-tier agencies are ANSA in Italy, efe in Spain, and Mena in Egypt. In addition, there are numerous national agencies that serve as important vital links, especially in the developing nations, between the major world agencies and the "retail" newspapers, broadcast stations, and other recipients of the reports of the AP, Reuters, and AFP. The world services sell their reports to the national agencies, which in turn distribute the news reports to local media that otherwise might not receive them. Finally, the national agencies stand as key gatekeepers (and potential censors), deciding which news can and cannot be distributed to the local media within their own nations.

Some of the great newspapers of the world—*The Times, The Daily Telegraph*, the *Financial Times, The Independent*, and *The Guardian* of London; *Le Monde* of France; *Frankfurter Allgemeine* of Germany; *Neue Zürcher Zeitung* of Switzerland; *Asahi* of Japan; *The New York Times, The Washington Post*, the *Los Angeles Times, The Wall Street Journal*, and others in the United States—maintain their own correspondents abroad. The same is true of the extensive broadcasting systems BBC, CBS, NBC, ABC, CNN, and others, as well as the leading news magazines such as *Time, Newsweek, The Economist, L'Express*, and *Der Spiegel*. Other important regional dailies are the *The Hindu* and *The Times* of India, *Al Ahram* of Egypt, and the *New Straits Times* of Singapore.

Several newspapers, such as *The New York Times, The Washington Post*, and the *Los Angeles Times*, as well as *The Guardian* of London, syndicate their news and sell it to other newspapers at home and abroad. As a result, their news stories and features supplement as well as compete with the world news agencies. It is well to remember that once a news event is reported—the death of a king or a major earthquake—this information becomes the common property of journalism and can be repeated anywhere; only the precise wording of a news story can be copyrighted, and this rarely becomes a factor in news flow.

A survey in 2002 reported on the foreign bureaus of major U.S. papers. *The New York Times* had forty reporters in twenty-six bureaus;

*The Washington Post* had twenty reporters in twenty-six bureaus; and the *Los Angeles Times* had twenty-one reporters in twenty-six bureaus. Knight-Ridder had fourteen reporters in fourteen bureaus. *USA Today* had four reporters in four bureaus. Regional papers with five or more bureaus included the *Chicago Tribune* (ten), *Newsday* (five), *The Dallas Morning News* (five), *The Baltimore Sun* (five), and *The Boston Globe* (five).

The expansion in overseas coverage has happened, in part, because of the expanded interest in overseas business and financial news, a key aspect of the global economy. This interest explains the 119 reporters in forty bureaus of *The Wall Street Journal*, with its business focus and overseas editions. Reuters and Bridge News (formerly Knight-Ridder financial news) have hundreds of overseas staffers to report specialized business news. Bloomberg News, another financial news service, has 226 reporters in sixty-two countries.

With the growing importance of broadcast media, people receive more and more of their news from electronic sources, especially television. As a result, two television news services, Reuters TV (formerly Visnews) and Associated Press Television News (APTN), as well as the great Western networks, have been playing an increasingly important role in the international news system. Live feeds from another continent are usually identifiable as the work of the network involved, but the source of the news on tape or film is not as evident. Most viewers are unaware that much of the foreign news viewed on television is supplied by two television news agencies, dominated by American and British interests.

Reuters TV, the biggest and best known, is the world's leading supplier of international news video and film for television, servicing more than 409 customers in eighty-three countries, and is distributed by both satellites and air-mailed videocassettes. Reuters TV says it reaches 1.5 billion people daily. In 1992, Reuters bought out its co-owners, NBC and BBC, and changed its name from Visnews. Reuters TV staffs thirty-eight bureaus and works with contract crews in about seventy countries.

The Avis of these services is APTN, also located in London, which remains a center and clearinghouse for international news exchanges. APTN was founded in 1994 as Associated Press Television, and in 1998 it merged with Worldwide TV News (WTN) to form APTN. Both services have exchange agreements with the U.S. networks, ABC, CBS, NBC, and CNN, all of which maintain several bureaus overseas. The U.S. networks sell some of their news products abroad and thus contribute to the interchange that makes the international news system work. Video news agencies like these do not produce programs that TV viewers can use. Rather, they provide footage of an event with only natural sound and very little editing. This is sent out via an encrypted video stream that is distributed on three satellites for global coverage.

Eurovision, the regional television exchange system in Western Europe, gets about 40 to 50 percent of its material from Reuters Television and APTN. The majority of television systems around the world depend on these two services for all of their world news on television. In numerous small African nations, often a lone television service depends on a five-minute package of world news from Reuters TV for its entire foreign coverage.

It can be said with some, but not much, exaggeration that a Westerner's right to know is the world's right to know. For any news story that gets into the European or U.S. news media can, and often does, flow rapidly around the world and can appear in local media anywhere if it gets by the various gatekeepers that select and reject the news of the day. Stories about civil war in Chechnya, the war in Iraq, or terrorist bombings in Egypt can and often will be read or viewed or listened to in Africa, Asia, and Latin America.

The domination of international news by the AP and other Western news organizations is often resented in other nations. The poorer nations particularly are dependent on the Western agencies and media to find out about themselves and their neighbors. They criticize what they consider a one-way news flow from North to South, from the rich to the poor. They resent the fact that Western journalists with Western values set the agenda for the world's news. (This is changing as Asian news media rise in influence.)

There is some basis to complaints about this Western-dominated system. But the West does not enjoy a closed monopoly of world news; any news organization is free to report world news, but few as yet have the capability and credibility for so doing. Moreover, far ranging and technically sophisticated as it is, the world's present news system is not as pervasive and efficient as it might be, considering the world's diversity and its need for information.

## Global Television News

The successful establishment of the twenty-four hour Cable News Network (CNN), with its global reach, has been a major innovation in international news as well as in competitive U.S. cable television news.

Ted Turner, the Atlanta, Georgia, broadcaster, launched the around-the-clock news service to attract viewers to cable television and to compete in news with the three major U.S. networks. Started in 1980, its growth and success have been impressive—and imitated. From a single network available to 1.7 million U.S. households to its current 23 networks reaching some 260 million households worldwide, CNN is seen in more than 200 countries. (CNN's domestic service reaches another 71 million homes.) So when a world crisis such as the 9/11 terror attacks occurs, CNN plays a major role in informing the world quickly. CNN and its companion cable service, Headline News, have an estimated value of $1.5 billion. CNN employs 1,800 staffers in nine domestic and nineteen overseas bureaus, all feeding their reports through Atlanta to CNN's widening global audience. In the 1990s, when CBS, NBC, and ABC were cutting back on overseas operations, CNN was opening new bureaus in such places as Nairobi, New Delhi, Frankfurt, Paris, and Beijing—at a cost of about $600,000 to open and staff each additional office overseas.

During an international crisis, CNN plays a special global role. Whereas ABC, CBS, and NBC will issue news bulletins and then go back to scheduled programming and perhaps do a late-evening wrap-up, CNN stays on the air for long stretches of time, continually updating the story. The three major networks' version of the story will be seen in the United States; CNN's version will be seen all over the world. Overseas, travelers often can watch CNN in their hotel rooms, foreign television services pick up the whole service or some news programs from CNN, and individual television viewers can get it off their satellite dishes or subscribe to the service locally.

During prolonged crises, such as the Gulf War, CNN can play a key role with its extensive coverage of all facets of a story. Indeed, CNN's international position often makes it a player in diplomacy as well as a reporter of major events. With its reports available in all world capitals, political leaders and diplomats watch closely and are willingly interviewed on CNN in order to get their views widely known. (CNN recognizes its near-diplomatic status, and reporters are aware of the danger of being manipulated by their interviewees, whether they be George W. Bush or a spokesman for Osama bin Laden.)

Recently, CNN has not been without its problems and its critics. When there is not an international crisis or a celebrity scandal or trial, viewership of CNN drops off sharply, and revenues from advertising have declined as well. During the O.J. Simpson trial, audiences soared when CNN provided gavel-to-gavel coverage, often to the neglect of foreign news coverage.

It can be argued that CNN is primarily a technological innovation in international news by reason of its ability to interconnect so many video sources, newsrooms, and foreign ministries to so many television sets in so many remote places in the world. In this regard, CNN has undoubtedly had a major impact on diplomacy as well as global news. Nonetheless, a television news channel of true global reach was an innovation whose time had come and, as proof of that, CNN now has serious competition at home and abroad.

In 1991, the BBC began its own World Service Television (WST), now called BBC World, and has been expanding it rapidly. Since 1997, BBC World has been challenging the dominance of CNN International. BBC World has a twenty-four hour international current affairs TV channel with BBC news, documentaries, interviews, and so on. Unlike the radio service, it is commercially funded and is widely carried on satellite and cable.

In what has been called the newest public utility, the 24/7 cable-news-television industry, CNN has been bucking stiff competition from MSNBC and Fox News Channel (FNC). MSNBC is owned jointly by NBC and Microsoft, and has averaged a higher daily audience than CNN. Fox News Channel, which appeals to a more conservative audience than the other two cable channels, has been making large gains. Since 9/11, the cable channels have been competing fiercely. During the first week of coverage, CNN pulled in a near-record number of viewers. CNN was first among all cable networks for the week of September 10–16, pulling in 3.07 million cable and satellite households. That was one million more households than second-place FNC. However, in early 2002, FNC pulled ahead of CNN and has stayed there ever since.

Both Rupert Murdoch, owner of FNC, and NBC have had their sights on global networks similar to CNN International and BBC World. Some experts argue that in normal times the overwhelming interests of audiences everywhere are not about global news per se but, in a more focused way, about their own region and locality. Yet as the most recent global crisis shows, global television news takes center stage once again by reporting, explaining, and influencing the world's response to great events.

The success of CNN and BBC World illustrates the ways that media technology can shape the contours and impact of international news— and will continue to do so. International radio broadcasts, both shortwave and medium wave, are also major purveyors of global news. But because of their roles in public diplomacy, the BBC World Service and the Voice of America are discussed in Chapter 11.

With the greatly enhanced technological reach of international communication, the location of a sender or receiver is no longer as important as it once was. The key gatekeepers of the world news system are still concentrated in New York City, London, Paris, and similar metropolitan centers, but it is not necessary to be in those cities to follow the news of the world. A shortwave radio or a satellite dish, and now a computer with an Internet connection, can keep a person almost anywhere in touch with the day's principal events. Furthermore, distance has become increasingly less a factor in the cost of long-distance news communication, whether it takes place through a private telephone, computer or fax messages, television reception, or news reports bounced off satellites. Essentially the same technological process (and at the same cost) is required to send a news flash via satellite from London to Paris as from London to Tokyo. And the greater the traffic on the system, the lower the unit cost of the messages sent. International communication is tied to computer technology, and in that explosive field the costs of computers are dropping as rapidly as their efficiency is increasing. In addition, the capacity of communication satellites to carry information is expanding. Much of the content of the international news system concerns popular culture—video, movies, music in its many forms, youth life styles and attire—all of which appeal to a global youth culture found literally everywhere. Besides traditional news, the system carries news about the widely known and admired icons of pop culture, the singers, musicians, dancers, rappers, and movie stars. The commonalities of this youth culture were well shown on July 3, 2005, by the Live 8 concerts in eight major industrial nations plus South Africa, in an effort to pressure leaders at the Group of 8, then meeting on aid, to mitigate poverty in Africa. Over a million young people attended, while another five million watched AOL's live video streams on their computers. The music, performers, and their message resonated around the world.

## Cracks in the Conduits

If technology is the good news, then performance in recent years is the bad news. In earlier years, the American "national media"—particularly

*The New York Times, The Washington Post,* the *Los Angeles Times, The Wall Street Journal,* CBS, NBC, ABC, *Time,* and *Newsweek*—which set the news agenda for other media, did much of the gathering of news from abroad with the help of news agencies.

But that situation changed around 1989 when the Cold War ended. The television networks and the news magazines gave much less attention to serious foreign news. One indicator: In its heyday, CBS maintained twenty-four foreign bureaus; by 2002, it had nine reporters in only four capitals: London, Moscow, Tel Aviv, and Tokyo. Dan Rather admitted to Harvard students, "Don't kid yourself, the trend line in American journalism is away from, not toward, increased foreign coverage."[3]

Max Frankel, former editor of *The New York Times,* wrote, "A great shroud has been drawn across the mind of America to make it forget that there is a world beyond its borders. The three main television networks obsessively focus their cameras on domestic tales and dramas as if the end of the Cold War rendered the rest of the planet irrelevant. Their news staffs occasionally visit some massacre, famine, or shipwreck and their anchors may parachute into Haiti or Kuwait for a photo op, but these spasms of interest only emphasize the networks' apparent belief that on most evenings the five billion folks out there don't matter one whit."[4]

Foreign news is expensive to gather and often not of interest unless American lives—as soldiers or terrorism victims—are at stake. Instead, network television and the news magazines shifted their resources and considerable talents into high-profile stories of scandal, celebrity, and sensation, such as stories of White House sex scandals, the violent death of Princess Diana, and the celebrity trials of O.J. Simpson and later Michael Jackson.

The content of *Time, Newsweek,* and *U.S. News and World Report* reflected the declining interest in global news. Throughout 1995, *Time* devoted 385 pages, or 14 percent of the magazine, to international news. *Newsweek* used 388 pages, or 12 percent of its coverage, and *U.S. News* had 386 pages of foreign news, or 14 percent. For all three magazines, this was a significant decline from ten years earlier. In 1985, *Time* had run 670 pages, or 24 percent, of foreign news; *Newsweek* had 590 pages, or 22 percent; and *U.S. News* 588 pages, or 22 percent.[5] There was evidence from polls as well that the public of Western nations had become less interested in foreign and any other kinds of news and were increasingly cynical about journalism.

However, a few major U.S. daily papers still report the world. The best and most comprehensive foreign reporting, some of very high quality, comes from just six daily newspaper groups, those owning *The New York Times*, *The Washington Post*, *The Wall Street Journal*, *Chicago Tribune* (including the *Los Angeles Times*), *The Christian Science Monitor*, and *The Baltimore Sun*, all of which maintain overseas news bureaus. These papers, whose total daily circulation is about 11 million, represent only about 20 percent of newspaper circulation of all U.S. dailies. This small group plus the AP and Reuters are the prime sources for foreign news. It should be noted that a good deal of serious foreign news is available to radio listeners of National Public Radio's two daily programs, *All Things Considered* and *Morning Edition*. Major British and European newspapers and broadcasters still cover world news in large part because their readers demand it.

But as the events of September 11, 2001, demonstrated, the news media of America and other Western nations responded, and responded magnificently, to the challenges of the new war on terrorism. Several months later, after the crisis had eased somewhat, the media, particularly television, went back to its old habits of not much news from abroad.

The elaborate international news system is still in place and is fully capable of handling any major news that breaks anywhere in the world.

## Notes

1.  Colin Cherry, *World Communication: Threat or Promise?* (New York: Wiley Interscience, 1971), 57–8.
2.  Joseph Pelton, "Heading for Information Overload," *Inter-Media*, Autumn 1988, 19.
3.  Stephen Hess, *International News & Foreign Correspondents* (Washington, D.C.: Brookings Institution, 1996), 61.
4.  Max Frankel, "The Shroud," *The New York Times Magazine*, November 27, 1994, 42.
5.  Ibid.

# Chapter 4

# The Internet, Comsats, and Bloggers

*We are laying the foundations for an international information highway system. In telecommunications we are moving to a single worldwide information network, just as economically we are becoming one global marketplace. We are moving toward the capability to communicate anything to anyone, anywhere, by any form— voice, data, text, or image—at the speed of light.*

—John Naisbitt

The so-called new media (some not so new)—camcorders, cellphones, satellite phones, bloggers on the Internet—have been transforming the traditional ways that news has been gathered and reported.

When the tsunami roared through Indian Ocean beaches, drowning thousands, in late 2004, the first video and photos the world received came from camcorders held by tourists caught in the deluge. Long before press photographers could reach the area, the vivid video was being viewed by millions around the world.

Similarly, when London subways were attacked by terrorists on July 7, 2005 (7/7), the first dramatic photos came from Londoners trapped underground, who recorded the scenes on their cellphones. Many of these dramatic pictures were quickly available to the world, not on television screens or in newspapers but on bloggers' websites.

In both cases, the news media's role of providing the "first draft of history" was being challenged by ordinary citizens with a gadget in their hands. The effect is to accelerate the speed with which news and pictures of great events travels about the globe. Compare these recent news stories with the U.S. presidential election of 1920—the first reported by radio. Station KDKA in Pittsburgh kept a few people informed about election tabulations and newspapers carried the final results the next day. But it was two weeks before many people in scattered rural areas learned the news that Warren Harding had defeated James Cox for the presidency. The drastic differences between then and now dramatize the reality that the mechanics of delivering the news to an interested public is a significant factor in the communication process. New technologies have been shaping and changing editorial content in diverse ways. News, particularly international news, has over the years been directly affected by each new invention. The postal service, telegraph, cable, telephone, and radio in turn have each greatly extended the reach of foreign correspondents and world news agencies and the speed with which they can deliver news, each innovation supplementing rather than replacing earlier methods of communication.

Like other institutions and organizations, the news media—newspapers, news services, radio stations, television, cable channels and networks, and news magazines—are being strikingly altered by the information revolution. News communication is being dramatically affected by ongoing revolutionary changes in communication satellites, computers, digitalization, miniaturization, and the Internet.

Stuart Loory pointed out that information was once transferred from one power center to another in Washington, D.C., by newspapers, but that recently, television news, mainly CNN, has been doing the job: "The executive and legislative branches increasingly exchange news and views via live, ubiquitous coverage."[1] Now, new technologies make it possible for international journalists to do for the entire world what domestic television and, to a lesser extent, print media do in Washington. "The corollary," Loory said, "is that television will have increasing significance for foreign policy making. Programs like ABC's 'Nightline' and 'Capital to Capital' and events like the 'spacebridge' [two-way live conversations between nations] have demonstrated the possibilities."[2] Here again, we see the steadily increasing importance of CNN, MSNBC, BBC World television, and other global news media.

To these media must now be added the Internet, which has been playing a facilitating and supplementary role in the rapid dissemination of a fast-breaking story—either a trivial Hollywood scandal or the ominous events of the latest terrorist attacks. Online news junkies have quick access not only to more news but also to a heady mix of unconfirmed rumor, conjecture, commentary, discussion, and conspiracy theories.

Sometimes, rumor and conjecture find their way into the legitimate news media. Further, the Internet and twenty-four hour cable news cycle can greatly accelerate a story, often to the detriment of traditional journalistic practices such as verifying sources and creating context. More and more people are getting their news from cable and the Internet.

## The Key Role of Satellites

In our concern with how international news moves about the globe, the significant changes initiated by communication satellites, a major by-product of the space age, must be recognized. Recently, there has been a quantum jump in the ability of people to talk to and see one another. Marshall McLuhan once wrote that we were experiencing a "global electronic village" being created by television. John Naisbitt countered that it is in fact the communication satellite that is "creating a super tribal community unlike any environment previously known to mankind since the Tower of Babel."[3]

In the past thirty-five years, global telecommunications by satellite have achieved remarkable results. Joseph Pelton pointed out that "trillions of dollars of electronic funds transfers and hundreds of millions of dollars of airline reservations flow through global networks each year. Billions of conversations carry on international business, diplomacy, finance, culture, and recreation as a matter of routine."[4] Included in these vast communication flows are, of course, the world's news in pictures, sounds, data, and words.

Our interest is with the impact of telecommunications on international news flow. And the most immediate short-term effect of Comsats (that is, communication satellites) is a reduction in the cost of long-distance communications and a corresponding increase in the amount of words, data, and images exchanged. In other words, more news is flowing at less expense. We have seen dramatic changes in long-distance telephone calls, which form the bulk of traffic on the INTELSAT system; that system is operated by a multinational consortium controlling long-distance point-to-point Comsat communications.

Arthur C. Clarke dismissed the notion that Comsats are merely an extension of existing communication devices and do not engender much change. He placed Comsats in the same class as the atomic bomb and automobile, "which represent a kind of quantum jump which causes a major restructuring of society." Clarke recalled a parliamentary commission in England 100 years ago when the chief engineer of the post office was asked to comment on the need for the latest American invention, the telephone. The engineer made this remarkable reply: "No Sir. The Americans may have need of the telephone—but we do not. We have plenty of messenger boys."[5]

That telephone, in time, came to have its own revolutionary impact on modern life, and now the personal letter has been replaced by the long-distance call as well as by fax and e-mail. And telephone services, as has been noted, constitute the primary activity today of communication satellites and are the major source of revenue for INTELSAT. (The telephone and its wireless version, it should be noted, are major tools as well in news gathering—formerly local tools but now used globally.)

At the end of the 1970s, the traffic of INTELSAT still consisted mostly of people talking to people, but since the mid-1980s, at least half the information volume has consisted of machines communicating with other machines. The mind-boggling information-carrying capacity of INTELSAT VI is driving this trend, and INTELSAT VII, launched in 1993, followed by INTELSAT VII-A, in 1995, have continued it. Pelton developed a term, TIUPIL, to show the relationship between human capabilities of processing information and the speed of the information machines—present and future. A "TIUPIL" represents the "Typical Information Use Per Individual Lifetime" and was defined as twenty billion bits of information: the total information received by a person who lives seventy years and processes some 27,000 written or spoken words a day. A TIUPIL can be transmitted on INTELSAT VII in a matter of just seven seconds, or about nine times a minute. "Soon we will have networks of satellites capable of sending up to 100 billion bits of information in a second. This means we will have machines capable of processing information thousands or even millions of times faster than the human brain," Pelton wrote. "If one asks why we need such high-speed machines, the answer is clearly for machine-to-machine communication. Once we have communication satellites and fiber optic cables capable of handling super high-definition, 3-D television, the meeting of telephone or human data requirements will be small potatoes indeed."[6]

Although they have been called microwave relay towers in the sky, Comsats do have broader, unique properties. They do not link just two points, but many. They can simultaneously receive and transmit to many places, sending a panoply of message forms—television, telephone, telex, photo facsimile, fax, and high-speed computer data. For example, an increased mobility of money is a result of the computer revolution.

Today, satellite systems are operational at the international (intercontinental) level, the regional (continental) level, and the domestic (national) level. Satellites extend the range of over-the-air broadcasting systems, but they have a much greater impact on satellite-cable networks. CNN and various other cable services, such as Home Box Office and other pay services, extend their reach dramatically by being tied in with cable services. In addition, numerous specialized satellite systems are functioning, such as those designed for military, data relay, and maritime and aeronautical purposes.

INTELSAT is the largest and oldest system, with fifteen satellites (plus backups) over the Pacific, Atlantic, and Indian Oceans. Some 120 nations, each with its own earth segment, belong to the consortium, and any two member countries can communicate directly without going through former colonial capitals. User countries, territories, and possessions total about 170, operating internationally on almost 1,500 preassigned pathways. INTELSAT also functions as the carrier for national domestic services in about thirty countries.

Comsats have greatly expanded the capacity of news media to move international news around the globe, but the ability of the satellites to relay color television signals, giving that medium a global impact, is what has made Comsat technology such a significant mass communication development. This is true even though television use accounts for a comparatively small proportion of the monthly revenue of INTELSAT.

When Early Bird, the first commercial Comsat, was launched in 1965, the principal television use was expected to be for occasional live events such as sports, state funerals, space missions, and the coverage of disasters and wars. Although reportage of such major events still accounts for much television traffic on INTELSAT, the most extensive and consistent use of the global system is for daily television news "packages" sent from one country to another. The U.S. networks—NBC, CBS, and ABC—plus CNN daily incorporate satellite news feeds from their correspondents in various parts of the world or, for special coverage, sporadically purchased from foreign broadcast news services, such as Reuters Television or APTN.

Innovations in communication technology are changing both the ways that global news is gathered and disseminated and the ways that individuals receive the news. The speed and scope of foreign news reporting is constantly expanding as the use of laptop computers is increasing. Foreign correspondents have long said that their worst problems are not censorship or other authoritarian restraints, but logistics— getting to the remote news scene, such as an earthquake in Peru or a civil war in Congo, and then getting the story out. The technology to solve part of that problem has been developed and increasingly utilized: especially small portable computers that can transmit stories over phone lines (or by wireless) directly to newsroom systems. Initially, these portables were used to cover golf matches, auto races, football and basketball games, and court trials, but now journalists covering the whole range of news carry them.

A major technological advance for television reporting was the development of new, highly portable "satellite uplinks," which can be disassembled, checked as baggage, and flown to the site of a breaking story in order to feed back live reports. A "flyaway" dish can become a temporary CNN or ABC bureau in just the time it takes to get one on the scene. Other innovations useful to reporters in the field (as well as to individual citizens) are the portable wireless telephone and the video telephone.

This advance means that an editor can telephone a foreign correspondent, whether he or she is covering a conference in Geneva or a war in Central Asia. And that correspondent can, if necessary, send in the story by his or her cordless telephone or by videophone to a television station.

Another significant aid for reporters today is databases, which are collections of text or numbers that are stored in computers. Online databases, of which there are now thousands, are mainly for the retrieval of information by researchers who can tap into a data bank through telephone lines attached to a computer terminal. Increasingly, newspapers and broadcasters have used such sources for investigative and general reporting. Distance is not a factor, for in a matter of minutes a U.S. reporter can gain access to anything printed in a British newspaper or a journal in Japan. Closer to home, the reporter can call up and scan the full text of about seventy dailies offered by various newspaper databases; such as the Nexis database, which carries more than 140 international newspapers, magazines, news services, and newsletters.

A further utilization of Comsats that is changing the structure of daily journalism is facsimile production and distribution of national and international newspapers, pioneered by *The Wall Street Journal.* Each day, a fax of every page of the paper is sent from its production plant in Chicopee, Massachusetts, to twelve or thirteen various printing plants around the country. The page-size fax pages are processed onto offset pages. *The Wall Street Journal* has extended this expertise to Asia for its subsidiary, *The Asian Wall Street Journal.* This kind of technological innovation, plus an informative, well-written news product, has moved *The Wall Street Journal* to 2,070,000 in circulation in 2005.

Another national daily newspaper, the Gannett Company's *USA Today,* has employed the same facsimile production methods, circulating 2,280,000 copies in 2005 from thirty U.S. printing sites. In 1985, *USA Today* began beaming facsimile pages of its international edition to Singapore for printing and distribution in the Far East. Other publications routinely utilize facsimile transmission technology, including the *International Herald Tribune* of Paris, *Die Zeit* of Hamburg, *China Daily,* *The Economist,* *Time,* and *Newsweek.* The national edition of *The New York Times* is printed in several regions of the United States to facilitate its same-day delivery across the nation.

## Personalized Media

Innovations in information media—personal computers with Internet connections, photocopiers, printers, fax capabilities, modems, videocassettes, cordless and mobile telephones, interactive television, databases, cable, and satellite connections—all often considered "personalized media," are having profound effects on the audience or recipients of international news. In fact, the term *audience* is itself becoming a bit obsolete, because it implies a mass of passive receivers of communication. Increasingly, personalized media are supplementing traditional media in the affluent West, but less so in developing countries.

In today's information societies, an individual is no longer a passive recipient of news or entertainment, but now is an "information seeker" who can select or choose his or her news or information from a widening variety of sources, many of which governments are unable or unwilling to control. Further, individuals themselves, such as those involved in computer networking, become sources of information; that is, communicators. Autocratic governments find it difficult to control personalized communications.

With a personal computer and a modem connected to a telephone or wireless, a person can tap into the fast-growing Internet system, providing access to thousands of databases, including news publications and other current information from home and abroad. Further, that receiver can become a sender by freely communicating with other computers through the Internet, e-mail, and various networks and bulletin boards.

Another recent innovation enables a traveler to receive at his or her hotel, for a price, a copy of his or her favorite newspaper when far from home. The technology, which allows anyone with an Internet connection and a printer to receive images of participating newspapers around the world, was developed by a Russian company, called IBS. Therefore, a hotel can receive copies of some eighty-three newspapers and, on request by a hotel guest, can print a copy of any of these on a laser printer.

The printed word has changed as well. Fax, the same technology that sends the *International Herald Tribune* from Paris to Hong Kong, sends millions of documents, letters, and messages across continents and oceans. Facsimile transmissions have played a role in challenging or even toppling unpopular regimes, from Iran to Panama to China to the collapsing Soviet Union. Not only does fax foster immediate human interaction across great distances, it also facilitates the vital flow of information into and out of repressive regimes.

Digital recorders, both video and audio, have greatly enhanced the ability of individuals to choose what they will hear or see and, as a result, have expanded rapidly in recent years even to remote corners of the Southern Hemisphere.

Much of the talk of an "information superhighway" involves the idea of a merging of computers, telephones, and televisions (video, text, and sound) to provide new delivery systems and content options. Two models for the so-called "infobahn" are offered: broadcast and the Internet. In the broadcast model, entertainment would be the driving force, leading to the 500-channel future, with features such as video on demand, interactive home shopping, entertainment, and advertising. The latter model is on the lines of the Internet, the vast computer/communications network begun in 1969 that now connects many millions worldwide. The two models exist and compete side by side.

## The Internet and International News Flow

The potential of the Internet for international news communication is beginning to be realized, but is still very much a work in progress. Daily, the Internet carries more news than 1,600 daily newspapers can provide to a worldwide audience of 40 to 50 million Internet users. More and more Internet users are getting their news online and from media in far-off places.

In 1990, twenty newspapers were available online; by 2000, 4,925 were worldwide, with 2,799 of them in the United States. Despite the recent fall of technology stocks and the demise of many dot coms, experts believe these numbers in time will only go up, and websites will carry more and more news to ever-larger audiences. Here and abroad, the print media as well as cable and network broadcasters are in hot pursuit for these proliferating Internet news seekers.

An Internet user in Pakistan, Paris, or Pretoria can read the online edition of *The New York Times*, *The Times* of London, or *Die Zeit* of Hamburg. Major newspapers and other news media, such as magazines, radio and television broadcasters, and cablecasters, from a variety of mostly Western nations—what was formerly called the "foreign press"—are available in ways never before possible for those with the means and inclination to log on. The impact on journalism education is obvious: Instead of going to a university library to peruse back copies of several dozen foreign newspapers, a journalism student today using his or her computer can read, study, and compare hundreds of publications and broadcasting outlets of many countries. Many other related sources are available as well. For example, by calling up www.memri.org, the website of the Mideast Media and Research Institute, a student can read translations from Arabic of what the Arab press and broadcasters are reporting and proclaiming about the war on terrorism.

The BBC's impressive utilization of the Internet has placed the broadcast giant in direct competition with British newspapers. Starting its online operations in 1998, the BBC now has 525 sites. It spends $27 million on its news website and this is backed by the BBC's vast news gathering resources, including 5,000 reporters scattered around the world, which is funded by its annual £2.8 million subsidy from the British government. The success of the BBC's news website clearly troubles British newspapers. Its audience has increased from 1.6 million unique weekly users in 2000 to 7.8 million in 2005. The news website has a breadth and depth that newspapers have difficulty keeping up with.[7]

The Associated Press has adopted the Internet to distribute its articles and photographs over the global Internet. In so doing, it has followed other mainline news organizations into uncharted journalistic territory. The AP's great rival, Reuters, announced in 2000 similar plans to reposition itself as a high-flying Internet player. Reuters plans to spend $802 million to shift its delivery systems to the Internet.

The Internet incorporates many elements of various print and electronic media that have preceded it. Computers can be used to send and receive text, sound, still images, and video clips. Yet for all its versatility, the Internet is not expected to replace its predecessors, but to take its place alongside them as a social, cultural, and economic force in its own right. No longer a curiosity, the Internet has become another way for to people find out what is happening in the world.

Much news or information on the Internet is of dubious value and may be deliberately wrong or misleading. During the weeks after the September 11 attacks, the Internet was overwhelmed with wild rumors, deliberate misinformation, and conspiracy theories. But the discriminating and critical viewer could still find solid, reliable information because the world's best news organizations—newspapers, news magazines, television, and radio services—were reporting the real news daily. (An important role for professional online news media is to act as a check on unreliable and unsubstantiated reports.)

The Internet has certain unique advantages. For example, CNN Interactive, which is one of the world's busiest news websites, with some 3.5 million "page views" a day, features extensive original coverage of environmental and ecological issues. Although Internet users are still comparatively small in numbers, many interactive news media go into depth on all kinds of stories that receive only a minute or two on television or a few paragraphs in a newspaper story. Cyberspace is not limited by the time restraints of broadcast news or the space limitations of the printed media.

Cybernews so far is complementing the traditional news media, but may soon become a new kind of journalism. John V. Pavlik wrote, "Since networked news can be interactive, on-demand, and customizable; since it can incorporate new combinations of text, images, moving images, and sound; since it can build new communities based on shared interests and concerns; since it has the almost unlimited space to offer levels of reportorial depth, texture, and context that are impossible in any other medium—new media can transform journalism."[8]

Perhaps the single most significant characteristic of the Internet is that it is a communication device that lets people share ideas (including news) on a global network. This feature suggests that international news communication has made tremendous strides in the past twenty-five or so years, which is the age of the personal computer. A PC with a modem, either hooked up to a telephone line or wireless, means that the world—literally the world—is more available than ever before. Not only individuals but professional news media now can reach and hold not just audiences or readers, but also communities of people with shared concerns literally anywhere in the world.

## Bloggers Join the Fray

Internet journalism and international news have been influenced by the rapidly growing army of bloggers. A "blog" (web and log) is technically someone's record of the websites he or she visits. Bloggers have been called one-person Internet blabbermouths, who pop off to anyone who will listen. They criticize each other but, more importantly, they take on the mainline media. Sometimes right and often wrong, they provide a kind of instant feedback loop for media corrections. They often write personal diaries and commentaries, with the best of them weighing on the pressing issues of the world. They report news items that the traditional media ignore or suppress, and they provide links to other bloggers with something to say. Anyone can be a blogger and no one is in charge.

Their sheer numbers are mind boggling: in mid-2005, a website, Technorati, reported an astonishing growth: nearly 80,000 new blogs are created every day and there are some 14.2 million in existence, and of these 55 per cent remain active. Some 900,000 new blog postings are added every day. Their influence is increasing—some are quoted on regular media and some media have their own blogs—and being on the Internet, their reach and influence can and does become global.

In Madrid, David and Alfonso Rojo publish the Periodista Digital, a widely read blog with 115,000 registered subscribers. Daily, about 4,000 people log on to headlines about the highs and lows of public life in Spain. Doreen Carvajal reported that "The Web is a sprawling space that has spawned new breeds of digital gadflies like the Rojos and an assortment of self-appointed cybermonitors of the conventional news media of Europe. Across the world, their sharp comments can evoke an array of reactions: amusement, insults, public outrage, blunt legal threats. Yet these websites and blogs are scoured by the policy makers and the political elite."[9]

A popular German blog, Bildblog, attracts 300,000 readers a month, mainly because of its fact-checking of Germany's largest daily, the tabloid *Bild*, with a 3.8 million circulation. Four journalists with other day jobs scrutinize *Bild* for errors and miscues. The site attracts about 10,000 visitors a day.

Richard Posner wrote that "in effect, the blogosphere is a collective enterprise—not 12 million separate enterprises but one enterprise with 12 million reporters, feature writers, and editorialists with very little little costs. It's as if Reuters or the AP had millions of reporters, many of them experts, all working for no salary for free newspapers that carried no advertising." If Posner is correct, the influence of the bloggers on international news media may be considerable, even if far flung and almost impossible to measure.[10]

Communications over the Internet have greatly multiplied and amplified the voices, information, exhortations, and diatribes passing through the world news prism. More people than ever before are getting information, tuning in, tuning out, and forming opinions. This is what freedom of expression is all about.

Thoughtful persons in mainstream journalism—the "news business"—are well aware of the importance as well as the many pitfalls for journalism on the Internet. Publishers, broadcasters, and journalists believe that the news media must be involved with the Internet, but neither they nor anyone else seems to know where this brave new world of communication is headed.

Internet journalism is still in its infancy and is continuing to expand as readers, especially younger ones, turn to the Internet for a fast take on the news. The beneficiaries of this continued audience growth continue to be the largest and best-known national news organizations —those that stress national and international news.

The Internet is still an ancillary news source for most people, after broadcasting and newspapers, yet the audience for news and information sites is growing. Some of the most frequently used U.S. news websites are www.msnbc.msn.com, www.cnn.com, www.nytimes.com, www.abcnews.go.com, www.usatoday.com, www.washingtonpost.com, www.time.com,    www.latimes.com,    www.foxnews.com,    and www.wsj.com.

## International Concerns about Cybernews

The rapid spread of interactive journalism has raised some nagging issues. For example, who will benefit and who will not? Globally, the information revolution has been flourishing mainly in America, Japan, Western Europe, and other industrialized countries. The poor nations want the new media, but lack the economic and social infrastructure to utilize and sustain them. Not many of Africa's fifty-four countries are linked to the Internet, and experts warn that unless Africa gets online quickly, what is already the world's poorest continent risks ever-greater marginalization. Without network connectivity, large areas of Africa will be prevented from participating in many evolving aspects of life on this planet. As in all nations, the younger, better educated, and more affluent are using the Internet; the poor, the undereducated, and the elderly have no way to access the information highway. But some major gains have been made in India and China.

Among Western democracies, there are unresolved questions about how much freedom of expression (including press freedom) can be legally permitted on what is being recognized as the most participatory marketplace of ideas the world has yet seen.

The Internet faces more draconian censorship from authoritarian regimes or despotic rulers. The small, affluent, and authoritarian nation of Singapore thinks it can control the technologies of freedom that threaten its one-party rule. To control television, satellite dishes have been banned, and the country has been wired for cable television, thus enabling the government to screen out objectionable material. Controlling cyberspace is more difficult, but Singapore is trying. Schools are equipped with computers, and Singaporeans are urged to link up with the Internet by dialing a local telephone number. Thus, the government can monitor Internet usage through the local servers. Local officials concede that some users can bypass this system by dialing into the Internet through foreign phone systems. Singapore is not expected to be able to sustain such controls over the flow of electronic information that is so essential for the global economy (for China's controls on the Internet, see Chapter 7).

## Implications of Rapid Change

To summarize, innovations in communication technology suggest certain broad trends for transnational journalism:

1.  The unit cost of international communication of news will continue to drop as usage of the world news systems increases, and as the efficiency, speed, and reach of the hardware become greater.

2.  Technology is making it possible to send and receive news and other essential information from almost anywhere in the world and with increasing speed. The continuing integration of computers with telecommunication means much more interactive, or two-way, communication.

3.  The two-way capability of cablevision, tied in with Comsats and personal computers on the Internet, means that information users can seek out or request specific kinds of information or news and not remain a passive mass audience. The two-way capability of telecommunications means that there will be more two-way flows of information, with consumers having more choice about what they receive. The trend toward such interactive communications systems is clear, as the rapid increase in the numbers of bloggers shows.

4.  Because of continuing technical improvements, the potential numbers of channels and sources of information are virtually unlimited, and the possible varieties and kinds of future "content" stagger the imagination.

5.  These personalized communications, typified by bloggers, the Internet, e-mail, fax, videocassettes, and cablevision, present a challenge to authoritarian governments, which traditionally control their newspapers and broadcasting. How does Big Brother stop someone from watching a pirated videocassette, or from calling up distant information on the Internet, or picking up news off a satellite, or receiving e-mail from a dissident group overseas?

6.  Finally, concern is growing about the effects of all this greatly expanded communication flow on its global audiences. Most people spend no more than an hour a day reading newspapers or getting the news from television or radio, but the news volume cascades on. David Shenk wrote that in the middle of the last century, "We began to produce information much faster than we could process it. We have moved from a state of information scarcity to a state of information surplus—from drought to flood in the geological blink of an eye." In his recent book, *Data Smog: Surviving the Information Glut*, Shenk argues that information overload is bad for your health, promoting stress, memory overload, compulsive behavior, and attention-deficit disorder. Shenk argues

that the well-known global village, created by mass communication, is at the same time growing increasingly fragmented and fractionalized as people, despairing of being able to master a grand overview, retreat into their own special interests. He argues that cyberspace, including the Internet, promotes a highly decentralized, deregulated society with little common discourse and minimal public infrastructure.[11]

Concerned persons are pondering the implications of all this. Society, in short, faces the danger of computer/communications technologies advancing faster than our ability to develop methods of controlling and using them for the general welfare of humankind. This has always been true of technologies, but today that gap is becoming ominously wide. Nonetheless, innovations in media technology will continue to shape international news. Julius Barnathan of ABC News sees the development of multilanguage broadcasts as an impending and important innovation. One video will be accompanied by as many as eight narrations.

Finally, Pelton of INTELSAT saw much more to come: "New and perhaps totally different architectures for space communications are likely to evolve in the 21st century and the long-term growth and development of space communication seem relatively well-assured. In short, the 21st century should see the beginning of the true long-term road to space communications, making it truly the beginning of the 'golden age' of space communications."[12]

## Notes

1. Stuart Loory, "News from the Global Village," *Gannett Center Journal*, Fall 1989, 167.
2. Ibid.
3. Joseph Pelton, "Heading for Information Overload," *Inter-Media*, Autumn 1988, 19.
4. Ibid.
5. Arthur C. Clarke, "Beyond Babel: The Century of the Communication Satellite," in *Process and Effects of Mass Communication*, W. Schram and D. Roberts, eds. (Urbana: University of Illinois Press, 1971), 952.
6. Pelton, "Heading for Information Overload."
7. "Old News and a New Contender," *The Economist*, June 18, 2005, 52.
8. Pelton, "Heading for Information Overload," 20.

9. Doreen Carvajal, "Europe Teems with Web Dailies That Twit the Mainstream Press," *The New York Times*, February 21, 2005, sec. C, 7.
10. Richard Posner, "Bad News," *The New York Times Book Review*, July 31, 2005, 1.
11. Michico Kakutani, "Data, Data, Everywhere, and All the World Did Shrink," *The New York Times*, July 8, 1997, sec. B, 6.
12. Pelton, "Heading for Information Overload," 21.

# Chapter 5

# The Impact of Great News Events

*Real news is covered the same way that real wars are won: by putting enough
boots on the ground.*

—Tim Rutten of the *Los Angeles Times*

Great news events of our times have given us insights into the role that
global news plays in assisting and accelerating political and social change.
Intensive television coverage of such an event as the air war over Kosovo
and Serbia does not determine the political outcome of such crises, but
reporting (or nonreporting) has a clear impact on public opinion, which
in turn may well influence decisions made by government leaders of
great nations.

Today, fast-moving changes are being shaped by transnational communication. Not only have speed and volume increased along with
greater geographical dispersal of international news flow, but the nature
and effects of the content have changed and diversified as well. Instead
of the mere words and numbers of yesteryear's news, today vivid color
video coverage of news events is now delivered to the world's news
publics, greatly increasing the impact of the message. As a result, a new
kind of audience involvement in world events has emerged. The propaganda maxim that the report of the event can be as important as the
event itself has greater impact than ever in the age of media events.

In this chapter, we will look at journalistic aspects of five great news
stories: the tsunami battering South Asia, the 9/11 attacks on the U.S.,
the collapse of Soviet communism, the 1991 failed coup in Moscow,
and interactions between terrorist attacks and global television.

## The Tsunami Batters South Asia, Killing Thousands

After an underground earthquake off the coast of Sumatra on the day after Christmas 2004, a giant wave radiated throughout the coastal areas of Indonesia, Thailand, Sri Lanka, India, numerous islands, and even to the coast of East Africa. The death toll climbed to over 220,000 dead or lost, and the homes and livelihoods of millions were devastated.

The disaster rippled beyond South Asia, making it a tragedy of global proportions. Among the casualties were thousands of vacationers of fifty nationalities from outside the area. The missing included 1,500 from Sweden, 700 to 800 from Norway, and over 100 each from New Zealand, Denmark, the Czech Republic, Italy, Germany, and Israel. The disaster's reach was an unsettling reminder that globalization can bring the world together in tragic ways.

The world's news media responded quickly, as thousands of images from around the region poured out to television networks. Video compression technology, fed by digital cameras and enabled by satellite and videophones, along with laptops with uplink capabilities, meant that the world was viewing the deadly aftermath just hours after it had ended.

Soon after that, real-time video footage of the tidal wave striking the shore, much of it taken by tourists on or near beaches in Thailand, began appearing on network broadcasts. In this disaster, there had been a reversal of the news-gathering process. Usually, reporters would get a story and then commission a photographer to go and get the pictures. In this case, the reporters were chasing the pictures and trying to create some context for what the viewers were seeing.

Some saw the tsunami story as a kind of tipping point in so-called "citizen journalism," of which bloggers are a part. Digital technologies—the Internet, e-mail, blogs, digital cameras, camera phones—have enabled people on the scene of a news event to share with professional journalists the capability to reach a wide audience, and show the world what they saw and experienced.

"Tsunami videos" proved a boon for bloggers trying to attract viewers. Dozens of locations on the Internet hosted amateur videos of the Indian Ocean disaster. Many video bloggers were deluged with requests to see more of the dramatic scenes. One blog created just after the disaster, Waveofdestruction.org, logged 682,366 unique visitors in four days. Another site, named "Cheese and Crackers," went from attracting about ten surfers a day to 640,000 visitors after showing the tsunami videos.

But the tidal wave and its follow-up stories of the relief and reconstruction efforts of the outside world were also a boon for the so-called "mainstream media." Tim Rutten, media critic of the *Los Angeles Times*, noted that the story vindicated the indispensability of the mainstream media. He said that in their response, "they have fulfilled the most basic of journalistic obligations—the duty of witness. They have placed the suffering and loss of millions before the conscience of the developed world, and the result has been a demonstration of human solidarity across national, religious and culture divides that seemed beyond reach just a month ago."[1]

Using front-page stories as a measure, in the first several days *The New York Times* published fifty-three stories on the tsunami, the *Los Angeles Times* thirty-eight and *The Washington Post* thirty-one. In Britain, the BBC had audience increases of as much as 50 percent for its regular nightly news programming. CNN, with its extensive overseas staff, saw its daily audience increase by 38 percent and its prime-time viewers grew by 46 percent. CNN had eighty journalists on the scene within days of the disaster and the BBC had 100 people in the field. Rutten commented that "Real news is covered the same way that real wars are won: by putting enough boots on the ground."[2]

Most of the world responded generously with money and assistance for disaster relief. Finally, the tsunami story was a truly global drama that had victims and heros but no villains—no human ones, anyway.

## The 9/11 Terror Attacks on the U.S.

The news of a single day has rarely had such a profound effect on modern history. December 11, 1941—the date of the surprise attack on Pearl Harbor that brought America into World War II—was such a day. September 11, 2001—the terrorist attacks by hijacked airliners into the World Trade Center towers in New York City and the Pentagon in Washington, D.C.—was another historic day that set off a global upheaval with still unforeseen repercussions. After the collapse of the two skyscrapers, the scarring of the Pentagon, the crashing of four airliners, and about 3,000 lives lost, Americans and many others worldwide no longer felt personally secure and safe from the threats of a dangerous world beyond their borders. The United States and its allies promptly embarked on a war against terrorism.

News coverage of the many facets of 9/11 was comprehensive and magnificent. In New York and Washington, D.C., journalists reported a local story of great national and international import. Global color television—nonstop and constantly updated—carried unfolding details to every corner of the world. Supplemented by radio, print media, the Internet and cellphones, much of the world saw and heard nearly the same video images and news reports that Americans received. And the U.S. audience was huge: 79.5 million viewers were watching news coverage on broadcast and cable television networks in prime time on September 11, according to Nielsen Media Research.[3]

On September 14, three days later, 39.5 million viewers tuned in to television news coverage in prime time. The Internet audience (which is international) was huge as well. The number of page turns (hits) on just www.cnn.com jumped to 162.4 million.

Moreover, that vast audience approved of the way both the U.S. government and the media had responded. According to a poll by the Pew Research Center for the People and the Press, 89 percent of people felt the media had done a good or excellent job in covering the attacks.[4] Professional journalists agreed.

So after more than a decade of looking inward and often ignoring the outside world, the news media, as well as thoughtful citizens, began showing a more serious interest in world affairs again; in particular, trying to understand radical Islam and the complex politics of the Middle East and Central Asia. The nature and motives of Osama bin Laden became a subject of intense public and media interest—at least for a while.

A Pew poll taken in October 2001 found that the terrorist attacks and the war in Afghanistan had created a new internationalist sentiment among the public. There was more support for a multilateral foreign policy than before 9/11, with roughly six-in-ten (59 percent) now saying that interests of the allies should be taken into account by U.S. policy makers. By a two-to-one margin, the public thought that taking an active role in the world, rather than becoming less involved, would be a more effective way of avoiding problems such as terrorism in the future. And support for assertive U.S. leadership also had grown.[5] These opinion shifts were dramatic, but did not last.

Since 9/11, the major national news media had been given a chance for redemption, reporting with great competence a global news story with many dimensions. Because of budget cuts and fewer overseas reporters and bureaus than earlier, the broadcast networks—ABC, NBC,

Fox, and CBS—were the least prepared for this new "asymmetrical" war against terrorism, which has no standing armies to confront: its enemies are hidden, subversive, and of differing nationalities, but are found in "training camps" in remote areas of the developing world—in Afghanistan, and maybe in Iraq, Syria, Somalia, and Sudan. Or, probably some terrorists have been living in the West for many years in deep cover and waiting for the chance to strike—a new challenge for reporting as well as for governmental counter-terrorism efforts.

The 9/11 events thrust CNN back into clear leadership among the twenty-four hour cable services, because of its wide reception overseas. CNN was expected to report on American retaliation to terrorism wherever and whenever it occurred. During the first weeks after 9/11, CNN's audience, normally about 600,000 to 800,000, jumped to three million U.S. listeners. (As time went on, these totals slipped.)

The 9/11 coverage on network television was important, unprecedented, and revealing about television news itself. Network news showed it could still mount a powerful system of news coverage; no U.S. network or cable system performed badly. Viewers depended on Tom Brokaw, Dan Rather, and Peter Jennings (all three no longer anchors) not only for news but for reassurance and solace. In the first weeks, television coverage was unabashedly patriotic, with American flags much in evidence, but the public apparently didn't mind. In those first days, television news ran up huge costs but carried few commercials. The major print media dispatched platoons of reporters and photographers to cover whatever could be found out in Afghanistan, Pakistan, or wherever. Similarly, many journalists from Europe followed suit.

Americans were also getting their news from other sources: BBC television reporters scored several major scoops in Afghanistan, because the British government was more forthcoming with news. Although the press received high marks for its initial war coverage, the news media still faced controversy when reporting news from the "homeland." Some thought that a few members of the press had forsaken their traditional skepticism and were too willing to be a pawn of government and accept only the official versions of events. But other critics argued that the press was unpatriotic at times—too sympathetic to war protesters, and tending to overplay stories about collateral damage to civilians and reports of atrocities by the U.S. military.

All agreed this was a different kind of war—if, indeed, it was a "war." For the first time since the end of the Cold War, the press had a major international news story to focus on—one with staying power.

## Electronic Execution of Soviet Communism

The collapse of communism in Central and Eastern Europe in 1989, along with the end of the Cold War, were two of the most significant political events since World War II (some said since 1848), and were all the more dramatic because they were so unexpected. Certainly Western mass communication—going over, under, and around the Iron Curtain—played a role in raising expectations and in breaking the communists' monopoly on information and popular culture.

Critic George Steiner commented on the impact of television soap operas:

> Once "Dallas" had come their way [it could be picked up several hundred kilometers east of Checkpoint Charlie], once tapes of Western soap operas and rock jamborees could be multiplied and sold beyond the "Dallas line," the cataclysm and saturnalia were inevitable. Television sparked the great wild surge toward a consumer economy, and television packaged (brilliantly) the actual rush. Why live by bread alone when there is peanut butter? Why endure as a Soviet satellite when the word "satellite" means cable television?[6]

The dramatic and sudden collapse of communism in Eastern Europe came after a generation of communication interactions between the Western nations and the socialist nations of Eastern Europe, the U.S.S.R., and the Third World—all set in the context of the Cold War. Recent economic successes of the West, along with the failures of socialist political economies, helped explain the media changes. Further, the sheer pervasiveness of Western communications accelerated modifications of and, in time, the abandonment of communism and its press theory.

Western journalism rode the crest of the technotronic revolution that had reshaped global mass communication during the past generation and created the information societies of the West. (One Russian general said that the U.S.S.R. lost the Cold War because it was hopelessly behind the West in computer technology.) Communication satellites, computerization, global television, high-speed data transfers, and especially new media products such as videocassette and audiocassette players, all spurred by profit-making opportunities, has led to a vast flood of Western television programs, movies, videocassettes, CDs (compact disks), and taped music recordings, moving inexorably from Western to Eastern Europe.

Grist for this vast mill has consisted of not only Western pop culture (movies, TV shows, music videos, and rock and other popular music) but also newspapers, magazines, and books. Western versions of the news, along with Western methods of news reporting and presentation, became widely accepted and emulated. The AP, Reuters, CNN, the BBC and Radio Free Europe, Radio Liberty, and the *International Herald Tribune*, among other media, added diversity to the monolithic news structure of the communist regimes. Whatever their shortcomings, Western media had a crucial advantage over communist media: They were not government controlled and hence they achieved a wide credibility. Consequently, centralized communist governments lost their monopoly over their own information.

Western news media acted as catalysts for political change in communist nations in several ways: People in Eastern Europe did listen to Western broadcasts, which carried both world news and news about the satellite nations themselves.

Much of this news went by shortwave radio, some by AM and FM broadcasting and, for East Germany, via television from West Berlin and the Federal Republic. German-language television was received all over the GDR (German Democratic Republic) except in low-lying Dresden, which was locally dubbed the "Valley of the Ignorant" because of the poor TV reception there.

Some observers believe the beginnings of the breakup of the communist empire in Eastern Europe began with the successes of the Solidarity trade union in Poland. The Polish communist regime's monopoly on news was broken in two ways: first, by the rise of alternative newspapers that challenged the government and supported Solidarity goals; and, second, by a triangular communication flow between the alternative papers, foreign reporters, and international broadcasters. It worked this way: Foreign journalists reported news of Solidarity to their Western media; these stories were beamed back to Poland via international shortwave radio, particularly by the BBC, Deutsche Welle, and Radio Free Europe; then the stories were also picked up by the alternative papers in Poland.

This communication model was followed again and again. Michael T. Kaufman, who covered Poland for *The New York Times*, wrote:

> It turned out that a few dissidents using non-violent means, and exploiting the freedom of the press and airwaves beyond their borders, could in this increasingly interconnected world bring down autocrat after autocrat. Foreign correspondents wrote for their own papers, but their reports

were translated and beamed back to countries where such information as they were writing was banned. The spread of portable radios and videos made such information much more accessible. The official press was forced to offer more information, more truth, as it was forced to compete for credibility with the outsiders. . . . Once informed, the people were mobilized. In most places, they marched and chanted and drew placards and with the world press watching such means proved sufficient to expose previous forbidden truths and to make revolutionary changes that had so recently seemed impossible.[7]

In the revolutionary events of 1989, the media played a variety of roles. One was to report that such things happen and that times are changing. Another was to show that the world was indeed watching and that the Berlin Wall could be turned into a sieve. A third purpose was to show potential demonstrators in other countries that the unthinkable was perfectly possible. So, uprisings in East Berlin, Budapest, Prague, and Bucharest all reinforced one another.

For William E. Henry of *Time*, the triumphs owed something to journalism but little to journalists:

> The function of news people was not sage or analyst but conduit, carrying the raw facts of an amazing reality to the startled citizenry in each revolutionary nation and to a waiting world beyond. . . . The thrills of 1989 and early 1990 came as useful reminders that the most interesting part of the news business is, in fact, the news. For broadcast journalists, events proved anew that the chief element of their much discussed power is the simple capacity to reach many people quickly—and in cases of true turmoil, with a verisimilitude no other medium offers. TV's basic function was as the great legitimizer.[8]

## The Failed Coup in Moscow

Communications was one of the major reasons why the right-wing coup d'etat failed to topple the Soviet government in August 1991. The nine coup leaders arrested Mikhail Gorbachev, closed down all but a handful of Communist Party media, and held a television press conference proclaiming the new government. They assumed that the nation would passively accept the changeover. However, the coup masterminds failed to understand how much the Soviet Union had changed in six years of *glasnost*. With a more open communication system and a new taste for free expression, the resistance in Moscow rallied around Boris Yeltsin. They used fax, photocopying machines, and cellphones to let fellow citizens know it was not too late to resist the coup. Inexplicably, the plotters shut down neither international telephone lines nor the satellite relay station, and they did not jam shortwave radio. No actions were taken against the large foreign press in Moscow, which sent out a flood of words and pictures to a disapproving world. CNN was even received in some Soviet republics. It was as if the coup leaders became immobilized, like deer before car headlamps, by the television camera lights recording and transmitting the events within the parliament and the street barricades outside. Soviet journalists, emboldened by *glasnost*, refused to accept the coup restrictions. Blocked at the printing plants, dozens of independent publications ran off photocopies and passed them out on street corners. Moscow's subway was quickly papered with handbills. Interfax, the independent news agency, distributed underground reports along with its own stories.

The impact of Western radio was even more impressive. The BBC doubled its Russian-language program to eighteen hours, its largest increase ever. It also relayed the banned broadcasts of a Moscow station. Radio Liberty's twenty-four hour broadcasts, in Russian and eleven other Soviet languages, reached an estimated audience of 50 million. Gorbachev later said he gratefully listened to the BBC, RL, and the Voice of America while under house arrest at his dacha in the Crimea.

As *Newsweek* commented, "The coup leaders apparently relied on popular indifference and fear of authority. But those are not the attributes of people in the know. And last week Russians proved that they have entered the information age."[9]

Ironically, the new communications openness that propelled Boris Yeltsin to political power after the failed coup also caused him severe political damage in the winter of 1994–5, when he sent the Russian army into Chechnya to put down a rebellion. In Moscow and throughout the nation, millions of Russians watched television pictures of the brutal suppression of the revolt and the killing of thousands of civilians. And many Russians did not like what they saw.

## Terrorism and Television

The very nature of global television and telecommunications, that can bring people closer together while sharing the mutual grief of tragic events, such as the assassination of John F. Kennedy or the tsunami disaster in South Asia, also can be manipulated to capture the world's attention. Unquestionably, certain acts of international terrorism, such as jet hijackings, political kidnappings, and civilian bombings as in Oklahoma City, are perpetrated primarily to capture time and space in the world's media. Terrorism has been called "propaganda of the deed"—violent criminal acts, usually directed at innocent civilians, performed by desperate people seeking a worldwide forum for their grievances. Experts disagree over terrorists' motives.

Terrorism, of course, is not new. But the flare-ups of the phenomenon since the 1960s—especially in the Middle East, Northern Ireland, Latin America, Turkey, Italy, West Germany, Spain, and now the United States and Britain—have been facilitated in part, some say, by global television coverage that beams images of terrorist violence into millions of television sets around the world. Many terrorist groups have mastered a basic lesson of this media age: Television news organizations can be manipulated into becoming the final link between the terrorists and their audiences and, as with all sensational crimes, the more outrageous and heinous the terrorist act, the greater attention it will receive in the world's news media. Walter Laqueur said, "The media are a terrorist's best friend. . . . Terrorists are the super-entertainers of our time."[10]

In this age of global television, the effects of 9/11 and the 7/7 attacks in London were deeply felt in many lands. Whether in Madrid, Jerusalem, Shanghai, or Jakarta, the news and video were filtered through the prisms of differing cultures, ethnicities, politics, and religion. But the most important reaction was in Washington, D.C., where the Bush administration, supported by U.S. public opinion, vowed to strike back hard at terrorism.

After 9/11, international terrorism became a major concern at the top of the foreign news agenda as well as the global political agenda. After being downplayed by news media for years, terrorism was major news again; the "acts of war" on September 11 immediately triggered a new kind of war with Islamic terrorists and any states supporting them. The risk of future attacks of such a devastating nature was raised from "possible" and "unlikely" to "probable" and "likely" in the minds of editors and security officials alike.

A positive result was that the American public woke up to the importance of foreign news; the nation was reminded that we live inseparably in one world—a world that can be threatening and dangerous.

The news media were reminded of the perils of neglecting foreign news since the 1989 fall of communism. Historians may be critical of American presidential leadership for failing to respond sharply to terrorist acts against America during the 1990s. And much of the news media, particularly local media and broadcast and cable television, can be faulted for not informing the public (and government) adequately about the growing dangers coming out of the Middle East conflicts: the bombing of Marine barracks in Lebanon; the bombing of Air Force living quarters in Saudi Arabia; the blowing up of U.S. embassies in Nairobi and Dar es Salaam; and the attack on the *U.S.S. Cole* in Yemen—all precursors to 9/11.

For the first time since 1812, when the British burned down the White House, Americans realized that their two-ocean defensive shield could be penetrated. (In 1941, Hawaii was still a territory.) People realized we were now vulnerable to bioterrorism and even nuclear attacks as well as suicide bombings. In addition, airliner hijackings returned to the news as a major threat to the security of commercial aviation. The possibility of being hijacked by suicidal terrorists who used the airliner as a deadly missile attack, killing all aboard, had hardly been imagined.

No doubt the vivid television pictures multiplied the psychological impact of the terror—the depression, sense of loss, and insecurity—felt by so many people. This, apparently, is what the terrorists intended, but did global television assist the terrorists in achieving their aims? Perhaps, but there was no choice. Acts of terrorism are major news and, of course, have to be reported.

Television can be faulted on how it handled early stories of the anthrax scare. Twenty-four hour cable television, with its built-in tendency to hype and exaggerate a story and jump to conclusions before the facts are fully in, was the worst culprit. Many in the public were unduly disturbed by the ways that the anthrax stories in Washington, D.C., and New Jersey were reported. At the same time, there was a lack of incisive and reliable information from public officials.

Be that as it may, terrorism and all its facets are news, and as such it poses worrisome questions for broadcast journalists: Does television coverage really encourage and aid the terrorists' cause? Is censorship of such dramatic events ever desirable? Raymond Tanter wrote, "Since terror is aimed at the media and not at the victim, success is defined in terms of media coverage. And there is no way in the West that you could not have media coverage, because you're dealing with a free society."[11]

Terrorism coverage is a journalistic problem of international scope, just as international terrorism itself is a transnational problem that individual nations cannot solve without international cooperation. Broadcast journalists argue about whether the violence would recede if television ignored or downplayed an act of terrorism. Most journalists doubt that self-censorship by news organizations is a good idea, or even possible, in such a highly competitive field. However, television organizations have established guidelines for reporting terrorism incidents in a more restrained and rational way.

Two other terrorist episodes involving the U.S. news media, one in Iran and the other in Lebanon, are instructive about the role of media in such crises.

## Hostages in Iran

The seizure of the U.S. embassy in Iran in November 1979, with more than fifty American citizens (virtually all diplomatic personnel) held hostage, added a new and deepening dimension to the history of terrorism and the media's increasingly blurred role as both reporter and participant.

For the first time, a sovereign government became an overt party to the terrorism by supporting, instead of ousting, the young militants who took over an embassy compound and imprisoned its personnel. The militants' stated purpose was to dramatize the grievances of Iranians against the deposed Shah Mohammad Reza Pahlavi and force the U.S. government to return him to Iran for trial. Most observers agreed that the militants and Iran's rulers expected that heavy media coverage of the outpouring of support for the terrorists by the huge demonstrating crowds around the embassy gates in Tehran would convince American and world public opinion of the justice of their cause.

The saturation coverage of that year's biggest story quickly engulfed the U.S. news media, especially television, in controversy and brought charges that they were being used and controlled by Iranian militants. Particularly controversial was an interview by NBC News with an American hostage under conditions dictated by the Iranian captors, conditions that both CBS and ABC had found unacceptable.

For the more than 300 foreign journalists working in Tehran in the first months of the crisis, there was indeed a thin line between being manipulated by the Iranian militants and responding to legitimate demands for the latest information from their own highly competitive news organizations and their publics at home. Indisputably, the Western journalists in Tehran were part of the story and, inevitably, part of the controversy.

## Replay in Beirut

In June 1985, TWA Flight 847 out of Athens was hijacked and its crews and passengers held captive in Beirut, Lebanon. For more than two weeks, the three U.S. networks devoted more than half of their evening news shows to the crisis. One study found that CBS, NBC, and ABC broadcast a total of 491 hostage stories over the seventeen-day crisis period, comprising about twelve hours of news time. In most newspapers, the story was on page one from June 15 to July 7. Indeed, the event looked like a replay of the Iranian story and one that the news business could not ignore. As before, television was accused of aiding and abetting the terrorists by sympathetically publicizing their cause. Prime Minister Margaret Thatcher of Britain proposed a voluntary media code of self-censorship during terrorist incidents. The idea was seconded by U.S. Attorney General Edwin Meese. Fred Friendly, a former president of CBS News, said the worst errors in coverage had been caused by a "haphazard frenzy of competition" and the compulsion to obtain "exclusives": "We have to learn that they (the terrorists) watch TV. We need to get across that you can't shoot your way onto our air," Friendly said.[12]

This time, however, a measure of restraint and responsibility by television news was evident in some quarters. Despite the many specific criticisms of television's coverage of this highly emotional story, there was general agreement that such stories must be covered, but with restraint and good judgment. After it was over, the *Columbia Journalism Review* commented, "One of the tasks of journalism is to provide an assessment independent of that of the government and to stand apart from, rather than incite, the jingoism and xenophobia that spread so rapidly in situations involving the seizure of American citizens. In the Beirut hostage-taking, as in Iran, such detachment was hard to find."[13]

Tom Wicker of *The New York Times* summed it up well:

But the real reason that television was properly present in Beirut, even at those bizarre "press conferences," is just that television exists; it has become a condition of being. It may on occasion be inconvenient, intrusive, and even harmful; but if because of government censorship or network self-censorship the hostage crisis had not been visible, real, on American screens, the outrage and outcry would have been a thousand times louder than what's now being heard, and rightly so; for we depend on television for perception as we depend on air for breath. And that's the way it is.[14]

As with much else in foreign news, a big story in one nation is not necessarily a big story somewhere else. And, further, actors in the same violent story can be called "terrorists" in one nation and "freedom fighters" in another. Yet, for Western news media, after 9/11, and London and Madrid, any terrorist attack will be an important news story.

## Notes

1.  Tim Rutten, "When Facts Trump Attitude," *Los Angeles Times*, www.latimes.com, January 8, 2005.
2.  Ibid.
3.  "Add It Up," *American Journalism Review*," November 2001, 11.
4.  Ibid.
5.  "America's New Internationalist Point of View," Pew Research Center for the People and the Press, online report, October 24, 2001.
6.  George Steiner, "B.B.", *New Yorker*, September 10, 1990, 113.
7.  Bernard Gwertzman and Michael Kaufmann, eds., *The Collapse of Communism* (New York: St. Martins Press, 1990), 352–3.
8.  William Henry, "The Television Screen is Mightier Than the Sword," *Time*, May 10, 1990, 51.
9.  "How Resistance Spread the Word," *Newsweek*, September 2, 1991, 39.
10. Neil Hickey, "Terrorism and Television," *TV Guide*, August 7, 1986, 2.
11. Ibid.
12. "Terror Coverage is Criticized," *The New York Times*, July 31, 1985, sec. A, 3.
13. Ibid.
14. Tom Wicker, "Not a Pseudo Event", *The New York Times*, 1985, sec. A, 27.

# Chapter 6

# Globalization of Media

*Mankind has become one, but not steadfastly one as communities or even as nations used to be, nor united through years of mutual experience . . . nor yet through a common native language, but surpassing all barriers, through international broadcasting and printing.*

—Alexander Solzhenitsyn

If Jules Verne's adventurous Phineas Fogg traveled around the world in eighty days again today, he would find that as an Englishman abroad he would have little trouble keeping up with the news and entertainment. At almost every stopover, he would be able to buy a copy of the *International Herald Tribune* or possibly the *Financial Times*, and at his hotel's newsstand he would have a choice of *The Economist*, *Time*, or *Newsweek*, among other English-language publications. In his hotel room, he would be able to watch the day's televised news either from CNN via cable and Comsat from Atlanta or BBC World. On the local television station, he could see a world news package of stories put together by Reuters Television outside London. And if he had a small shortwave radio, he would be reassured by listening to the BBC World Service from Bush House in London or the Voice of America. Also, on local television, he would likely find reruns of his favorite British programs, and if he sought out a local movie theater, he likely would have a choice of current Hollywood productions. Chances are that a local bookstore or airport newsstand would have a wide selection of English-language magazines and paperback books. Finally, if he has a laptop computer or cellphone, he could send and receive e-mail messages.

The increasing availability of such Western publications and electronic media fare (most of it in English, the *lingua franca* of international communication) is an example of the way the major institutions of news communication—world news services, satellite services, broadcast systems, great newspapers and magazines—have become increasingly internationalized or globalized in recent years. Globalization offers business opportunities for media corporations to make money overseas. This is facilitated by innovations in media technology (facsimile printing and satellite distribution in particular) and a growing elite cosmopolitan audience, as well as other social and political realities. Whatever the cause, the fact is that more and more of the activities of the major news media now transcend parochial or national concerns and serve broader transnational purposes.

Out of the capitalistic West have been arising various media conglomerates that some critics feel may dominate, if not unduly influence, much of international communication and entertainment in the near future. Frequently mentioned among these "media baronies" are those of Rupert Murdoch of Australia, Britain, and America; Silvio Berlusconi of Italy; Time Warner, Disney Company (ABC), and Viacom (CBS) of the United States; the Bertelsmann group of Germany; and Sony and Fujisankei of Japan—all multimedia and multinational.

Whether this trend toward fewer, bigger, and more like-minded media of global communication is good or bad usually depends on the critic's personal tastes and ideology. But the globalization of mass communication is proceeding in response to the needs and economic opportunities of a shrinking world. The transnational media are doing more than seizing the chance for greater profits from new markets, albeit those factors are obviously important. Whether viewed as another example of Western "media imperialism" or as a significant contribution to global understanding and integration, the international media are becoming increasingly cosmopolitan, speaking English, and catering to an internationally minded audience concerned about world affairs.

## An American in Paris

The daily, ink-on-newsprint newspaper is still a major prop of journalism: There are more than 8,000 dailies worldwide and many thousands more weekly journals. A few of the more serious "prestige" papers attract readers far beyond their national borders. Not many Westerners read foreign publications, so they are unaware of the extent to which people abroad depend on newspapers and magazines published in other countries. The intellectually demanding *Le Monde* of Paris, famous for its analyses of world affairs, is widely read in the Arab world and francophone Africa. The London-based *Financial Times* uses a plant in Frankfurt to print nearly 53,000 copies daily of an edition described as "Europe's business paper" and has a U.S. edition printed in New York City for American readers. Gannett distributes in Europe copies of *USA Today* printed in Switzerland; the only difference is that the weather maps are of Europe and Asia. Britain's *Guardian, Independent,* and *Daily Telegraph* are found on many foreign newsstands, as are Germany's *Frankfurter Allegemeine* and Switzerland's *Neue Zürcher Zeitung.*

But the newspaper that has evolved furthest toward becoming a truly global daily is the *International Herald Tribune* of Paris. The IHT is the sole survivor of several English-language papers, including the *Chicago Tribune,* the *Daily Mail* (of London), the *New York Herald,* and *The New York Times,* that earlier published Paris or European editions for English-speaking travelers. Started by James Gordon Bennett in 1887 as the Paris edition of the *New York Herald,* the IHT has outlived its parents and today is fully owned by *The New York Times* company. The IHT is produced by an editorial staff of forty, including copyboys and clerks. Much of its copy comes from *The New York Times,* the *Los Angeles Times, The Washington Post,* and news services. As of recently, much more of the paper is staff written. Averaging about sixteen pages a day, the *Herald Tribune* in 2005 sold 240,918 copies six days a week in 181 countries (in Europe alone, sales were about 135,000), and no single country accounted for more than 15 percent of the total. This marvel of distribution appears daily on some 8,500 newsstands all over Europe, supplied by editions printed in Paris, London, the Hague, Marseilles, Rome, and Zurich; and more recently in Hong Kong and Singapore. African and Middle Eastern subscribers are served by mail; distribution in North America, Latin America, and the Caribbean comes from a Miami printing plant. The IHT thus has become the first newspaper in history to publish the same edition simultaneously on all continents.

Although it remains an American newspaper in outlook and perspective, it has gradually acquired an important non-American readership. Nearly half its readers are an elite group of European internationalists— businesspeople, diplomats, and journalists fluent in English. These non-

American readers are part of an "international information elite" who, regardless of geographic location, share a similar rich fund of common experience, ideas, ways of thinking, and approaches to dealing with international problems.

Numerous other publications, particularly magazines, have reached and helped shape this international information elite. Hearst Magazines International has successfully published magazines abroad, with sixty-four foreign language editions of eight magazines. In 1995, its leaders, *Cosmopolitan*, *Esquire*, *Good Housekeeping*, and *Popular Mechanics*, were distributed in fourteen languages to sixty countries.[1]

Another success, *Reader's Digest*, established its first foreign edition in Britain in 1938. By 1995, there were forty-seven international editions printed in eighteen languages. Almost 13 million copies a month are sold abroad. In some countries, including nearly all Spanish-speaking countries, the *Reader's Digest* is the most popular magazine. So successful has been its adaptation to foreign soil that many readers are unaware that the *Digest* is not an indigenous publication. Although studies show that *Digest* readers abroad belong to a "quality audience" of the affluent, the well-educated, and the well-informed, it is not that same audience of decision makers who read *Time* and *Newsweek*, which are primarily news media.

*Time* and *Newsweek*, besides spawning such notable imitations as *Der Spiegel* in Germany and *L'Express* in France, have been successful as transnational publications, and both can claim strong appeal to that internationally minded readership. *Time* has, over the years, evolved into a multinational news medium for a multinational audience. *Time*'s total circulation was 5,190,000 in 2005. Of that, *Time* Canada's share was about 225,000; *Time* Europe's (including Africa and the Middle East) about 555,000; the edition for the Pacific region about 136,000; and for Latin America 90,744.[2]

*Newsweek*, with a foreign readership of about one-third of its total 1998 circulation of 3.25 million and with a European circulation of 300,000, has done much the same thing overseas. *Newsweek International* has carried hundreds of exclusive stories and featured numerous covers, all different from the domestic edition. Whereas *Time* tailored its overseas editions to regional interests, *Newsweek* tried to be more global in its approach. Only about 15 percent of its readers abroad are Americans; the rest are from 150 countries.

A major competitor of the news magazines abroad is *The Wall Street Journal*. With a satellite-assisted leap across the Pacific, the highly successful

*Journal* launched, in 1976, an Asian edition in Hong Kong that covers a sixteen-country business beat from Manila to Karachi. Smaller than the domestic edition, *The Asian Wall Street Journal* tries for the same mix of authoritative business and political news, a risky experiment for a region with so little press freedom. And pressures have been applied, mostly by Singapore's authoritarian ruler, Lee Kuan Yew. In November 1985, the editor of *The Asian Wall Street Journal* apologized to a Singapore court for any possibility of contempt of court raised by a *Journal* editorial commenting on Singapore politics. The incident prompted questions about the appropriate responses when a foreign court challenges the editorial freedom of an American newspaper published abroad. By mid-1990, after three years of harassment and a lengthy legal dispute with Lee, the *Journal* announced that it was ending circulation in the island republic.

The *Wall Street Journal* also has a European edition, printed in the Netherlands and written and edited in Brussels, Belgium. The paper, which can be purchased on the day of publication throughout Britain and continental Europe, is edited for the international business executive doing business in Europe. Major competitors are two highly regarded British business publications, *The Economist* and the *Financial Times*.

In Latin America, following the invasion of cable television, American newspapers and magazines have been gaining many new readers in the region. Magazine publishers have launched Spanish-language editions of *Newsweek, Glamour, Discover, People, National Geographic,* and *Rolling Stone.* The *Miami Herald* has become the international English newspaper of Latin America, with ten regional printing plants and an overseas circulation of about 35,000 to 40,000. Brazilian sales of *Reader's Digest* in Portuguese jumped from 35,000 to 600,000 in two years.

## Changes in World News Services

The subtle changes in the world news services as they have expanded abroad are further evidence of this growing globalization of transnational media. Although they claim to "cover the world," the agencies historically have tended to serve primarily their own national clients and those in their spheres of influence; that is, Reuters serviced British media and the British Commonwealth, AFP worked mainly for the French press and overseas French territories, and UPI (in its prime), in addition to its U.S. clients, long had strong connections in Latin America. But these world agencies have become more international in scope, selling their services to whoever will buy, wherever they may be.

In addition, the personnel of world agencies have become significantly internationalized. Formerly, the AP, for example, boasted that its news from abroad was reported by American AP correspondents who had experience in running an AP bureau in the U.S. The agency would not depend on foreign nationals to provide news from their own countries for AP use in the United States. That has changed. With the increased professionalism of journalists abroad, news agencies not only find it more economic to use qualified local journalists, but also may get better reporting from staffers who know their own country, its language, and its social and political traditions. In late 2005, the AP planned to introduce an Internet database system called eAP that will deliver news photos, and video and sound clips, with identifying codes that will enable the AP to track how many times articles are used by a client.

Another facet of internationalization is foreign syndication of news by major daily papers. The New York Times News Service sends more than 50,000 words daily to 550 clients, of which 130 are newspapers abroad. Its close competitor is the Los Angeles Times/Washington Post News Service, which transmits about 60,000 words daily to fifty nations or about 600 newspapers, half of which are outside the United States. This total includes papers in West Germany and elsewhere that receive the dpa (Deutsche Presse Agentur), with which the service is affiliated.

As noted previously, there is syndication as well of television news film and videotapes, especially those of America's NBC, CNN, CBS, and ABC, and Britain's BBC and ITN, most of it distributed by two Anglo-American firms—Reuters Television and Associated Press Television News—via videotape and satellite (and sometimes by airmail) to almost every television service in the world. There is probably more international cooperation than competition in the transnational video news business, in part because most nations have only one government-controlled television service. Unlike the print media, which usually carry a credit line on agency reports or syndicated material, syndicated television news is usually presented anonymously. Whether watching news from Cairo or Shanghai, the viewer is rarely informed who supplied foreign video.

## Advertising Goes Worldwide

Advertising, too, has followed the global trend. Recent "megamergers" among advertising and marketing services companies point up how internationalized Madison Avenue, the symbolic home of American advertising, has become. The biggest merger in advertising history took place when Saatchi & Saatchi of London agreed to buy Ted Bates Worldwide for $450 million. Saatchi & Saatchi thus became the world's biggest agency, with U.S. billings of $4.6 billion and world billings of $7.6 billion. (In 1995, Saatchi & Saatchi changed its name to Cordiant, after founders Maurice and Charles Saatchi left the firm in a bitter departure.) The second largest advertising empire was created with the amalgamation of three other major concerns—Doyle Dane Bernbach Group, BBDO International, and Needham Harper Worldwide—which, combined, had world billings of $5 billion and U.S. billings of $3.7 billion.[3] Later, the United Kingdom's WPP agency bought out two American giants: J. Walter Thompson and Olgilvy and Mather.

Agency executives involved in these mergers cited the industry's understanding of the need to offer clients worldwide service as a primary motivation. As an executive of Young & Rubicam pointed out, "There is a trend toward global assignment of agencies. If you don't have a complete set of worldwide resources, you're in danger of being left out in terms of getting the best clients."[4]

Implied is the view that transnational advertising agencies would be in a position to channel standardized advertising from transnational corporations into transnational media with minimum effort. The same commercial—whether for Coke or McDonald's—could just be translated into many languages and placed in media anywhere in the world. However, this "global sell" theory has not worked out, according to Alvin Toffler, who wrote, "What's wrong with the global sell theory is that it makes little distinction between the world's regions and markets. Some are still in a pre-mass–market condition; others are still at the mass-market stage; and some are already experiencing the de-massification characteristic of an advanced economy."[5] Due to cultural preferences, widespread consumer differences about products persist, as do attitudes toward food, beauty, work, play, love, and politics. Toffler concluded that "globalization is not the same as homogeneity. Instead of a single global village, as forecast by Marshall McLuhan, we are likely to see a multiplicity of quite different global villages—all wired into the new media system, but all straining to retain or enhance their cultural, ethnic, national, and political individuality."[6]

## Media Changes in Europe

The increasing economic integration of the European Community plus the demassification and deregulation of broadcast media are rapidly internationalizing much of mass communication in Western Europe. Although Europeans, like people everywhere, prefer to read, view, and listen to news and entertainment in their home or native languages, the push toward transnational communication is still strong. This is due to the rapid expansion of cable and satellite options for viewers, as well as increased numbers of private or commercial television and radio channels and the increasing popularity of VCRs, DVDs, and the Internet.

As noted previously, major American and British print and broadcasting organizations are each trying to increase their readers and audiences in European nations. And other media conglomerates in France, Germany, Italy, and Japan are buying up media properties abroad. Deregulation and privatization of radio and television and the expansion of cable and pay television, assisted by satellite distribution, also have added potentially important new daily news outlets in English as well as many more entertainment options for Europeans. Europe's broadcasting systems, formerly run by governments or by public corporations (paid for by special taxes or fees), have heretofore generally offered high-quality programming but with limited choices. But Western Europe is now following the deregulated American models, with greatly increased choices. As a result, there has been a rush for the huge profits to be made. Adherents of Europe's tradition of public service broadcasting feel that programming quality will be sacrificed by deregulation and commercialization. The money to be made from advertising, viewer fees, and revenues from movies and video programs is expected to run into the billions.

Western Europe nations, particularly France, concerned about the influence and popularity of American movies and television shows with European audiences, have established quotas on imports and subsidized their own productions. However, another quieter invasion has taken place: American companies have infiltrated nearly every corner of the

European television business. Time Warner, Viacom, Disney/ABC, Cox Cable, NBC, and others are getting involved in European-based television programming, in broadcast stations, in cable and satellite networks, and in the coming convergence of telecommunications and entertainment. And they see a huge market: 350 million people in twelve major Western European nations and 650 million overall west of Russia, many of them hungry for televised news and entertainment.

## Expanding Media Baronies

Many of the innovative changes in European media, as elsewhere, are being made by the transnational media conglomerates, themselves a by-product of rapid changes in international communication. There is growing concern as well about the economic, and potentially political, influence wielded by these powerful forces in global communication. The prototype of the media barons is Rupert Murdoch with his News Corporation. With 150 media properties in Australia, the U.S., and Britain, Murdoch has been carefully assembling a vertically integrated global media empire. In the United States, he owns the Fox television network, the *New York Post*, and *TV Guide*. In addition, he has a significant share of Twentieth Century Fox Broadcasting, which produces TV shows and owns thousands of hours of films and television programs. In Europe, he has pioneered in satellite broadcasting and owns 90 percent of the British Sky Broadcasting channel (a satellite television system), a new sports network, and a twenty-four hour news channel that draws from his two London papers, *The Times* and *The Sunday Times*. He owns direct broadcast satellite services in Britain, Italy, Hong Kong, Japan, and Mexico; he owns two-thirds of daily newspaper circulation in Australia; and he owns HarperCollins Publishers, *New York* and *Seventeen* magazines, and other British papers, including *The Sun* and the *News of the World*. Constantly juggling his properties (and his considerable debts), his News Corporation, which had revenues of less than $1 billion in 1980, had expanded its revenues to $14 billion in 2000.

Murdoch's current strategy apparently is to own every major form of programming—news, sports, films, and children's shows—and beam them via satellites or television stations he owns or controls to homes in the U.S., Europe, Asia, and South America. He recently said, "We want to put our programming everywhere and distribute everybody's product around the world."[7] Most recently, he seems to be concentrating his efforts on global interactive satellite systems.

Murdoch's media acquisitions have apparently influenced several major U.S. media mergers, all of which have had implications for the future of international communications. In August 1995, the Walt Disney Company announced its purchase of Capital Cities/ABC, in a deal valued at $19 billion. The merger brought together ABC—then the most profitable television network, including its highly regarded news organization (Peter Jennings then as anchor)—and its ESPN sports cable service with an entertainment giant: Disney's Hollywood film and television studios, cartoon characters, theme parks, and so on, and the merchandise they generate. (In one recent year, the Disney Company sold more than $15 billion worth of Disney merchandise worldwide, a total more than seven times the global box-office receipts for Disney movies.) Disney is more interested in content, especially game parks, movies, and consumer goods, than in conduits (cable or satellites). For 2000, Disney's total revenue was $25.8 billion, putting it in second place among media giants.

The real giant among the mega-media companies was AOL Time Warner, whose 2000 total revenues hit $36 billion, well ahead of Disney. Viacom (CBS) stood in third place at $20 billion, followed by Vivendi/Universal at $18 billion, Bertelsmann at $16 billion, and Murdoch's News Corporation at $14 billion. However, the bursting of the dot com bubble in late 2000 hit AOL Time Warner hard, wiping out almost $200 billion in shareholder value. Time Warner shed AOL and has since come back. However, the French-controlled Vivendi/Universal conglomerate went under.

Another major merger began with Westinghouse's takeover of CBS Inc., creating the nation's largest broadcast station group, with thirty-nine radio and sixteen television stations reaching 32 percent of the nation. About the same time, Viacom, a hot cable company, bought a legendary Hollywood studio, Paramount Communications, for $8.2 billion. Several years later, Viacom bought the CBS Corporation for $37.3 billion, creating the world's second-largest media company. In May 2000, the FCC approved the Viacom/CBS merger and for its money CBS brought to the merger $1.9 billion in radio properties, including 190 radio stations; $4.4 billion in television holdings, including the CBS network, CBS Entertainment, CBS sports, and seventeen television stations; and $546 million in cable properties.

These megamergers positioned the resulting giants—Time Warner, Disney/ABC, Viacom (CBS), and Murdoch—to better penetrate and dominate the growing international markets for television, movies, news, sports, records, and other media programs. At the time of its merger with ABC, Disney president Michael Eisner spoke glowingly of India's huge middle class of 250 million as a great potential audience for Disney movies, cartoons, news, and sports programs. NBA and NFL games have been gaining large audiences overseas; hence the importance of the ESPN networks. Critics noted that news organizations (and journalists), such as *Time* magazine and CNN, or ABC News or CBS News, were just small players within these entertainment giants.

The keen competition among CNN, MSNBC, and Fox News Channel (FNC) to dominate a twenty-four hour cable news channel in the U.S. (see Chapter 3, "The International News System") has strong international potential as well. Broadcast networks have been looking to international markets as a way of gaining hundreds of millions of new viewers. NBC's international holdings currently are about 20 percent of the network's worth of $10 to $20 billion; in the next ten years, half of the network's value is expected to come from international holdings. As predicted, Asia is becoming the main area of global audience growth, because about 25 percent of the continent's vast population is expected to receive cable before long. By contrast, the U.S. market, with cable in 65 million of its 97 million households, is nearing saturation. Numbers of cable viewers are expected to rise abroad in time for the startup of NBC Europe as well as related NBC services in Latin America. Since 9/11, the war on terrorism for a while gave an impetus to twenty-four hour global news, and competition has become much more intense.

## Other European Baronies

Among European media groups with far-reaching holdings is Bertelsmann A.G. of Germany. From a Bible-publishing house, Bertelsmann grew into a media giant with book and record clubs in Germany, Spain, Brazil, the United States, and eighteen other countries. Bertelsmann owns Bantam, Doubleday, and Dell publishing in the United States, and Plaza y Janes book publishers in Spain, in addition to thirty-seven magazines in five countries, record labels such as RCA/Ariola, and a number of radio and television properties. In 1998, Bertelsmann shocked

U.S. book publishers by buying Random House for an estimated $1.4 billion, consolidating its claim as the world's largest English-language publisher of trade books. Considered the crown jewel of American book publishers, Random House had $1.1 billion in sales in 1996. With the sale, half of the top twenty U.S. publishing firms, with a 28 percent share of the total U.S. market, were in foreign hands. With $15.5 billion total revenue in 2000, Bertelsmann ranked as the world's fifth largest media conglomerate.

Possibly the most swashbuckling of the media barons has been Italy's Silvio Berlusconi, who built a multibillion-dollar media television and newspaper empire, Fininvest, of unusual power and influence. With 42 percent of Italy's advertising market and 16 percent of daily newspaper circulation, he has concentrated his power more into a single market than any of the aforementioned barons. He owns Italy's three main private television channels, Rete 4, Canale 4, and Italia 1, as well as *Il Giornale*, a leading Milan paper, two leading news weeklies, thirteen regional dailies, and a large book publisher plus television holdings in France and Germany. Using his extensive media power, Berlusconi became Prime Minister of Italy in April 1994. The media-baron-turned-politician promised a revolution of prosperity and clean dealing. However, he was soon in trouble and in November 1994, the fifty-eight-year-old billionaire was forced to resign when charged with corruption. In 1998, he was convicted on corruption charges. However, by May 2001, Berlusconi was voted back into power as Italy's Prime Minister—a position he lost in 2006.

## Diffusion of Mass Culture

A major impact of these global media giants comes from their diffusion of the popular culture of the West to all—literally all—corners of the world, with profound influences that can only be described as revolutionary. The world is beginning to share a common popular culture. Much of the diversity of the world's cultures and languages is being lost forever. This trend is part of a long-term historical process that predates modern media, but in recent years the pace has accelerated.

American films regularly acquire more than 50 percent of the French market; about 50 percent of the Italian, Dutch, and Danish markets; 60 percent of the German markets; and 80 percent of the British markets.

Recently, among the world's 100 most attended films, eighty-eight were American. Seventy-five percent of all imported television programs come from America. Millions in Europe can now watch *Oprah Winfrey*, subtitled or dubbed. American basketball, played in 192 countries, may become the world's most popular sport. The NBA finals have been broadcast in 109 countries in twenty languages. Here are random examples of U.S. mass culture abroad: *Dallas* has been seen in ninety-eight countries; 40 percent of television programming in New Zealand is American; Mickey Mouse and Donald Duck, dubbed in Mandarin, have been seen weekly in China; *Sesame Street* has been seen in 184 countries; and the hottest game show on French television is *La Roule de la Fortune*. Popular culture also conveys life styles. Like their Russian counterparts, young Chinese prefer American jeans and T-shirts as well as rock music. Young people in Germany are using such slang terms as "rap music," "body building," "windsurfing," and "computer hacking"—and, what is more, they are doing these activities.

One of the most powerful influences on global youth culture has been Music Television, or MTV, which first appeared on U.S. cable in 1981. Since then, it has grown into a global phenomenon reaching into about 250 million homes worldwide and still expanding. Despite criticism and unease from some members of the older generation, the recording business, by hitching would-be music hits to television, has found a marketing tool that has brought it unprecedented profits. Much of MTV's success is based on adapting the musical programming to the musical tastes of the teenagers of the region receiving it. The West, it has been said, won not only the Cold War but also the battle for the world's leisure time. Popular culture has been one of America's most lucrative exports, but observers say that the worst, instead of the best, of American culture seems to be flooding the world. Critic Michiko Kakutani commented, "Some of America's culture exports are so awful that you suspect that we are using the rest of the world as a vast toxic waste dump and charging for the privilege."[8] Chinese pop singers produce songs so similar to those in the West that you have to listen carefully to find that the lyrics are in Chinese.

## The Videocassette and DVD Revolution

The global dissemination of popular culture, especially movies and music videos, was first greatly facilitated by the rapid spread of videocassette recordings and videocassette recorders to play them on. (The VCRs have been largely replaced recently by digital video disks (DVDs), but the impact and effects are similar.) The terms "explosion" and "revolution" have been used to describe this phenomenon. In less than a decade, the VCR and videotape penetrated remote areas that the printing press and other information devices had not successfully reached after centuries. The spread has been to poor nations as well as well as the affluent West, but for different reasons. Depending on culture and political traditions, VCRs can have profound effects not only on viewers but also on broadcasting and other media. Widespread use of VCRs can challenge the usual system of government control of television by providing diversity of views and variety in entertainment. (The use of audiocassettes has done much the same thing to radio broadcasting.) VCRs circumvent the utilization of broadcast television for development and political control by bringing about a de facto decentralization of media. People in poor countries, including youth, now often have the freedom to view what they want to see—not what Big Brother, or even their parents, think is best for them. And apparently what they want are movies, pop music, and videos from the West. In Saudi Arabia, the only choice for viewers of over-the-air television has long been the puritanical, heavily censored and dull programming of government television. (For example, religious orthodoxy requires that a Saudi woman's face may not be shown on television.) As a result, VCRs and DVDs have proliferated by showing much of the forbidden fruit of Western movies, including X-rated videos, most of them smuggled into the country.

In India, many people, annoyed by the inadequacies of state-run broadcasting, have turned to private enterprise "alternative television" news on videocassettes. The producer of "Business Plus", a monthly tape on political and economic issues, said India has the only private-view news magazines in the world. The tapes, made in English and Hindi, rent for about 60 cents a day or sell for about $8. The audience, though small, is composed of middle-class, cosmopolitan Indians dissatisfied with the vacuity of official news and documentaries. The trend toward news-oriented videotapes began earlier with "Newstrack," a fast-paced monthly video of investigative reporting with a segmented format like that of "Sixty Minutes."

Throughout emerging nations, small shops renting or selling videotapes (and later DVDs) from the West have become commonplace. In the remote nation of Bhutan, on India's northern border, people had been watching videos on television sets for years before the nation had an over-the-air television service. To a Westerner, the VCR is an easy way to watch a movie or record a television program for later viewing, but to many millions in developing nations, VCRs and DVDs are a means of gaining alternative news sources or viewing sometimes prohibited Western entertainment shows—activities that authoritarian countries have largely failed to censor or control.

## English as the Media Language

Effective communication across national borders, regardless of other cultural and political differences, certainly requires that sender and receiver communicate in a mutually understandable language. More and more, that language is English, which is clearly the leading tongue of international communication today.

Among the "Big Ten" world languages, English usually ranks third, with about 300 million native speakers in twelve countries, after Mandarin Chinese, with about 885 million, and Spanish, with 332 million native speakers. English is ahead of Russian with its 282 million speakers, Arabic, with 220 million, and German, with 118 million. Furthermore, English is the most widely used geographically, and for about 400 million educated persons around the world, English is their second language. Several hundred million more people have some knowledge of English, which has official or semi-official status in some sixty countries. What is more, this number includes most of the world's leaders. (If a leader wants to get on global TV, he or she had better know English.) In all, there are about one billion English speakers in the world, and the number is rapidly increasing.

Unquestionably, English has become the global language of science and technology. More than 80 percent of all information stored in 100 million computers around the world is in English, and 80 percent of all scientific papers are published first in English. English is the language of the information age: Computers talk to each other in English. The Internet today reverberates with many languages, many of which can be translated into English by computer programs. English is the most-taught language in the world; it is not really replacing other languages but, rather, supplementing them.

In many developing nations, English is the language of education, providing an entrée to knowledge and information. But one unfortunate result is that many native English speakers, especially Americans, have much less incentive than, say, Israelis, Dutch, or Swedes to learn other peoples' languages. Currently, the U.S. government has an acute shortage of Arabic speakers. Few Americans even learn to speak Spanish, although it is widely spoken here. The nation's Hispanics numbered 35.3 million in 2000, and to inform and entertain them were thirty daily newspapers, 265 weeklies, 352 magazines, and 594 radio stations —all in Spanish.

Globally, English has also become the leading media language for international communication. Most of the world's news is carried in English. Most news agencies carry some of their news in English. Six of the world's biggest broadcasters—the BBC, CBS, NBC, ABC, CNN, and CBC—reach a potential audience of about 300 million people through English-language broadcasting.

The imperialism of nineteenth-century Britain was a major reason that so many people from Singapore to India to Kenya to Nigeria to Bermuda converse today in English. Not unrelated is the phenomenon of numerous English-language daily newspapers flourishing today in countries where English is neither the official nor even the most widely used language. Beginning with the *Chronicle of Gibraltar* in 1801, English-language dailies, catering to expatriates, the foreign community, and local educated elites, have long survived, if not always flourished, in such diverse metropolises as Mexico City, Caracas, Paris, Jerusalem, Taipei, Rome, Athens, Cairo, Beirut, Manila, Bangkok, Singapore, and Tokyo, as well as throughout India and Pakistan and the former British territories of Africa, such as Nigeria, Ghana, Sierra Leone, South Africa, Uganda, Kenya, Tanzania, Zimbabwe, and Zambia. In parts of polyglot Africa, English has almost evolved into another African language because of the role it plays in education, commerce, and mass communication.

Most of the "content" of mass culture that moves across national borders is in English. Jeremy Tunstall has said that English is the language best suited for "comic strips, headlines, riveting first sentences, photo captions, dubbing, subtitling, pop songs, billboards, disc-jockey banter, news flashes, and sung commercials."[9] One appeal of English as an international language is that it is easy to speak badly.

This thrust of English as a world media language has become self-generating, and any educated person of whatever nationality who wishes to participate in this shrinking and interdependent world finds it useful to know English. In fact, because English is now spoken as a second language by more people around the globe than by the British and the

Americans combined, it must now be considered as belonging to the world, as indeed it does. For when two persons of differing linguistic backgrounds are able to converse in person or through computers, the chances are they will be using English.

## Notes

1. Deidre Carmody, "Magazines Find Green Pastures Abroad," *The New York Times*, March 20, 1995, sec. C, 5.
2. *1998 IMS Directory of Publications* (Fort Washington, PA: IMS Press, 1998), 727–8.
3. Richard W. Stevenson, "Ad Agency Mergers Changing the Business," *The New York Times*, May 13, 1986, 1.
4. Ibid.
5. Alvin Toffler, *PowerShift* (New York: Bantam Books, 1990), 340.
6. Toffler, *PowerShift*, 341.
7. Ken Auletta, "Leviathan", *New Yorker*, October 29, 2001, 50.
8. Michiko Kakutani, "Taking Out the Trash," *The New York Times Magazine*, June 8, 1997, 31.
9. Jeremy Tunstall, *The Media Are American: Anglo-American Media in the World* (London: Constable, 1977), 128.

# Chapter 7

# China: Caged Media in a Free Economy

*I am the best journalist in China.*
> —Zhao Yan, imprisoned Chinese journalist

*No sex, No violence, No news.*
> —motto of foreign TV channel licensed for China

China is a nation that wants the benefits of an open, capitalist economy for its 1.3 billion people, but still wants to tightly control its media. For the past thirty years, the Chinese leadership—nominally still Communist but in fact strongly committed to a capitalist economy that it calls "market socialism"—has been unsure about how to carry this off. After a visit to China, one American editor asked, "Can China run a free market economy without a free market in ideas?"[1] Many suggest it is impossible to do so. It is, some insist, just a matter of time before the Chinese people add democracy to the list of modern life styles imported from the West.[2]

China does not reject the idea of press freedom. Its 1912 constitution granted its citizens freedom of speech and press, but the constitution included a list of situations in which government could restrict this freedom.

The Chinese call this "a pragmatic approach" to freedom of the press. This approach includes strong opposition to the notion of press "freedom to spread lies and rumors."[3] This "pragmatic approach" to press freedom has meant that China's leaders have alternately encouraged its media to be independent—at least economically independent—but then cracked down when that independence seemed to threaten those in control.

The confusion shows when two respected news organizations present conflicting reports on China's media in the same week. The BBC (British Broadcasting Corporation) reported "sweeping changes across the media industry," including "hard-hitting investigations" of corruption.[4] That same week, *The Economist* reported on "China's Media: Back on the Leash."[5]

## An End to Media Subsidies

Both reports agree on the cause of the apparent contradiction. The Chinese government has transformed almost all the nation's subsidized media from being a huge financial drain into a profit-making global industry. This means advertising, which implies popular content that attracts lots of readers, listeners, and viewers. But Chinese Communist officials do not want any content, popular or not, domestic or foreign, that could threaten their grip on power. Foreign media conglomerates can, for example, bring entertainment or sports programs into China via satellite. But China forced media mogul Rupert Murdoch's STAR-TV to drop all BBC news reports when they criticized China's human rights record.[6] This move came after Murdoch angered Beijing by predicting that satellite TV would put totalitarian regimes out of business. A Murdoch company also canceled a planned book by Hong Kong's last British governor and instead published an English translation of the life of Chinese leader Deng Xiaoping. In case the Chinese did not fully understand that Murdoch was really sorry for his comments, his Phoenix TV telecast a twelve-part program on Deng's life made by China Central Television (CCTV).[7] Despite Murdoch's efforts to avoid offending Chinese officials, even he runs into suddenly shifting media policies. In 2005, his News Corporation thought it was about to win permission for a TV cable channel filled with programs from his STAR-TV subsidiary and get a bigger piece of the $19 billion advertisers were spending on China's commercial TV. In August 2005, the Chinese government denied approval for that channel, for a Viacom plan to co-produce children's programs with a Chinese company, and for a Disney channel that was to follow the September opening of Disney's theme park in Hong Kong.[8] Murdoch's view of China's media policy after years of negotiation with their government: Beijing is "quite paranoid about what gets through."[9]

Western media conglomerates try hard to satisfy Chinese authorities. This is a major reason the Chinese think it is safe to allow some foreign television channels in the country. Or at least some parts of the country. AOL–Time Warner got permission in 2001 to start a Mandarin-language channel in a limited area of southern China. In return, AOL agreed to carry CCTV's English-language channel on its cable systems in New York, Los Angeles, and Houston. For China, AOL chose to pick up a Singapore TV channel. Its motto: "No sex, No violence, No news."[10]

## Hong Kong's Allure

The allure of Hong Kong forced China to let Western TV into its southeast, mainly into booming Guangdong province, just next to the former British colony. Hong Kong's Western values, including democracy and an independent media, are apparent on Hong Kong television.[11] A dozen daily newspapers and six broadcast stations with news programs guarantee some serious competition for news, in spite of pressures from the mainland and even nervous Hong Kong media owners.[12] Large numbers of people in southeast China were watching Western-style Hong Kong TV programs, since their antennas and illegal satellite dishes could easily pick them up. By 2005, China had authorized six foreign companies to beam twenty-four hour channels to southeast China. Government officials hoped these TV channels would lure Chinese viewers from Hong Kong television, while the channel owners would protect their licenses by carefully avoiding any antigovernment programs. Like audiences everywhere, however, Chinese TV viewers will abandon channels that block important news. When New York's World Trade Center was destroyed by suicide bombers on September 11, 2001, CCTV in Beijing kept the tragedy off all of China's television channels for nearly an hour, while awaiting the Ministry of Information's guidance on how to react. But the news was out via the Internet, telephone, and other channels. People near Hong Kong quickly switched to its Phoenix channel. In Shanghai and other cities, Chinese students and others pooled their money to rent rooms at tourist hotels where they could get international channels such as the BBC and CNN. By the time CCTV got on the air with a muted report, it had lost much of its audience. In fact, Phoenix pulled away so much of CCTV's audience that Phoenix executives carefully understated how many mainland viewers it had, so as not to offend and embarrass CCTV.

Furious CCTV news executives got the Ministry to reconsider its policy that requires that major news must get advance clearance.[13]

Increasingly, Chinese citizens are getting access to foreign TV programs. Some believe that television has become the main source of information from outside China. One survey found Chinese adolescents were watching, on average, two American movies or television programs a week.[14] Foreign films and TV programs screened by the censors are available on many channels, dubbed in Chinese or with Chinese subtitles. But most Chinese get their foreign movies from street vendors and small shops selling pirated copies. They come with a choice of Chinese-language tracks, such as Mandarin and Cantonese. U.S. industry experts estimate that 85 percent of DVDs, videotapes, and CDs sold in China are pirated copies that the censor never gets to review.[15] This influx of foreign ideas has drastically reduced the power of China's rulers to isolate and dominate society. Television has, in fact, forced changes in China's economic and political policies. As one media executive said, "Even if the Chinese tried to keep foreign cultural icons out, piracy would make them available."[16]

## The Mongolian Cow Sour Yoghurt *Super Girl* Contest

Despite all the media controls, even some television shows produced in China can upset government officials. In summer 2005, a wildly popular singing contest attracted record audiences and a rebuke from *China Daily*, the official government newspaper. *Super Girl*, a Chinese version of *American Idol*, had more than 400 million viewers for its finale. Most viewers no doubt just saw this as TV entertainment, but some people said the show made a political statement as well, because of how the winner, a singer from rural Hunan province, was chosen. The winner, Lu Yuchin, was popularly elected by 3.5 million cellphone voters.[17] In a nation where most public meetings are banned, fans formed clubs to collect votes for their favorites. The contest originated with a provincial television station in rural Hunan, far from the watchful eyes of the Ministry of Information, and was sponsored by a local dairy. Thus the official name of the show: *The Mongolian Cow Sour Yoghurt Super Girl Contest*. China Central Television (CCTV) was startled by the huge numbers of viewers that the program drew, an audience larger than CCTV gets even for its Chinese New Year extravaganzas. It said the show had "debased Chinese culture." *China Daily* commented: "How come an imitation of a democratic system ends up selecting the singer who has the least ability to carry a tune?" Some thought Beijing was upset because the program introduced a huge Chinese audience to the idea of an election with numerous competing candidates. Others said CCTV was upset because the show cut into its own advertising revenues. Either way, *Super Girl* could be a threat to China's official mass media.[18]

## China's "Oprah Winfrey"

Another very popular TV program is *A Date with Chen Luyu*, a Chinese Oprah Winfrey. All sorts of celebrities and ordinary people share her sofa and talk about their lives on the Phoenix satellite channel, the first foreign-funded station authorized to reach mainland audiences. Chen Luyu insists that her program: ". . . is not about politics. My viewers don't want to listen to things like that, so I don't do shows like that." Her program is, however, a window on what concerns Chinese citizens. Inevitably, the talk includes comments on such topics as crime, corruption, and even AIDS, formerly taboo subjects. Chinese officials and perhaps the hostess herself want to avoid controversial topics. But she and even Chinese officials know that if all controversial topics are kept off the air, programs will soon lose their audiences.[19]

## A New Transparency

Despite their desire for tight media control, China's rulers want to create at least the appearance of transparency and more openness to the public and the media. In 2005, the State Information Office told Communist Party officials to start holding news conferences.[20] This is a big change. In China, journalists can be severely criticized for seeking even routine information from Party officials. A Hong Kong reporter who asked when the Premier would hold a planned news conference was told it was "secret information." And almost anything can be declared a state secret in China. When scores of children died from poisoning at a school near Nanjing in 2002, Chinese officials ordered the death toll be kept secret. Instead, they insisted that the media report on the arrest of the suspect and official efforts to prevent a similar tragedy in the future. Official media followed the rules, but foreign journalists traveled to Nanjing with and without permission to get the facts. Only in September 2005 did China announce that the death toll, at least in natural disasters, would no longer be considered a "state secret."

The announcement was made by the National Administration for State Secrets, a government agency that oversees the vast amount of information considered secret, at a news conference. No foreign journalists were invited to the conference.[21]

Even though the print media are directly owned by the government, controlling Chinese journalists has not always been easy. There are probably 100,000 people in China who say they are "journalists" and the number is growing.[22] In 2003, one Chinese journalism professor found more than 300 schools in China claiming to have a journalism program although, as in many countries, most of the graduates will not wind up as journalists. The top requirement for Chinese journalists, according to the Communist Party's Handbook for Journalists, is "faithfully propagating and carrying out the Party's principles and policies." But a major survey found many journalism students in China still thought they could fill the classic "watchdog" role and report government corruption.[23] And this role is actually recognized in the Chinese media system. Back in 1986, Communist Party Secretary Hu Yaobang told editors that they should include stories on problems in China, but 80 percent of their articles should focus on China's achievements.[24] In 2004, the Communist Party listed the press as one of the eight major means for overseeing party and government officials.[25] Despite such official pronouncements, however, being a "watchdog" journalist in China can be very risky.

## "The Best Journalist in China"

Zhao Yan, aged forty-three, says he is "the best" journalist in China.[26] That may explain why he was whisked off to prison from a Shanghai Pizza Hut in September 2004 and charged with leaking state secrets. Zhao was arrested shortly after he turned on his cellphone, a lapse that he thinks led State Security police to him. Zhao worked for a decade for *China Reform*, a newspaper with a reputation for exposing official corruption. While there, Zhao called himself "an anticorruption warrior." But in 2003 government officials began pressuring *China Reform* to tone down its exposés. Its chief editorial writer was detained by the police. Zhao decided it was time to move on and took a job with the Beijing bureau of *The New York Times*.

Working for a foreign publication can be dangerous for a Chinese journalist. The government has sometimes charged these journalists with being spies. Ching Cheong, a reporter for Singapore's *Straits Times*, was charged with spying for Taiwan in August 2005. He apparently obtained documents showing discord among the Chinese leadership over Tiananmen Square. Nearly two decades later, Chinese officials remain very sensitive to any reference to this 1989 student protest that the Chinese military brutally suppressed. Another journalist, Shi Tao, was sentenced to ten years in prison for emailing a dissident in the United States that his paper, the *Hunan Business News*, could not report on any demonstrations on the anniversary of the Tiananmen Square student protests. Chinese censors spotted Shi's message when someone posted it on a website.[27]

Just what secret Zhao is charged with revealing is unclear, since a year later no official charges had been filed. Zhao did tell a *Times* reporter that ex-president Jiang Zemin and his successor, Hu Jintao, were having a dispute over promoting a general. This wound up as one sentence toward the end of a *Times* story. Suggestions of any disagreements within the Chinese leadership always bring strong reaction from officials. Editors are routinely warned before Communist Party meetings that they are not to speculate on who might wind up in leadership positions. China's leaders believe they can handle the social and economic strains that are testing them, as long as there is no sign of disunity.[28]

While continuing to label as much information as possible "secret," the government is also cracking down on journalists who want to find information on their own. Chinese journalists have found that their newspapers were much more willing to print exposés if their stories exposed distant corruption. But in 2005 the Chinese government officially banned all "yidi baodao," or "reports from nonlocal places." From now on, Chinese journalists will have to stick close to home.[29]

Foreign journalists in China have faced restrictions on their own travel, but have regularly evaded them. *The New York Times*, London's *Guardian*, and other foreign publications reported regularly from all over China. Some of their stories came from tips from Chinese journalists who were not allowed to report the story. The *South China Morning Post*, published in Hong Kong, frequently was able to break stories that Chinese papers were forbidden to report, because their reporters could travel to cities and towns all over China. The *Oriental Daily News* of Hong Kong was a regular source of information about the mainland because of its contacts, and it frequently reported news that was blacked out by mainland media.[30] *Apple Daily*, a popular, pro-democracy Chinese-language tabloid in Hong Kong, that carried lots of news from mainland China, said its reporters were being denied visas for China because of its anticorruption articles. It also said advertisers reported they were under pressure to withhold advertising.[31]

## Exposing Corruption

Stories exposing corruption can be published even in mainland China if the editors are careful in choosing the right targets and the right time. *People's Daily*, the government's flagship newspaper, launched an anticorruption campaign in 1983 when the government decided corrupt local officials had to be curbed. Provincial papers soon felt free to do their own exposés, and as the scandals grew readership leaped ahead. Before long, Party leaders complained that the press attacks were too harsh and directed editors to cut back on the exposés.[32] This pattern of government supporting anticorruption exposés and then shutting them down has continued for decades. In 2003, for example, the *Southern Metropolitan Daily* reported the death in police custody of a graphic designer arrested because he lacked the proper ID. It became a national story and within two months the Chinese government said it would replace the regulations that allowed police to make such arrests. Soon after this, however, three senior editors of *Southern Metropolitan Daily* were arrested. The official charge was embezzlement, but many journalists believed the charges were trumped up in order to punish them for pushing their criticism too far.[33]

## Exposing Business Corruption

Most of China's many thousands of magazines stick with safe topics such as sports, fashion, entertainment, and accounting. But some have found they are well placed to play the role of government critic with relative safety.

*Caijing* (Finance and Economy), a bimonthly business magazine published in Beijing, has regularly exposed government as well as private corruption. Articles have reported on stock market manipulation, corruption at government-owned banks, and government attempts to cover up the 2003 outbreak of SARS (Severe Acute Respiratory Syndrome). *Caijing* Editor Hu Shuli got her start as a journalist writing for the Communist Party's *Workers' Daily*. Even there, she wrote and got published stories about corrupt local officials. She joined journalists who demonstrated to support the 1989 student protests in Tiananmen Square, but found her paper would not publish anything on them. Shortly after, she moved to the *China Business Times* and then to *Caijing*.

Since she became editor of *Caijing*, Hu's journal has exposed so many corrupt private and government officials that a magazine profile called her "the most dangerous woman in China."[34] *Caijing* first reached a broad national audience with an exposé of backroom dealings by some of China's leading fund managers in 2000. Another major story involved accounting fraud at a blue-chip Chinese company. The mainstream media would not touch the story, even though an insider provided all the information necessary to verify the fraud. *Caijing* broke the story along with *Southern Weekend*, another, muckraking, newspaper that is read all over China. Only when the company came forth with a formal announcement of an internal investigation did the mainstream media run the story.

In China, even during times of relative media freedom, only a handful of media outlets will venture to report on corruption or other sensitive matters even within government limits. The rest of the media follow after explicit government approval.[35] Because of *Caijing*'s reporting, it has become required reading in the Chinese business community. But it is not just reporting on sensitive business stories that earned *Caijing* its reputation as one of the most important publications in China. When the World Health Organization reported in March 2003 that the SARS epidemic had crossed from Hong Kong to the mainland, *Caijing* leaped on the story as a major threat to business and people in China. Ignoring government denials, *Caijing* produced four special weekly issues on SARS. For these and other stories, the World Press Review in 2003 named Hu International Editor of the Year.[36] This international recognition and *Caijing*'s owner, Beijing's Stock Exchange, may shield Hu from government crackdowns. Also, from her early years on the more directly government-controlled *Workers' Daily*, she knows the limits on journalism in China. "I know how to measure the boundary lines," she said. "We go up to the line and we might even push it. But we never cross it."[37] But sometimes that line may be difficult even for Editor Hu to see. In June 2002, *Caijing* lost a defamation suit to a company for reporting alleged financial irregularities. The head of the company was the niece of former President Deng Xiaoping.

"*Caijing* is about as good as it gets in China," says Orville Schell, Dean of the Graduate School of Journalism at the University of California, Berkeley. "And, they've picked the perfect niche—business—which gives them the maximum latitude to do investigative work in China."[38]

But some see even *Caijing* becoming more cautious in current climate. After all, although owned by the Beijing Stock Exchange, it is still a government publication. Some staff members have been called in for "self-criticism."

## A Muckraker in the South

*Caijing* may have some protection from the Beijing Stock Exchange, but being in China's capital means its editors are always being closely watched by the state censors. Being distant from Beijing does give editors some advantages. *Southern Weekend*, 2,000 miles to the south in booming Guangdong province, has a national reputation for aggressive reporting and exposing government corruption. *Southern Weekend* says it has to be aggressive to compete with the nearby Hong Kong media. Time and again, it has tested the limits of reporting and thus gained a national audience. You can find *Southern Weekend* on newsstands all over China. A news vendor in Lanzhou, more than 2,000 miles away in northwest China, said he could sell more copies of *Southern Weekend* if he could get them from the state news agency.[39] *Southern Weekend* has made a few missteps. In 2002, the paper was ordered to pull a story about alleged corruption at Project Hope, a charity run by the Communist Youth League. Officials did not deny there was corruption, but feared that the exposé would dry up contributions for some important charities. Another publication known for aggressive reporting on farm protests is *Freezing Point*, a supplement to the widely read *China Youth Daily*. The government shut down *Freezing Point* early in 2006. There were so many protests, however, that *Freezing Point* was allowed to start publishing again, but Chinese officials refused to reinstate *Freezing Point*'s nationally known editor, Li Datong. Li was already in trouble, because six months earlier he had posted a letter on the publication's website criticizing the Propaganda Department for planning to dock reporters' salaries if they strayed from the Communist Party's line. Joseph Kahn, *New York Times* Bureau Chief in Beijing, said strong editors like Li will still keep pushing the limits in China and may eventually win the battle for more press freedom.[40]

Even if journalists are unable to report stories in their own publication, the news often gets out anyway. When a flood in central China killed eighty miners, local officials tried to cover it up with bribes and threats. Local media were afraid to report it. Journalists who covered the story, however, quickly leaked the information to distant publications and Internet websites. The major Communist Party publications recognize that they will lose their readers if they do not do some hard reporting of their own. After the mine disaster news got out to the public, the *People's Daily* jumped in with a series of articles. But Xinhua (New China), the nationwide news agency, ignored the story.

All the Chinese media ignore serious public protests, even when they turn violent and people are killed. The Chinese media were silent about a violent demonstration in December 2005, against construction of a power plant, that left twenty or more people dead. Four days later, Xinhua released a story reporting three deaths after villagers in the southern town "assaulted the police."[41]

## China's Tabloid Press

When the Communist leaders told government newspapers they had to start paying their own way, Chinese editors got much more freedom to publish material that would attract readers. Officials pushed this policy even further in 2003, when it told government offices they were no longer required to subscribe to official publications they had been receiving, but generally filing away unread, for years. Even Communist Party publications had to find a market. A new type of paper, the evening tabloid, has appeared in most Chinese cities. The Communist Party or the local government still owns the paper, but the editors can publish almost anything they think will attract readers. The editors have quickly adopted the same content that Western tabloids had shown could attract city readers: crime, sex, entertainment, features, color, short but graphic articles, and even some stories about corruption. Since most sales have been by street vendors, editors have provided such sensational headlines as "He Insulted Her; She Axed Him."

The tabloids are generally evening papers, while the morning papers remain tightly government controlled. As a result, the tabloids, which vary in format but have the same racy content, have surged ahead of the official morning papers in circulation and advertising revenue. Even the *People's Daily*, the major official government newspaper, lost 75 percent of its circulation in the 1990s.[42] Some journalists despair that the tabloids spell the death of "serious" journalism in China and suggest editors won't risk their economic success by challenging any but the most corrupt local officials. This is a "new opium for the masses," say some critics, who also charge that the tabloid journalists take bribes or charge fees to get stories into their newspapers.[43]

The Party finds it increasingly difficult to dictate to the editors of these self-supporting publications. One Shanghai newspaper editor said he never reads Ministry of Information material. Still, there are limits on all these editors, who get reminded at times that they are running government-owned publications. In 2003, the lead story in one issue of the English-language *Shanghai Daily* was the Academy Awards from Hollywood, while it ignored a Communist Party declaration that *China Daily* headlined. Party leaders reportedly called from Beijing and the Party report was in the next day's paper—but not on page one.

## A New Cultural Appeal

Perhaps the most dramatic example of a Chinese publications shifting from the government subsidy model to going after readers on its own is *China Culture Gazette*. It changed from a boring and money-losing Ministry of Culture magazine to a hot-selling industry leader, *Culture Weekend*. The secret: celebrity interviews and nudes, most of them Westerners. *Culture Weekend* even changed color from red to yellow. A "yellow" publication or film in China is X-rated. The Ministry was furious, but the editor pointed out that the huge sales were the only thing that prevented the magazine from closing, since the government had chopped its subsidy. *Culture Weekend* kept publishing and other publications started providing a diet of girls in bikinis, movie stars, and pop singers. Again, editor Zhang Zuomin knew the limits: "I will not run anything antiparty in my paper," he said, "and I will not run pornography."[44]

## Talk Radio

Competing with the tabloid press for the audience in China's cities is another Western import, talk radio. Radio reaches 95 percent or more of the Chinese people.[45] Much of it is the usual mix of music, weather, official news, and various special programs for farmers, women, children, and other groups. In China's cities, radio has been heavily influenced by Western content and formats. In Shanghai, your taxi driver will likely be listening to a mix of Western and Chinese pop music on an FM station that identifies itself (in English!) as "Your favorite music radio." The 1970s Carpenters' recording "Yesterday Once More" serves as the station's theme song. But it is talk radio that is, as one Chinese author put it, presenting a vivid picture. Talk radio is one of the few channels available to most Chinese for giving their opinions in public. It also sets up a different relationship between the media and the audience, since call-in listeners can often pick the topic and set the tone and direction of the discussion.

The programs generally focus on local issues (complaints about potholes, broken street lights, etc.), social issues (rude behavior on subways and buses), and the inevitable personal problems (inattentive husbands and unfaithful wives). Again, it was competition from Hong Kong that got talk radio started in mainland China. Hong Kong radio talk shows were attracting large audiences in southeast China, so in 1986 the government set up a mainland station to compete for listeners. The Chinese call-in programs proved hugely popular and soon won back the audience from the Hong Kong stations, winning official praise for "breaking the domination of foreign radio." Other talk radio stations were soon established in China's major cities and one other effect was soon clear: The new talk radio stations attracted far more listeners than the official stations that were filled with official propaganda and dreary programs. And talk radio hosts soon learned that some provocative dialogue on a sensitive issue could push up listenership in hurry. These hosts soon became local celebrities. Advertisers clamored to buy time on their programs.[46]

Programs to deal with special problems soon developed. Some hosts regularly helped dissatisfied customers get refunds from merchants, others collected complaints about the health system. Public officials, including city mayors, were invited on to answer citizen complaints. Late-night programs brought on physicians, psychologists, and other specialists to deal with personal problems of callers. Among the most popular programs was *Secret Whispers*, a late night show on Shanghai East Radio, a government station with a strong commercial base. The program tried to answer callers' questions about sex, a topic virtually ignored in both families and schools in China. A survey of callers found that, in Shanghai at least, sex and money were the most popular topics. One Shanghai talk show reportedly attracted 4,000 calls a minute. Inevitably, some callers want to talk about generally sensitive topics, such as government corruption or the gap between rich and poor in China. When ex-President Clinton took calls on a Shanghai radio station in 1998, a caller managed to get in complaints about the high levels of pollution in China's cities. Since most shows are live, hosts have to be ready to redirect the discussion but still not discourage other callers. And some topics are just not open for discussion, at least not on China's radio stations: A Beijing host quickly cut off callers who wanted to talk about legalizing prostitution and easing the policy of one couple, one child. Program hosts fend off critics by arguing that their programs are educational and also frequently bring on guests who support official policies. The call-in radio programs suggest a different level of public participation in public issues in China. It is a channel for public debate and discussion that is essentially beyond government control.

## New Threats: Cellphones and the Internet

Perhaps even bigger threats to China's rulers are cellphones and the Internet. China has more than 100 million Internet users and 350 million mobile phone users. They represent, in fact, an instant communication network. Internet cafés with rows of computers are found in China's cities. The government reportedly has 50,000 people constantly monitoring websites for any political threat.[47] Young people, especially in China's cities, use their mobile phones for both e-mail and text messaging. Government tries to monitor messages that go to large groups, but the speed of cellphone messaging makes it very difficult. In April

2005, huge crowds gathered for anti-Japanese demonstrations, despite government efforts to mute the protests. The Chinese authorities have been aggressive in their efforts to block and counter websites they consider unfriendly. They once planted a People's Republic flag on a Taiwan website.[48] The government censors are especially on guard against Falun Gong, a cult movement once supported by the government but banned in 1996. In March 2002, Fulan Gong supporters hacked into a city cable network in Changchun, the birthplace of the movement, and broadcast an hour of Fulan Gong material and attacks on the Chinese government to an estimated 300,000 homes.[49] China also pressures Internet providers, including Yahoo and Google, to identify the sources of any messages officials consider subversive and to block unwelcome sites or information. A Google search outside China for photos of Tiananmen Square, for example, produces images of the 1989 student uprising, but Google search results within China show tourists taking photographs.[50]

Despite these efforts, the Chinese authorities find it impossible to monitor all websites. One BBC journalist in Beijing typed the words "Dalai Lama" into his search engine in English and Chinese with no results. "Human rights" also drew a blank. The Chinese censors also successfully blocked access to the BBC Chinese Service and the main BBC website. When the journalist switched to other international news websites, however, he quickly got access.[51] An American journalist also found that a carefully worded message can get by the censor. He posted a message in a Chinese Internet chat room calling for multiparty elections, citing the example of Taiwan. The censor erased it within ten minutes. But then the journalist changed the tone to suggest that China's Communist leaders might allow multiparty elections "in 20 years." The censor either missed this message or let it pass. In fact, there are so many Internet messages to monitor that the censors reportedly only delete messages that seem to represent a serious threat.[52] One indication of the problem is that even though China tries to suppress evidence of homosexuality in the country, one study reported 250 gay-themed websites in China.[53]

But even though Chinese authorities are constantly alert to keep the Internet under control, they will encourage Internet use when it serves their purposes. The Internet has, for example, become an accepted channel for dissent, because it is much preferable to more threatening public demonstrations. In 2000, the government ordered all government agencies to set up websites to receive complaints. The Ministry of Foreign

Affairs website got 1.2 million complaints in three years, mostly saying that China was not acting strongly enough in world affairs.

"Policy-makers can't make decisions based on public opinion, but they can't ignore it either," said Li Minggang, who runs the Ministry of Foreign Affairs website.[54] Even nongovernment websites can have a place under China's media policy at times. When China's Railway Ministry let a Japanese company bid to build a new Beijing–Shanghai express train, a Patriots' Alliance website sprang up to protest dealing with China's former enemy. Within ten days, its online petition had 87,320 protesting signatures, reflecting anti-Japanese feelings that remain strong more than sixty years after the end of Japan's World War II occupation. The Chinese government quickly rejected the Japanese proposal. But the government's attitude changed when the Patriots' online rhetoric turned to Taiwan. Chinese officials feared that the Patriots' anti-Taiwan messages would help the most anti-Communist candidates in the upcoming election on that still-defiant island, that China hopes to integrate peacefully with the mainland just as it did Hong Kong. Meanwhile, the Patriots' Alliance website, attracting 80,000 visitors a day by 2004, branched out and even got a local government commendation for leading a clothing drive for the poor. Website owner Lu Yunfei believes he deserves government support: "We're doing this for the public good," he said, "so how could the government oppose it?"[55]

### New Internet Controls

Overall though, Chinese authorities want to control the Internet just as they control all other media in China. In September 2005, the government decreed that newspaper and magazine websites must "give priority" to news and commentary from official sources. Search engines such as www.sohu.com and www.sina.com, which had been posting private criticisms of government in their chat rooms, were ordered to block such comments and instead post only opinion pieces from government. "The foremost responsibility of news sites on the Internet," the regulations stated, "is to serve the people, serve socialism, guide public opinion in the right direction, and uphold the interests of the country and the public good."[56] Foreign Internet providers were ordered to reveal the identities of users and popular student bulletin boards to block access by off-campus computers. Despite student protests, bloggers were now required to register their real names. The new rules were seen as helping officials track down the authors of antigovernment statements.[57] Students, of course, are quick to seek and often find ways to outwit the Internet censors. In 2005, China banned Wikipedia, an online encyclopedia that users can edit. But a Chinese hacker in North Carolina, named Bill Xia, came up with a program called Freegate that links computers inside China with servers in the U.S. At least temporarily, this makes Wikipedia available via Chinese computers.[58]

But the Chinese authorities keep trying to limit Internet access, and have recently introduced some new "Internet cops," Jingjing and Chacha. These are animated icons used in the southern city of Shenzhen, a hotbed of unauthorized Internet activity just across from Hong Kong. Xu Qian, one of the 100 staff of Shenzhen's Internet Surveillance Center, says of Jingjing, "He is just like a policeman, interactively moving along with you. Wherever you go, he is watching you."[59]

## The Bloggers

Government officials have become increasingly annoyed with bloggers. They are largely individuals who have no connection to traditional media and suddenly appear and disappear before authorities can find out who they are. Li Xinde traveled around the country with a digital camera and a laptop computer, looking into reports of corruption. He then posted his stories on his website and left town before local authorities could find him.[60] There may be five million bloggers in China and two million have accounts with Bokee (Chinese for "blog"), a firm set up by a young entrepreneur to serve China's bloggers. By mid-2005, Bokee had a staff of 200, with advertisers including IBM. Founder Fang Xingdong does not want any problems with Chinese authorities and has a staff of ten on guard day and night to intercept "sensitive content, including anything remotely critical of the government."[61] A very popular blogger is "Aggressive Little Snake," whose "The Dog Newspaper" website won a German prize for best blog.

Chinese officials strongly discourage public discussions of human rights, so "The Dog Newspaper" campaigns for the rights of canines. Bokee has already attracted investors from both China and overseas, and next year hopes to be listed on a U.S. stock exchange. Bokee's marketing director is Mu Zimel, whose lurid sex diary attracted millions until it was banned by the government.

Chinese officials have always tried to keep explicit sexual material from the public, but over the centuries have failed. Mian Mian's 2003 novel *Candy*, promoted as "a blast of sex, drugs and rock 'n' roll" among modern China's youth, was banned by the government and as a result had a huge black market sale. The Chinese government banned the film *Farewell My Concubine* and were embarrassed by its worldwide success. To the Chinese government, the film is doubly disturbing. It paints a stark picture of the turmoil of the 1966–76 Cultural Revolution and its main character is a homosexual Chinese opera star. Still, Chinese officials give great leeway to the top film producers in China, partly because they are well known to international audiences who can influence decisions that affect China. The ban on *Farewell My Concubine* was lifted during a Chinese campaign to have the Olympics staged in Beijing. Meanwhile, Chinese filmmakers have gone to Hong Kong and elsewhere to escape the Beijing censors. Beijing gets very upset when these unapproved and uncensored films win international prizes as "Chinese films."[62] But when there are no politics involved, Chinese censors seem to have become more willing to let sex into public view. Fashion magazines with scantily clad women on the covers plus "candid talk about sex" on the pages between fill city newsstands throughout China. "We court the metrosexual," said Jin Jin, editor of *FHM* magazine.[63]

Despite the sometimes antigovernment bravado, however, there is little chance of any revolutionary change in China's press. The Tiananmen Square protests and their tragic end frightened many Chinese. They saw the abyss of civil war again opening up, and many Chinese believe radical political change is too dangerous. Editor Chen Xilin of *China Business Times* said of the student protesters who died: "Tragic, yes, but that's history. The new elite is a lot smarter, and one thing is certain about the future of China: it belongs to smart people."[64] China's economic boom is muting the most serious protests and most people, especially the younger generation, see this as more important than rapid political change. Some of the Tiananmen Square student protesters are now wearing business suits and are part of China's middle class. Even Mian Mian, denounced less than a decade ago as "a poster child for spiritual pollution" by the Chinese government, is fitting into the new China. Her latest novel, *Panda Sex*, uses the notoriously sex-shy bear as a symbol to suggest that getting ahead in life may be more important than either politics or sex. China's media leaders and foreign media moguls seem to agree on the political point, but sex is likely to continue to be a headache for Chinese censors, since newsstand sex sells well. China's media seem to be accepting a period of continued economic boom, but very gradual political change, in the country. A huge media role in the economic boom and a cautious approach to political issues seems to be the compromise that most accept. Perhaps this compromise is symbolized by a best-selling music cassette, "Red Sun." It features old hymns praising Communist leader Mao Tse Tung set to soft rock rhythms.

## Notes

1.  Max Frankel, "Word and Image: A Great, Irrelevant Wall," *The New York Times Magazine*, October 25, 1998, 36.
2.  Thomas L. McPhail, *Global Communication: Theories, Stakeholders, and Trends* (Boston: Allyn & Bacon, 2002), 86.
3.  Tsan-kuo Chang and Zixue Tai, "Freedom of the Press in the Eyes of the Dragon: A Matter of Chinese Relativism and Pragmatism," in *International Communication: Concepts and Cases*, K. Anokwa, C.A. Lin, and M.B. Salwen, eds. (Belmont, CA: Wadsworth, 2003), 24.
4.  Dan Griffiths, "China's Breakneck Media Revolution," http://news.bbc.co.uk, August 20, 2005.
5.  "China's Media: Back on the Leash," *The Economist*, August 18, 2005, 50.
6.  "The End of the Affair," *The Economist*, September 24, 2005, 80.
7.  Daya Kishan Thussu, *International Communication: Continuity and Change* (New York: Oxford University Press, 2000), 214.
8.  Geoffrey A. Fowler and Kathy Chen, "China Blocks News Corp. Plan for TV Channel," *The Wall Street Journal*, August 25, 2005, sec. B, 1.
9.  Howard W. French, "Fashion Magazines Rush to Mold China's Sense of Style," *The New York Times*, October 3, 2005, sec. A, 10.
10. John Jirik, "China's News Media and the Case of CCTV-9," in *International News in the Twenty-First Century*, C. Paterson and A. Sreberny, eds. (Eastleigh, U.K.: John Libbey/Luton Press, 2004), 133.
11. Kara Chan and Hong Cheng, "One Country, Two Systems," *Gazette*, 64(4), 2002, 385–400.
12. Doreen Weisenhaus, "Hong Kong's Free Press: Overshadowed by Beijing," *IPI Global Journalist*, 18(1), 2005, 22–3.
13. Li Yi, "How Chinese Television and News Media Presented the U.S. 9-11 Tragedy," cited in Jirik, "China's News Media and the Case of CCTV-9."
14. Qingwen Dong, Alexis Tan, and Xiaobing Cao, "Socialization Effects of American Television and Movies in China," in *Communication and Culture:*

*China and the World Entering the 21st Century*, D.R. Heisey and W. Gong, eds. (Amsterdam: Editions Rodopi, 1994), 314.

15. Geoffrey A. Fowler and Jason Dean, "Media Counter Piracy in China in New Ways," *The Wall Street Journal*, September 25, 2005, sec. B, 1.

16. Geraldine Fabrikant, "Media Executives Court China, but Still Run into Obstacles," *The New York Times*, August 29, 2005, sec. C, 1.

17. Jim Yardley, "An Unlikely Pop Icon Worries China," *International Herald Tribune*, http://iht.com, August 4, 2005.

18. Robert Marquand, "In China, It's Mongolian Cow Yogurt Super Girl," *Christian Science Monitor*, www.csmonitor.com, August 29, 2005.

19. "China's New Faces," BBC World, http://news.bbc.co.uk, September 17, 2005.

20. Chang Weimin, "China's ruling Party opening up to the world," *China Daily*, reported on http://news.bbc.co.uk, September 5, 2005.

21. Joseph Kahn, "China's State Secrets Will Guard One Less: Death Tolls," *The New York Times*, September 13, 2005, sec. A, 5.

22. Chongshan Chen, Jian-Hua Zhu, and Wei Wu, "The Chinese Journalist," in *The Global Journalist*, D.H. Weaver, ed. (Cresskill, NJ: Hampton Press, 1998), 9.

23. Wei Win and David Weaver, "Making Chinese Journalists for the Next Millennium," *Gazette*, 60(6), 1998, 513–29.

24. "China: The Media," Section 15 in *Library of Congress Country Studies*, October 3, 2005.

25. Yao Qingjiang and Josie Liu, "The Winding Road: Journalists Struggle for Press Reform in China," *IPI Global Journalist*, 18(1), 2005, 20–1.

26. Jim Yardley, "Secrecy Veils China's Jailing of a Journalist," *The New York Times*, August 31, 2005, sec. A, 1.

27. Trina Rosenberg, "Building the Great Firewall of China, with Foreign Help," *The New York Times*, September 18, 2005, sec. WK, 11.

28. "A Dragon Out of Puff," *The Economist*, June 15, 2002, 18.

29. "China's Media: Back on the Leash."

30. "Student Riot," Associated Press report credited to *Oriental Daily News*, published in *Milwaukee Journal Sentinel*, July 3, 2005, sec. A, 10.

31. Weisenhaus, "Hong Kong's Free Press: Overshadowed by Beijing."

32. Judith Shapiro and Lian Heng, *Cold Winds, Warm Winds: Intellectual Life in China Today* (Middletown, CT: Wesleyan University Press, 1986), 121–44.

33. Yao and Liu, "The Winding Road."

34. "International Editor of the Year," *World Press Review*, October 2003, 20–1.

35. Bill Savadove, "Mainland Press Pushes the Envelope," *South China Morning Post*, September 9, 2002, sec. A, 20.

36. "International Editor of the Year."

37. David Barboza, "Pushing (and Toeing) the Line in China," *The New York Times*, April 18, 2005, sec. C, 3.
38. Ibid.
39. Author interview, October 24, 2002.
40. "A Free and Fettered Press," National Public Radio, February 19, 2006; http://onthemedia.org
41. Howard W. French, "Beijing Casts Net of Silence over Protest," *The New York Times*, December 14, 2005, sec. A, 3.
42. Chengju Huang, "China's State-Run Tabloids: The Rise of 'City News-papers'," *Gazette*, 63(5), 2001, 435–50.
43. Jianying Zha, *China Pop: How Soap Operas, Tabloids, and Bestsellers are Transforming a Culture* (New York: The New Press, 1995), 107.
44. Ibid.
45. Anju Chaudhary and Anne Cooper Chen, "Asia and the Pacific," in *Global Journalism: A Survey of International Communication*, 2nd edn, J.C. Merrill, ed. (New York: Longman, 1991), 240.
46. Hua Xu, "Talk Radio in Urban China: Implications for the Public Sphere," in Heisey and Gong, *Communication and Culture*, 329.
47. Jim Yardley, "A Hundred Cellphones Bloom: And Chinese Take to the Streets," *The New York Times*, April 25, 2005, sec. A, 1.
48. Bridgette L. Nacos, *Mass-Mediated Terrorism* (New York: Rowman & Littlefield, 2002), 106.
49. Yuezhi Zhao, "Fulan Gong, Identity and the Struggle Over Meaning Inside and Outside China," in *Contesting Media Power: Alternative Media in a Networked World*, N. Couldry and J. Curran, eds. (New York: Rowman & Littlefield, 2003), 209.
50. Joseph Kahn, "So Long, Dalai Lama: Google Adapts to China," *The New York Times*, February 12, 2006, sec. WK, 5.
51. Griffiths, "China's Breakneck Media Revolution."
52. Nicholas Kristof, "Death from a Thousand Blogs," *The New York Times*, May 24, 2005, sec. A, 25.
53. Larry Gross, "The Gay Global Village in Cyberspace," in Couldry and Curran, *Contrasting Media Power*, 267.
54. Charles Hutzler, "Yuppies in China Protest Via the Web—And Get Away With It," *The New York Times*, March 19, 2004, sec. A, 4.
55. Ibid.
56. Joseph Kahn, "China Tightens its Restrictions for News Media on the Internet," *The New York Times*, September 26, 2005, sec. A, 9.
57. Paul Mooney, "Chinese Students Protest Web Limits," *Chronicle of Higher Education*, April 1, 2005, sec. A, 50.
58. Geoffrey A. Fowler, "Chinese Censors of Internet Face 'Hacktivists' in U.S.," *The Wall Street Journal*, February 13, 2006, sec. A, 1.

59. Mure Dickie, "China's Virtual Cops Pinpoint Web Dissent," *Financial Times*, February 18, 2006, 3.
60. Kristof, "Death from a Thousand Blogs."
61. Jamil Anderlini, "Blog founder seeks success writ large," *South China Morning Post*, July 12, 2005, www.asiamedia.ucla.edu/eastasia.asp·
62. Zha, *China Pop*, 103.
63. French, "Fashion Magazines Rush to Mold China's Sense of Style."
64. Zha, *China Pop*, 108.

# Chapter 8

# The Evolving Media of the Arabs and Africa

*There is always something new out of Africa.*
—Pliny the Elder (A.D. 23–79)

Broadly speaking, the media of mass communication are unevenly distributed around the world. There are far more newspapers, magazines and journals, broadcast and cable TV, AM and FM radio stations, Internet users, movie theaters, and cellphones per capita in the affluent industrialized Western nations than in the struggling, developing nations of the "South." In the West, media are plentiful throughout a nation; in poor countries, media are found mainly in the capital or large cities, and rural areas are media starved. That picture, although generally accurate, is an incomplete one, however, for the proliferating "new media," so integral to the Information Age, are today found throughout the world. Although they do not yet exist in great numbers, these new media are being utilized in surprising and useful ways to assist poor nations in their long ascent to modernization and democracy.

In this chapter, we look at recent dramatic changes in the media of the Arab nations of the Middle East and their impact on the current war in Iraq. In the last section, we will examine some encouraging trends in Africa—the most media-deficient region of the world. Quiet media revolutions are changing some societies just as, in the 1960s, the small, battery-powered transistor radio changed much of Africa by broadcasting news, information, and music to rural peoples in remote areas that had never known mass communication.

## Arabs Receive Satellite Television News

Throughout the twentieth century, the predominant press model for twenty Arabic-speaking nations was authoritarian. The press, television, radio, and national news agencies from the monarchies of Morocco and Saudi Arabia to the secular states of Egypt and Syria were firmly controlled by their governments. Further, there was little regional communication in Arabic, with the exception of the Voice of the Arabs radio broadcasts out of Nasser's Egypt.

Television viewers were accustomed to stale, heavily censored, state-controlled television and had little access to independent and reliable news in Arabic. All that changed in 1996, when Al Jazeera began broadcasting out of the tiny oil sheikdom of Qatar on the Persian Gulf. The Doha-based satellite channel was in the vanguard of big changes and became the most freewheeling station in the Arab world, delighting millions of viewers across the Middle East and annoying many Arab governments. Their audience has been estimated at 30 to 50 million viewers.

Al Jazeera has become the Arab world's CNN, with round-the-clock, all-news and public affairs programs reaching multitudes in twenty Arab states, mostly through private satellite dishes, which can be purchased for less than $100. Millions of Arab families now own TV dishes, whether in the slums of Cairo or the mansions of Kuwait. Al Jazeera has also become available in Britain and the U.S., where many thousands of viewers pay $30 a month to receive a multi-channel Arabic "package."

With more than 350 editors, anchors, and technicians and more than thirty-five bureaus around the world, the network often focused on subjects considered subversive in most Arab nations: persecution of political dissidents; the absence of democratic institutions; the inequality of women; torture; polygamy; and rival interpretations of Islamic teachings. Its talk shows have infuriated Arab rulers by bringing to its studios political dissidents from Egypt, Saudi Arabia, Algeria, Syria, Morocco, Jordan, and Iraq. The network has built a reputation for independent, groundbreaking reporting that contrasted markedly with other Arabic-language stations. Broadcast by satellite, Al Jazeera has been difficult to censor, although Arab nations have tried. Algeria's regime reportedly shut off electricity in parts of the country rather than allow television sets to pick up a debate on the country's bloody civil war.

Al Jazeera has even scooped governments that control their own media. In 1999, it broadcast in advance of the Iraqi media Saddam Hussein's Army Day speech, in which he called on Arabs to overthrow their leaders if they were allied with the United States. Al Jazeera has relentlessly reported strife in the occupied territories of Israel and has kept the Palestinian cause very much alive in living rooms of the Muslim world.

After September 11, Al Jazeera became a central player in the emerging Middle East propaganda war. The network gained access to news sources in Afghanistan and during the first weeks of the war had the only television footage from inside Afghanistan. Britain's Prime Minister, Tony Blair, has been interviewed, as has Secretary of State Colin Powell. But as the war went on, U.S. policy makers grew troubled by the frequent rebroadcasts of Al Jazeera's exclusive December 1998 interview with Osama bin Laden, in which he urged Muslims to "target all Americans," and by the anti-American oratory of many of its analysts, guests, and callers on its popular talk shows.

Nonetheless, the station's Arab viewers are able to see things they are not supposed to see. For the first time, Arabs with a satellite dish can have access to uncensored news. The station offered silent footage of Bright Star, a joint Egyptian–American military exercise off the coast of Egypt—a potent commentary on the cooperation of the Egyptian military with the Pentagon. The station also gets credit for being one of the few Arab television stations to interview Israelis.

The Arab world's most-watched station regularly evoked the wrath of the Bush administration, as when they ran video taken by insurgents when they shot down a Bulgarian helicopter, killing six Americans. Yet in 2005, Al Jazeera had become a leading vehicle for the region's budding reform movements. Giving voice to reformers, for example, after the assassination of former Lebanon prime minister, Rafiq Hariri, it aired ten straight hours of footage from Lebanon as street protesters demanded the country's government expel the occupying Syrian troops. Because of intensified coverage of Middle East reform movements, its correspondents have been barred in Saudi Arabia, Kuwait, Algeria, and Tunisia, all autocratic governments, as well as in Iraq.

As Robin Wright of *The Washington Post* reported, "Al Jazeera's popularity has given rise to 100 satellite channels in the region. Together they are called the most dynamic force for political change in the Middle East. They offer a locus for the Arab street to vent, formulate, and discuss public affairs. One report said, 'all in all, Arab satellite stations have pushed ajar the door of democracy and flanked state monopoly on media'.[1] Al Jazeera staffers say they are responsible for the rising ripple of activism in the Middle East, including the ousting of the pro-Syrian government in Lebanon. One editor said "It was really remarkable. It was the first time people in this region have been able to topple a government. We were all captivated." Syrian troops tried to physically block Al Jazeera camera operators from covering their withdrawal from Lebanon.[2]

In July 2005, the network said it planned to introduce an English-language satellite channel, competing with CNN International and BBC World. Prominent Brit David Frost has signed on to anchor a regular news program. The goal is to reach not just Western audiences but also English-speaking Muslims in Asia and in the West. In 2005, there were reports that due to intense pressure from the Bush administration on Qatar, a crucial American ally in the Persian Gulf, the network was being put up for sale.

## Al Jazeera Only Part of the Story

Satellite television has changed communication in the region. With a $100 satellite setup, the average Arab citizen can now tune into at least three satellites, each carrying hundreds of channels. A few include a growing number of independent news channels. Because they can originate anywhere, they are difficult to censor. In addition to Al Jazeera, there are four other major satellite news channels:

- Al Arabiya is the second largest satellite station and is owned by the Middle East Broadcasting Center, which is itself owned by a Saudi billionaire. So the channel is supportive of the Saudi government and is considered a quieter competitor to Al Jazeera.
- Al Alam is a popular channel supported by the Iranian government and is critical of the U.S. government and the Iraq war. The channel considers itself an answer to what it considers the "American cultural invasion."
- Al Ekhbariya is aimed at a Saudi audience and was begun last year as an alternative to Al Jazeera. The channel offers news and talk shows twenty-four hours a day, delivered in an official and rather flat manner.
- Al Hurra is an American-backed channel that copies the formats of Al Jazeera and Al Arabiya, but has been struggling to build an

audience. It is considered to have high production values and polished presentations, but is widely considered as American propaganda.

These Arab-based television news channels broadcast to Arabs in Europe and sometimes run afoul of European governments. In December 2004, the highest court in France banned the television channel Al Manar, ruling that the Beirut-based broadcaster had repeatedly violated France's hate laws by making anti-semitic comments. The popular channel was run by the Hezbollah militia.

The Arabic press reaches far fewer people than television, tends to be local, and is much more susceptible to government censorship. As a result, some Arab papers are published in Europe. Several papers stand out because of their influence. *Al Sharq Al Awsat*, one of the oldest and most influential, is published by a private company based in London and is widely distributed. A supporter of the Saudi government, the paper maintains an even and balanced approach. *Al Hayat* is clearly an Arab nationalist paper; it is also published in London and owned by a Saudi prince. It is more critical of Saudi Arabia than its rivals and is staffed mainly by Lebanese. *Okaz* is Saudi Arabia's most visible paper and, though independent, is considered a spokesman for the Saudi government and is an agenda setter for other Saudi media. *Al Ahram* of Cairo has long been considered an important Arab paper, even though it is backed by the Egyptian government. It favors democratic reforms, but is not pro-U.S. In addition, the Internet offers hundreds of Arabic websites—gossip, music, e-mail, and chat sites. Also, numerous online news sites try to attract Arab readers. Arabs now receive much more locally produced television programming, Internet offerings, and websites than even a few years ago. A few optimistic observers believe these communication flows may lead to more open and possibly democratic societies.

## The Dark Side of the Arabic Internet

As a communication tool, the Internet has proved to be a lethal and effective weapon for Islamic terrorists in their "long war" with the West. Never before has a guerrilla organization so effectively utilized new media—the Internet, e-mail, blogs, camcorders, and cellphones—to carry on its real-time war along with an electronic jihad. The information wing of Abu Musab Zarqawi in Iraq has used a whole gamut of communication devices in its struggles. Essentially, the Islamic jihadists utilize the Internet in four basic ways: to send propaganda and ideological appeals to potential followers everywhere; to inform and control terrorist cells and give specific commands for terrorist acts; to raise funds for terrorist activities; and to shock the world with vivid camcorder videos of gruesome acts, such as bombings, beheadings, and graphic images of innocent victims.

## Africa Flirts with the New Media

In the 50 years since political independence from colonialism, the forty plus new nations of Africa have lagged behind the West in acquiring daily newspapers, radio and television broadcasting stations, motion pictures, magazines and book publishing, and news agencies as well as telecommunications generally. However, during this new century and in numerous places, Africans—despite their enormous problems and the difficulties of their harsh environment—have begun to adopt and adapt such media as cellphones, FM radio, VCRs and DVDs, and computer-assisted global communication. Though modest in scope, these activities contribute to individual and national development and may have long-term consequences.

## Cellphones in Rural Africa and India

Mobile phones, or cellphones, have proliferated throughout the Western world in recent years and, for journalists, have proved to be exceedingly useful tools to file stories from remote places, or to keep in touch with their editors or colleagues. But the use of cellphones has grown even faster in developing nations and contributes to economic development.

For example, sales of cellphones have been increasing rapidly in rural India, where unexpected uses have been found for them. In the seas off Kerala state, crowded with fishing boats, fishermen use cellphones to keep in touch with the dozen-odd seafood markets, checking prices at different ports. Since acquiring the mobile service, fishermen have markedly increased their profits and efficiency. The 5,000 fishermen who work off the coast are not alone in embracing wireless technology. From garment workers in the south to farmers in the Punjab, rural India has discovered the convenience of doing business on mobile phones. Many people in rural areas have no alternative. Half of India's 660,000 villages have never been wired for fixed-line service, and those connected have had outdated equipment and long waits for service.

In Africa, lack of telecommunications has sorely frustrated the rise of television broadcasting and landline telephone service Lately, we've seen how the videocassettes and compact disks have largely bypassed television, which, like telephone service, has been confined to urban areas, often only in the country's capital. And now, rather unexpectedly, cellphones have catapulted rural Africa into the twenty-first century. During recent years, from 1999 through 2004, Africa has become the fastest growing cellphone market anywhere. Africa's mobile subscribers jumped an average of 58 percent annually, from 7.5 million to 76.8 million. The next fastest expanding region was Asia, which grew annually at 34 percent in the same period.

Africans, most living on $2 a day, were not considered rabid telephone users. But when African nations began to privatize their telephone monopolies in the mid-1990s, the use of cellphones exploded after competitive operators began to sell air time in smaller, cheaper units. Now, one in eleven Africans is a mobile subscriber. Africa has an average of just one landline for every 33 people, but cellphones are enabling millions of people to skip a technological generation and go straight from letter writing to instant communications. The technology is, for many, a social and economic godsend. One program in South Africa allows about 100 farmers in a remote area to learn the prevailing prices for produce in major markets, which is crucial information for dealing with middlemen. Health-care workers elsewhere in South Africa summon ambulances to distant clinics by way of cellphones.[3]

## FM Radio and Political Change in Ghana

In sub-Saharan Africa, radio has long been the most potent mass medium, reaching far more people than newspapers or television. But in most African countries, AM radio has been a heavy-handed government monopoly. However, in Ghana, a West African nation of 26 million, a significant change took place in 1995 when the previous government, led by President Jerry Rawlings, gave up its monopoly on the airwaves and permitted the establishment of private FM radio stations. After that, more than forty FM stations cropped up around Ghana, broadcasting in

English and Ghanaian languages. The stations offered local music and their own news, and most importantly, they broadcast hours and hours of live talk radio, during which Ghanaians could tell government and anyone else what was on their minds.

The resulting national dialogue that took place over FM radio enabled presidential challenger J.A. Kufuor to win an election over Rawlings, whose tired and corrupt party had controlled the country for twenty years. This was the first-ever peaceful transition from one elected civilian government to another in Ghana. Observers said that when people saw something that concerned them, they called in to their FM station, which gave the public a voice. Politicians could hear ordinary people talk about many problems—unemployment, corruption, food prices. People were fed up and they told each other about it. Of Ghana's ten provinces, eight had these flourishing FM stations, and in all these provinces, Kufuor won. In the two provinces without FM stations, the incumbent Rawlings won. Since the election, the FM stations, all run by young Ghanaians who had worked or been educated in the West, have been trying to force more transparency on the new government. One official said, "The minute people were able to talk freely—and anonymously—on the radio and ask what officials were up to was the beginning of accountability for government in Ghana."[4] Finally, the four most democratic nations in West Africa today—Ghana, Mali, Senegal, and Benin—all have flourishing FM radio stations.

## Job Outsourcing and Satellite Channels

Africa has taken two small but significant steps to participating in global communication: telemarketing jobs and contributing to U.S. cable programming. Kenya's international call center—KenCall—has about 200 telephone operators, who are kept busy dialing customers in Britain and the U.S. This is a growth industry in Africa, and in 2005 there were an estimated 54,000 call-center jobs in Africa out of a total six million such jobs worldwide, most of them in India. But the prospects for growth are good, because so many Africans are educated in either English or French. So far, South Africa is ahead of the others, with an estimated 500 call centers employing about 31,000 people. In West Africa, Ghana has lured an outsourcing company based in Dallas that employs about 2,000 Ghanaians to process health claims for Aetna and other insurers.

Another international connection for Africa with the greater world has been the launching in 2005 of the Africa Channel on cable television in the United States. A purpose of the project is to overcome some of the many stereotypes about Africa in the West. The backers have secured rights to 1,200 hours of movies, music, and reality and variety shows that have already been broadcast in Africa, principally in South Africa. Some features, including a daily current events program, "Africa Today," will be produced specially for the twenty-four hour channel.

## Africa In and Out of the News Spotlight

For twelve days in March 1998, American newspapers and television news were full of stories and video about Ghana, Uganda, Rwanda, South Africa, Botswana, and Senegal—all stops on President Bill Clinton's tour of Africa, with an entourage of 800, including more than 200 journalists. For that brief time, the public was deluged with considerable information about that complex and troubled region. But after Clinton returned to Washington, D.C., the news spigot from Africa was abruptly shut off. This reaffirmed a journalistic truism about Africa: The continent usually makes news when a famous personage comes calling, such as President Carter did in 1978 or Pope John Paul II did in 1982 and 1998. Africa gets our attention as well when American soldiers' lives are at risk in Africa, as in 1992, when U.S. Marines landed in Somalia.

Yet most of the time, sub-Saharan Africa, except for South Africa, continues to be the least reported region of the world. One reason is that Africa's own news media, which are weak and usually government controlled, have not been effective in reporting reliable news to Africans, much less to the outside world, and generally are not much help either to foreign journalists trying to report from Africa.

During the 1960s and 1970s, independent black Africa received special attention in the Western press as some forty new nations with promising futures stepped onto the world's stage. But as many of these countries foundered and regressed, and as the Cold War waned, the global media's interest in Africa dropped sharply. These days, there is a grudging consensus among journalists that Africa is badly neglected in global news. Jim Hoagland of *The Washington Post* said Africa has gotten short shrift in the media for a long time, and David Gergen of *U.S. News* commented,

"The history of American media has been one of general inattention to Africa, except when there's been a major famine or conflict."[5]

*Africa's Media Image*, a book edited by Beverly Hawk, with contributions by Africanists and journalists with African experience, gives detailed analyses of shortcomings of Western reporting of major African news stories over the past generation, confirming a near-unanimous view of African specialists that Western news media need to do better. News flows out of Africa to Europe and America in much the same ways that it does from other developing nations in Latin America, Asia, and the Middle East, with many of the same traits.

### Parachute Journalism

A story breaks that captures the world's attention: widespread famine in Niger or Ethiopia, genocidal warfare in Sudan or Rwanda, civil war in Congo. The foreign press arrives, often in large numbers, covers the story, shoots pictures and video, and then abruptly leaves. This kind of reporting, typically seen on television, fails to provide needed context and follow-up that such stories require for public understanding.

### Declining Coverage

Since the end of the Cold War, much less news has been coming out of Africa, as many civil wars and upheavals have ended. Many small nations, among them Benin, Botswana, Burkina Faso, Mali, Burundi, Guinea, Niger, Lesotho, and Togo, not only have rarely had resident Western correspondents but also are seldom visited by Western reporters passing through the region. A few years ago, armed conflicts were going on at the same time in Angola, Chad, Djibouti, Ethiopia, Liberia, Rwanda, Somalia, Sudan, and Western Sahara, but little reporting about these wars appeared in the U.S. news media. On June 8, 1998, Nigeria's military dictator, Sani Abacha, died unexpectedly. This major story from Africa's most populous nation received only brief mention on the evening television news. The next day, *The New York Times* and *The Washington Post* both gave the story several pages of coverage.

### Barriers to Reporting

Journalists in Africa face barriers not found elsewhere. Few foreign correspondents know the many local languages, although knowledge of

English and French is usually sufficient for dealing with news sources. Distances are greater, communications less reliable, and air travel inconvenient and often haphazard. Reporters sometimes have to fly through London or Paris to get from one African capital to another. African governments often treat reporters badly; some at times just bar all foreign reporters. Often, reporters may be permitted in, but access to news sources or officials is severely limited.

### Failures to Report Bad News

By gathering news that authorities do not want reported, correspondents face the threat of expulsion. Over the years, many Western reporters have been forced out of Africa and refused visas when they sought reentry. Because of this possibility, some journalists believe that sometimes the bad news does not get reported. A British journalist, Ian Smiley, suggested that such self-censorship was a standard feature of reporting throughout the Third World and was nowhere more rigorously observed than in Africa.

Because of this reluctance to report fully, a darker side of Africa may be ignored. True, the coverage has been thin and violence prone, but the need may not be just to provide more positive, cheerful, and sympathetic coverage. The need may be for more realistic and thorough coverage of the continent's deepening crisis. Not much of this gloomy scenario gets into daily news reports.

Two respected journalists have sounded warnings. Robert Kaplan painted a disturbing picture of West Africa which, he said, is "becoming the symbol of worldwide demographic, environmental, and societal stress, in which criminal anarchy emerges as the real 'strategic' danger. Disease, overpopulation, unprovoked crime, scarcity of resources, refugee migrations, the increasing erosion of nation-states and international borders, and the empowerment of private armies, security firms, and international drug cartels are now most tellingly demonstrated through a West African prism."[6]

Columnist William Pfaff voiced similar concerns: "The destitution of Africa has been an all but forbidden topic in political discourse. The time has arrived, however, for honest and dispassionate discussion of this immense human tragedy, for which the Western countries bear a grave, if partial, responsibility and which will worsen if not addressed. Much of Africa needs, to put it plainly, what one could call a disinterested neocolonialism."[7]

These are controversial views, and some argue that they show a lack of belief in the survival skills of ordinary people, and may convince the concerned and sympathetic outsiders to give up on Africa. The plight of Africa reflects a central quandary about reporting Africa. Despite the steady decline in news about Africa, the U.S. media's selective, violence-ridden reports have painted a negative and discouraging picture. Yet, if Kaplan and Pfaff are correct, the reality may be bleaker than we believed, and there indeed may be a need for Western nations to intervene. That is not something the Western publics want to hear.

Finally, considering the erratic and sparse coverage of Africa on television and in the news magazines, it is imperative that the handful of prestigious newspapers not dilute their African coverage. Three papers, *The New York Times*, *The Washington Post*, and the *Los Angeles Times*, continue to produce superior daily reporting out of Africa. Several British papers do an excellent job covering Africa.

## Notes

1. Robin Wright, "Al Jazeera Puts Focus on Reform," *The Washington Post*, May 8, 2005, sec. A, 16.
2. Ibid.
3. Sharon LaFraniere, "Cellphones Catapult Rural Africa to 21st Century," *The New York Times*, August 25, 2005, sec. A, 1.
4. Thomas Friedman, "Low Tech Democracy," *The New York Times*, May 1, 2001, sec. A, 27.
5. Beverly Hawk, *Africa's Media Image* (New York: Praeger, 1992), 224.
6. Robert Kaplan, "The Coming Anarchy", *The Atlantic Monthly*, February 1994, 44–76.
7. William Pfaff, "A New Colonialism," *Foreign Affairs*, January/February 1995, 2–6.

# Chapter 9

# Foreign News in Flux

*The cause of the decline and fall of the Roman Empire lay in the fact that there were no newspapers of the day. Because there were no newspapers, there was no way by which the dwellers in the far-flung nation and the empire could find out was going on at the center.*

—H.G. Wells

*The press should be free to go where it wants, when it wants, to see, hear and photograph what it believes is in the public interest.*

—Walter Cronkite

The craft of gathering foreign news by journalists stationed overseas has been undergoing substantial changes in recent years. Because of financial cost cutting and new technologies, less news is reported from abroad and by very different methods. The foreign correspondent—that widely traveled and glamorous specialist of journalism—is becoming a different breed of reporter from the old days of the Cold War. The public today seems less interested in foreign news, and editors and broadcasters are giving them a lot less of it.

This describes foreign affairs journalism *before* the momentous events of September 11, 2001. For some time, foreign news dominated the media and the public could not seem to get enough of it. Covering the multifaceted war on terrorism and maintaining reporters overseas was very expensive. Television broadcasters lost nearly $100 million a day in local and national advertising because of extended coverage in the first few days that often ran without commercial breaks. Expenses of reopening bureaus, staffing them, and using the latest technologies to send words and images cost news organizations about $25 million in the first week, as journalists arrived in Pakistan, Afghanistan, Tajikistan, Yemen, and Bahrain. Setup costs for satellite communications equipment can be as much as $70,000 for each uplink and about that much a week to maintain it. As the crisis seemed to ease, audience ratings for war news were starting to drop and television executives hinted that cutbacks might be coming.

The shock of 9/11 triggered one significant shift: Most Americans were turning to cable news for daily reports about terrorism and the war, and the number has increased since mid-September 2001. A Pew Center survey found that fully 53 percent of respondents cited cable as their primary source for news on the crisis, versus 17 percent for network television and 18 percent for local television. The number relying mostly on newspapers for war news since 9/11 has increased from 11 percent to 34 percent. All types of media could take comfort in the fact that 66 percent of respondents say they are more interested in news now than before 9/11. But this unprecedented foreign news glut, with high public interest, did not last.

During the decade before 9/11, the news media were indifferent to foreign news at a time when ethnic conflicts killed millions and globalization touched most American communities. A Harvard study found that during the 1970s, network television devoted 45 percent of its total coverage to international news. By 1995, foreign news represented only 13.5 percent of total coverage. Budgets and staff were cut, bureaus closed, and the media emphasized shifts to economic and entertainment/trivia concerns.

Yet serious journalists and editors have long argued that foreign news is important and should be reported thoroughly and well. Many of the best and brightest journalists have spent part of their careers in what must be among the most demanding jobs in journalism. Transnational news gathering is an exacting occupation for the professional newsmen and newswomen who put together the various stories, reports, rumors, and educated guesses that make up the daily international news file. To them, theirs is a difficult, dangerous, and badly misunderstood enterprise. They understand its shortcomings and difficulties far better, they believe, than politically motivated critics or cost-conscious media owners.

In a real sense, the world's ability to learn the news about itself depends on what gets into the news flow in the fifteen or twenty open societies with highly developed media systems. After an important story appears, for example, in New York, London, Paris, Rome, or Tokyo, it immediately starts flowing through the arteries of the world's news system and will be widely reported elsewhere—but not everywhere, and certainly not every story; the majority of non-Western governments act as gatekeepers, screening news in and out of their nations. These political controls, as well as poverty and illiteracy, deprive the great majority of the world's peoples from learning even the barest outline of major current events. But any major story that "breaks" in the West has at least the possibility of being reported throughout the world.

To the few thousand foreign correspondents, the world's nations are strung out on a continuum from "free" or open at one end to "not free" or closed at the other, and with many variations in between. To illustrate, the Associated Press has little difficulty gathering news in open Sweden, because several newspapers there take AP services and share their own news and photos with the agency. In addition, AP correspondents can use other Swedish media as sources and can develop their own stories or easily gain access to public officials.

Sudan, like other developing nations, offers a different kind of challenge. AP has no clients in Sudan, largely because the Sudan News Agency lacks the hard currency to buy the Comsat-beamed AP world service. The local media are subject to official controls, and AP cannot justify the expense of maintaining a full-time correspondent in Khartoum. Therefore, AP "covers" Sudan by using a local stringer (a part-timer who is paid for what news is used). Periodically, AP may send a staff correspondent to Sudan to do background or round up stories. At other times, AP may try to report on events in Sudan from Nairobi, in neighboring Kenya. Yet as recent events in Sudan have illustrated, the world knew too little about a state that condoned, if not encouraged, genocide against its own people. Despite the efforts of a few hardy reporters who managed to get into Darfur to report the atrocities against helpless civilians, the United Nations has still not taken effective action to halt the genocide.

At the "not free" end of the continuum are a few countries that for years barred all foreign journalists and news agencies. In the Cold War days, when something important happened in Tirana, Albania, for instance, AP and the world usually found out about it belatedly from a government-controlled Albanian radio broadcast monitored abroad, or from travelers or diplomats leaving the country. Albania has since opened, and Western analysts were surprised that Albanian refugees knew about the collapse of communism, which they learned about by listening carefully to English broadcasts on the BBC and VOA. Much news of the turmoil in Africa is often reported from the safety of neighboring countries.

A foreign correspondent often defines a country as free or not free according to how much difficulty he or she has in reporting events there. This may sound narrow and self-serving, but it has validity: the freedom of access that a foreign reporter enjoys is usually directly related to the amount of independence and access enjoyed by local journalists themselves. If local journalists are harassed or news media controlled by a particular government, so very likely will be the foreign journalists.

With the availability of impressive gadgets used by today's foreign correspondents—satellite telephones, videophones, laptop computers, reliable phone lines (or better yet cellphones), and faxes—the reporter abroad is better able to do his or her job. An important new gadget is the video telephone so widely used in Afghanistan. Even so, collecting news throughout the world is still an erratic and imperfect process. Some significant events are either not reported or reported long after the fact. Certain areas of the world, such as central Africa, rarely get into the world news flow.

In the dangerous and confusing post Cold War world, foreign reporters and news organizations went through an identity crisis over what is news. As John Walcott of *Newsweek* said, "The Cold War provided us with a coherent global road map, in terms of what to cover and how to cover it."[1] The press is not used to reacting to a world full of conflicts and violent encounters that, as George Kennan put it, offer no "great and all absorbing focal points for American policy."[2] Now the war on terrorism has provided for some nations a focus for global news comparable to that of the Cold War.

A key challenge is disagreements between journalists and government officials over the very nature of news. To journalists, news is the first, fragmentary, and incomplete report of a significant event or happening that editors think will be of interest or importance to their readers or listeners. To many government officials, news is "positive" information that reflects favorably on their nation (and hence themselves) and serves their country's general interests and goals. Yet those same leaders want to know all that is happening elsewhere that affects their own interests and country. An AP man said that news is what a government official wants to read about somewhere else, whereas propaganda is what the official wants the world to read about his or her country. Politicians and government leaders in every nation attempt to manage or manipulate the news so that it favors their causes, their programs, their image.

Any major news story is perceived differently by the press in almost every country for these reasons: Media everywhere tend to have a "bias of nationalism" that affects the way a story is reported. What has been called "journalism as politics" permeates foreign news in subtle ways. Moreover, the maxim "all news is local" has validity because editors usually respond more fully to what happens nearby or what affects local interests.

Certainly, before 9/11 the news media, especially television and news magazines, had been paying less attention to foreign news. Always expensive to cover, the consensus in the news business had been that you can expect international news to turn a profit only when it is really domestic news in a foreign setting, such as a U.S. military intervention, when it is "our boys" who are "over there," as in Afghanistan or Iraq.

## TV News in Decline: The CBS Case

CBS News, long famed for its international coverage, once maintained twenty-four foreign bureaus. By 2005, it had reporters in only four capitals: London, Moscow, Tel Aviv, and Tokyo. Dan Rather told a group of Harvard students, "Don't kid yourself. The trend line in American journalism is away from, not toward, increased foreign coverage. Foreign coverage requires the most space and the most air time because you are dealing with complicated situations, in which you have to explain a lot. And then there's always somebody around who says people don't give a damn about this stuff anyway . . . 'If you have to do something foreign, Dan, for heaven's sake, keep it short'."[3]

Tom Fenton, a former CBS reporter, recently wrote that foreign news is down 70 to 80 percent since the early 1980s, supplemented by "junk news" and "tabloidism." Meanwhile, the all news cable channels—once our great hope—degenerate to celebrity and commentary formulas, offering little credible reporting. One of the most alarming comments in Fenton's book: "In the three months leading up to September 11, the phrase 'Al Qaeda' was never mentioned on any of the three evening news broadcasts—not once. I, and scores of my fellow American foreign correspondents, had been tracking stories about Al Qaeda and its allies for more than a decade. But we rarely reported what we knew on network news—because, much of the time, our bosses didn't consider such developments newsworthy."[4] Fenton said CBS relies increasingly on information supplied by video wire services and overseas broadcasters. It's television's equivalent of outsourcing.

The three major news magazines, each of which has long emphasized foreign news gathered by its own overseas correspondents, reflected the declining interest in international news. Throughout 1995, *Time* devoted 385 pages to international news, or about 14 percent of the magazine, yet ten years earlier, in 1985, *Time* published 670 pages of foreign news, or 24 percent of its news content. Circulation for *Time*, *Newsweek*, and *U.S. News* is sharply up with war news but, ominously, advertising revenue was lagging during 2001.

## Changing Correspondents

"What is commonly referred to as the world flow of information," AP correspondent Mort Rosenblum wrote, "is more a series of trickles and spurts. News is moved across borders by a surprisingly thin network of correspondents. . . . The smaller countries are squeezed into rapid trips during lulls between major stories in the larger countries." Rosenblum quoted a comment from a Latin American academic that "news breaks in South America along the direct line of the international airline route."[5]

In some places it may seem that way, and yet the total flood of daily news reports from abroad is immense. One study estimated that the big four agencies send out about 33 million words a day, with 17 million from AP, 11 million from UPI, 3.4 million from AFP, and 1.5 million from Reuters. Among the smaller agencies, dpa of Germany was set at 115,000, ANSA of Italy at 300,000, and efe of Spain at 500,000.

Considering the demand for foreign news and the difficulties of reporting from far-flung places, there are probably too few correspondents stationed overseas. Rising costs and inflation have made maintenance of a staffer overseas quite expensive. Estimates for maintaining a newspaper bureau overseas (that is, at least one reporter) for a year range from $150,000 to $250,000, and the costs keep going up. A television bureau can cost more than $1 million a year. It is not surprising, therefore, that many news media rely on the news agencies for their foreign news. In most countries, that means the Associated Press and Reuters. High costs help explain the drop in overseas television bureaus.

AP and other news agencies are using more and more "locals"—nationals of countries they cover. Western journalism is increasingly relying on foreign nationals to help report the news. Foreign journalists are not only less expensive, but often have a grasp of local languages and knowledge of their own countries that U.S. journalists cannot match. Journalist Scott Schuster attributed the trend to a global acceptance of English as a media language and the global influence of American journalistic methods: "American influence is most profound among broadcasters, and foreign broadcast journalists need only to turn on their TV sets to receive lessons on how to do the news American-style," he said. Schuster goes on:

> American methods of news production are being adopted all across Western Europe and in many Third World countries. . . . During the coming decade journalistic styles in both print and broadcast media are likely to experience continuing international homogenization. The nationality of the reporter will no longer be an issue. Brits will cover Britain. Ghanaians will cover Ghana, and a large number of American journalists will become "foreign correspondents"—covering America for foreign media.[6]

Increasingly, to deal with rising costs and tighter budgets, news media are relying on stringers or freelancers. A study by Stephen Hess of the Brookings Institution of 404 foreign correspondents working for U.S. news media found that 26 percent are freelancers. Moreover, many of these are underemployed, with 40 percent saying they do other work as well. All suffer the usual fate of freelancers: low pay, no benefits, and a precarious relationship with their employers.[7] Hess found six types of stringers: "spouses" of other correspondents; "experts," who know languages and the area; "adventurers," like Oriana Fallaci; "flingers," a person on a fling who might start a serious career; "ideologues" or "sympathizers," who are often British; and the "residents," who are often longtime residents and write occasional stories.

Although stringers and freelancers remain marginal, many prominent journalists started their careers that way, including Stanley Karnow, Elie Abel, Robert Kaiser, Elizabeth Pond, Caryle Murphy, and Daniel Schorr.

A significant change has been the increasing number of women among foreign correspondents, especially today as war reporters. Before 1970, their numbers were small, although there had been a few famous names: Dorothy Thompson, Martha Gellhorn, Marguerite Higgins, and Gloria Emerson. Hess found that, by the 1970s, about 16 percent of new foreign reporters were women; this doubled during the 1980s to about 33 percent. This ratio of two men for every woman was also found in Washington media as well as in U.S. journalism generally.

Some women correspondents have earned outstanding reputations, including Caryle Murphy and Robin Wright of *The Washington Post*, syndicated columnist Georgie Ann Geyer, and Elaine Sciolino of *The New York Times*. Christiane Amanpour of CNN has become a kind of celebrity because of her aggressive and frankly partisan reporting of such stories as the first Iraq war, civil upheaval in Africa, civil war in Bosnia, and wars in Afghanistan and Iraq. A significant number of women have been covering the Iraq war for Western media.

Foreign correspondents today are better educated, know more foreign languages, and have higher-status backgrounds than their predecessors. Current salaries range from about $50,000 to $90,000, with more experienced reporters earning even more.

American reporters working abroad have been steadily increasing in number. A 1969 study found 929 Americans working abroad, including broadcasting. By 1972, the number had dropped to 797; by 1975, there were only 676. But in 1990, there were 1,734 and, in 1993, the total neared 2,000.[8] A big part of the increase was due to more staffing abroad by business and economic publications and news services such as Reuters, Bloomberg, and Dow Jones, which have flourished as globalization spreads.

Bureaus located in key capitals are a good indicator of a news medium's commitment to foreign coverage. And some papers, such as *The New York Times*, have more than one reporter per bureau, such as in Moscow. Among U.S. dailies maintaining overseas bureaus in 2002 were *The New York Times*, with twenty-six bureaus and forty reporters; the *Los Angeles Times*, with twenty-one bureaus and twenty-six reporters; *The Washington Post*, with twenty bureaus and twenty-six reporters; and *The Wall Street Journal*, with forty bureaus and 119 reporters (including Asian and European edition staffs). *Time* had seventeen bureaus and nineteen reporters and *Newsweek* had eleven offices and sixteen reporters. Among the bureaus of U.S. television broadcasters, CNN led the pack with thirty; NBC had five; ABC had six, and CBS had four.

When not reporting a war, the networks increasingly seem to be relying on news film supplied by the syndicates, Reuters Television, APTV News, and other foreign broadcasters for international coverage. These less costly ways of collecting news have undermined the credibility of some foreign news. A few years ago, if you saw a foreign news story on NBC News, chances are that it was reported by an NBC reporter at the scene, with film shot by an NBC crew. Now, you can't be sure. The networks are relying more on less expensive, and often less experienced, freelancers and independent contractors whose products are rarely identified on the air, leaving the impression that the story was reported by network staffers. This practice gives rise to a growing concern about quality control. "By the time the tape gets on the air, nobody has the foggiest idea who made it and whether the pictures were staged," contended Tom Wolzien, a former NBC news executive.[9] More loss of authenticity results when U.S. network correspondents, based in London, add voice-overs to stories they did not cover. Bert Quint, former CBS correspondent said, "There's no reason to believe the person [doing the voice-over] because odds are he or she was not within 3,000 miles of where the story occurred."[10]

Not only are foreign correspondents comparatively few, they are unevenly distributed as well. One study found that more than half of all American reporters abroad were stationed in nineteen European countries. During the Persian Gulf crisis, more than 800 Western reporters descended on the region, but few were experts on Middle Eastern affairs. Many of the hundreds covering the wars in Afghanistan and Central Asia have had no previous overseas experience. Such "parachute journalism" does not always provide informed coverage, because so many of these reporters lack previous experience or understanding of the area about which they are reporting.

For readers and listeners, serious questions have been raised about the quantity and quality of foreign news. The debate tends to be circular. AP and other agencies have long maintained that their services gather ample amounts of foreign news, but that their newspaper and broadcast clients do not use very much of it. The media clients in turn argue that their readers and viewers are not very much interested in foreign news. Yet critics say that Americans are uninformed about the world because their news media report so little about it. The widespread shock and fear felt by many Americans after the September 11 terror attacks was in part related to their lack of knowledge about terrorism and the Middle East.

Certainly the generalization that the majority of the public, with access to the world's most pervasive media, are ill informed about world affairs has substance. A panel at Columbia's School of Journalism criticized the audience:

There is a crisis in international news reporting in the United States—and not one that should simply be blamed on the reporters, the gate-keepers, or the owners. We know there is stagnation, and even shrinkage, in the number of international stories in the media and the number of correspondents in the field for most U.S. media outlets. But the primary reason for this decline is an audience that expresses less and less interest in the international stories that do appear. What we're increasingly missing, as a culture, is connective tissue to bind us to the rest of the world.[11]

Foreigners traveling in the American heartland are uniformly impressed by the lack of world news in local media and the ignorance shown by most Americans about the outside world. By contrast, the average German, Dane, or Israeli knows more global news because his or her media carry more. Part of the problem is that Americans, like Russians and Chinese, have a continental outlook, living as they do in the midst of a vast land mass that encourages a self-centered, isolationist view of the world. With two friendly neighbors and protected by two oceans, Americans are slow to recognize their interdependence with others. The shock of 9/11 may have modified that mind set, but only temporarily.

The public's interest in foreign news has its ups and downs, depending on the perceived impact of any current crisis on their lives. During the Vietnam War, much concern was focused on happenings in Southeast Asia, but not in Latin America or Africa, where news coverage dropped off. After Vietnam, foreign concerns receded as the nation became enthralled by Watergate and its aftermath. But after the rapid increases and then decreases in the price of foreign oil, the Soviet incursion into Afghanistan, continuing Arab/Israeli conflict, and a rising level of terrorism directed against Americans, the average American's interest (if not knowledge) in foreign news, especially that of the Middle East, clearly increased. Then, during the summer of 1990, after Iraq invaded Kuwait and American forces were moved into Saudi Arabia before war began in January 1991, American and European interest in and anxiety about the Persian Gulf soared.

In late 1994 and early 1995, interest in foreign news plummeted as the U.S. news media became mesmerized with the murder trial of O.J. Simpson and the domestic politics of the Republicans' legislative zeal in Washington, D.C., after winning control of Congress in the November 1994 elections.

In 1998, the nation's prosperity and the continuing story about President Clinton's personal problems seemed to push foreign news off the nation's news agenda, at least for a while. The continuing crises in the former Yugoslavia, Iraq, and Israel and the teetering Asian and Russian economies did not go away; they just seemed less urgent and less visible. By mid-1998, nuclear tests by India and Pakistan and the possibility of war in South Asia brought a heightened interest in foreign news. The aerial war over Kosovo and Serbia led by America and NATO held the spotlight while it lasted. But the terror attacks of 9/11 have brought an abrupt, if temporary, change in Americans' attitude toward the outside world. Many were clearly frightened and saw themselves as vulnerable to the perils faced by Israelis and many Europeans.

Some critics believed that television had profoundly affected the public's news perceptions. Neil Postman believes television projects a "peek-a-boo" world, "where now this event, now that, pops into view for a moment, then vanishes again. It is a world without much sense or coherence. . . . Americans know of a lot of things but about almost nothing. Someone is considered well informed who simply knows that a plane was hijacked or that there was an earthquake in Mexico City."[12]

Despite ignorance of the world, there is a growing recognition that perhaps the term "foreign news" is a misnomer and that in our interdependent world we are potentially affected by any event almost anywhere. Failing overseas economies can threaten the U.S. stock market and prosperity. American workers who lose jobs in manufacturing due to cheap foreign imports, or farmers unable to sell wheat abroad due to the overvalued dollar, are becoming more knowledgeable about world economic trends. And the Iraq war and other turmoil reminded Westerners of their dependence on Middle Eastern oil and the lack of a conservation policy to deal with that dependence. Since 9/11, many Americans for the first time have believed they could die in a terrorist attack.

The reporting of foreign news has been criticized as being too crisis oriented. An ABC News poll found that among viewers polled, 55 percent agreed, "Television news only does stories about foreign countries when there's a war or some other violent crisis going on."[13] Media critic Hodding Carter said the networks "concentrate on showing kids throwing rocks at troops or guns going off or planes bombing or rubble falling. These are the repetitive images that block out the complexities." In addition, he cited the "extraordinary lack of continuity and perspective, which is the shadow of all television news."[14] Inevitably, much of what happens in the world will go unnoted. Wherever he or she may be, the average person obviously does not have the time or interest to follow all the news from everywhere. As one editor asked, "Who wants to read about Zaire if there is nothing going on there?" Gerald Long of Reuters explained more fully: "The prevalent school of journalism throughout the world is a 'journalism of exception.' In other words, you don't report that everything is fine in Pakistan. You report that there has been an air crash."[15] This approach contributes to an inevitable imbalance and distortion of reality.

The journalism of exception—reporting civil unrest, the coup d'etat, the train wreck, the drought—is at the root of much hostility and antagonism toward Western reporting. Journalists who work abroad say it is difficult to gain access to many parts of the world, particularly Africa, the Middle East, and Asia.

Journalists had particular difficulty in reporting the eight-year conflict between Iran and Iraq and the prolonged civil war involving Serbia, Bosnia, Croatia, and Kosovo. In its early stages, the war in Afghanistan was dangerous and challenging to report. Before 9/11, in India, the foreign cable networks, CNN and the BBC's World Service Television, became a target for Indian politicians looking for scapegoats to blame for secessionist movements, religious strife, and natural disasters. India's own television network, Doordarshan, owned and controlled by the government, is well known for delaying and sanitizing news broadcasts. CNN and the BBC came to India in 1991 while reporting the first Gulf war and later aggressively reported the razing of the Babri Mosque in late 1993 by Hindu fundamentalists, which led to national riots in which 1,800 died. In response, Indian political leaders of both left and right demanded strong action against the networks. However, when things go in favor of the politicians, they praise foreign coverage.[16]

A major point of contention, as mentioned, is that most governments believe the press, including foreign reporters, should serve the host country's national aims, whereas the Western press believes it must decide for itself what news to report. And each foreign reporter will report his or her version of events, as colored by the culture and traditions of his own national media.

## Physical and Psychological Dangers

Foreign correspondents often risk their lives to cover wars, civil unrest, and other forms of violence. Within unstable nations, journalists, both foreign and domestic, are often singled out as targets for arrest, beatings, or assassination. Sometimes they are just in the wrong place at the wrong time.

Algeria, beset by a long struggle between an authoritarian government and a militant Islamic opposition, has proved a deadly place to report the news: As of January 1998, 70,000 to 80,000 people had been massacred. Since 1993, some sixty Algerian journalists have been murdered because of their profession. In 2001, two more Algerians were slain. Many Algerian journalists have gone underground, fled into exile, or left the profession.

The admirable Committee to Protect Journalists keeps track of such violence, and reported that during the first nine months of 2005, thirty-three journalists had been killed worldwide while trying to do their job. In the Iraq war, fifty-three journalists were killed between the start of the war in March 2003 and September 2005.

During the past decade (1994–2005), CPJ reported that 341 journalists had been killed while carrying out their work. Most of those killed since 1995 did not die in cross-fire, but 247 journalists or 72 percent were murdered, often in reprisal for a story. In twenty-three cases since 1995, journalists were kidnapped, often taken alive by militants or government forces and subsequently killed. The kidnapping and murder of *Wall Street Journal* reporter Daniel Pearl in early 2002 highlighted this terrible phenomenon. In several cases, notably in Algeria and Turkey, journalists have simply "disappeared" after being taken into government custody.

The deadliest country for journalists in the past decade has been Iraq, where thirty-eight journalists and eighteen media support workers have been killed. Next comes Algeria, where thirty-three journalists have died since 1995. Russia is next; twenty-nine journalists have died since 1995. Some of these died covering the war with Chechnya, but at least eleven reporters have been murdered in contract-style killings in the four years since President Putin took power. Paul Klebnikov, the American-born editor of *Forbes Russia*, was gunned down outside his office in Moscow in July 2004. In Colombia, thirty journalists have been killed. A rash of journalist murders in the Philippines during 2004 brought the ten-year total to twenty-two. Sixteen journalists have been killed in India since 1995, many victims in the dispute over Kashmir.

In the opening days of the war in Afghanistan, eight journalists and cameramen were slain in a period of about a week, one of the highest tolls in the shortest time span for journalists. In contrast, during the same period, no U.S. military fatalities had been reported in that country since U.S. Special Forces began operating about a month earlier. That all fatalities were non-American journalists was a reminder of how committed many news organizations around the world were to the pursuit of the story.

Governments and warring armies are not the only foes of press freedom; sometimes terrorists and thugs attack the press. Louis Boccardi, then president of AP, said, "On the international scene, the world continues to grow more difficult to cover. The physical dangers abound. Dozens of journalists have been killed in the last few years and many more injured in the pursuit of a story, their story, wherever it was."[17]

Finally, it should be said that the Western practice of "journalism of exception" continues to rankle critics of the press everywhere. In America, many feel that the media report far too much negative news. But as Daniel Patrick Moynihan once said, "It is the mark of a democracy that its press is filled with bad news. When one comes to a country where the press is filled with good news, one can be pretty sure that the jails are filled with good men."

The reporting of modern wars—their own wars—have presented special challenges to American and British news media and to reporters who cover them. That problem is discussed in the next chapter.

## Notes

1.  Leon Hadar, "Covering the New World Disorder," *Columbia Journalism Review*, July/August 1994, 27.
2.  Ibid.
3.  Stephen Hess, *International News & Foreign Correspondents* (Washington, D.C.: Brookings Institution, 1996), 61.
4.  Tom Fenton, *Bad News* (New York: Regan Books, 2005), 4.
5.  Mort Rosenblum, *Who Stole the News?* (New York: John Wiley, 1993), 20.
6.  Scott Schuster, "Foreign Competition Hits the News," *Columbia Journalism Review*, May/June 1988, 45.
7.  Stephen Hess, "The Cheaper Solution," *American Journalism Review*, April 1994, 27.
8.  Michael Parks, "Foreign News: What's Next?, *Columbia Journalism Review*, January/February 2002, 54.
9.  Hess, *International News & Foreign Correspondents*, 100.

10. Ibid.
11. "World News: Truth or Consequences," *Columbia Journalism Review*, January/February 1995, 4.
12. Sally Bedell Smith, "How New Technologies are Starting to Change the Nation's Viewing Habits," *The New York Times*, October 9, 1985, sec. A, 10.
13. Sally Bedell Smith, "Why TV News Can't Be a Complete View of the World," *The New York Times*, August 8, 1982, entertainment section, 1.
14. Ibid.
15. Rosemary Righter, *Whose News: Politics, the Press and the Third World* (New York: Times Books, 1978), 70.
16. Arthur J. Pais, "Anger in India," *Columbia Journalism Review*, May/June 1993, 17.
17. Mark Fitzgerald, "A Dangerous Affair," *Editor & Publisher*, November 2, 1985, 18.

# Chapter 10

# War Reporting under Fire

*The first casualty when war comes is truth.*

—Senator Hiram Johnson, 1917

Four recent wars—the 1991 first Gulf war, the aerial war over Serbia and Kosovo, and the Afghan and Iraq conflicts—have dramatically altered the ways that armed conflicts are reported to the world. Although long-standing frictions and suspicions persist between the press and military officials, the use of new communication technologies has altered journalism for better or worse.

In the brief Gulf war, television and especially CNN turned much of the world into a global community witnessing a televised real-time war, as the brief conflict evolved from armed confrontation to spectacular aerial bombardment and finally to lightning ground warfare. The war became the biggest global news story in years, and telling it utilized the full resources of the U.S. and European news media as well as much of the international news system. More than 1,600 print and broadcast journalists were on hand to report it.

The 1999 NATO bombing campaign against Serbia, whose ground forces were mauling Kosovo civilians, was a new kind of war: an effort, mainly by U.S. air power, to bomb a nation into submission without deploying ground troops or even incurring casualties. As in the first Gulf war, the press accused the military of withholding news and of "spinning" combat reports for political and strategic reasons. The seventy-eight days of NATO bombing finally forced Yugoslavian dictator Slobodan Milosevic to yield and permit 16,000 NATO soldiers to chase the fleeing Serbian forces out of Kosovo and thus bring relief to the battered ethnic Albanians. In that last war of the twentieth century, global news coverage was greatly facilitated by the satellite telephone, twenty-four hour cable TV coverage, and, for the first time, the Internet.

During the opening months of the war against the Taliban in Afghanistan, press and military relationships were still evolving. The Bush administration made it clear that the press would receive less access to combat-related information than in previous conflicts. Yet the news media, here and abroad, poured out a steady torrent of news, speculation, commentary, and pictures about this many-faceted conflict. The world of 2001 was more completely "wired" for 24/7 coverage and journalists from many nations flocked to the region. The Iraq war, launched with great fanfare in spring 2003, at first dominated the world's front pages and television screens as the U.S. and its coalition forces quickly overwhelmed the army of Saddam Hussein and captured Baghdad. Then, when the blitzkreig morphed into a tortuous insurgency that after two and a half years (and counting) still had no end in sight, most of the world paid less and less attention. But for reporters still in Iraq, their work became increasingly dangerous and difficult.

The role of the news media in reporting and explaining Iraq has gone through changes. Wars, particularly when they involve Western powers, are always at the top of the news agendas for foreign nations. And as the world becomes more interconnected by global communications, many more people in more places are paying close attention through the news media.

## Background of Press Controls

How did the relations between American journalists and the U.S. military become so abrasive? In World War I, some 500 American correspondents covered the conflict for newspapers, magazines, and press associations in France and, unlike British and French reporters, they were free to go to the front lines without military escorts. Still, everything written by such star reporters as Richard Harding Davis, Will Irwin, or Floyd Gibbons was passed through the censorship of the press section of the Military Intelligence Service. Details about specific battles, numbers of casualties, and names of units could be released only after being mentioned in official communiqués.

U.S. military censorship followed the same general pattern in World War II, with the added feature of controlling radio broadcasts. The Office of Censorship was headed by Byron Price, a former AP editor, who handled with distinction the most difficult part of his job: the direction of voluntary press censorship that applied to print media outside the combat zones. In far-flung combat "theaters," reporters were generally free to move about and join military units but were always subject to possible censorship. About 500 full-time American reporters were abroad at any one time, and provided coverage that many considered the best and fullest ever seen. With mobile units and tape recordings, radio coverage greatly increased. Relations between the military and reporters were mutually trusting and supportive. Despite occasional conflicts over withheld information, everyone seemed to be on the same team. During the Korean war, the press–government relations were pretty much the same.

The change began in the 1960s Vietnam War when relations soured and reached their lowest ebb. Reporters and camera crews, working within military guidelines, were given free access without field censorship to roam Vietnam; some called it the best-reported war in history. Yet many in the U.S. military believed critical press reporting contributed to the American defeat by over-stressing negative aspects, including graphic pictures of dead and wounded, highlighting scandals such as the My Lai massacre, and misinterpreting key events, such as the Tet offensive, which the military pronounced a defeat for North Vietnam, and not a Vietcong victory as the press reported. Such reports, the military argued, aided the antiwar movement at home.

The war reporters felt that the U.S. military had misled and lied to them in Vietnam and that officials consistently painted a much rosier picture of the war than the facts justified. Given the record of deception, the press, it was argued, was correct in being skeptical of the military. A view prevailed within the military that the free rein given reporters in Vietnam led to reporting that seriously damaged morale and turned American public opinion against its own troops. If news or information is a weapon, then, the generals argued, it should be controlled as part of the war effort.

The brief war in 1982 between Britain and Argentina over the Falkland Islands in the South Atlantic provided a model for the Pentagon on how to manage the press during wartime. Only British reporters were permitted to accompany the task force, and these reporters were carefully selected. The seventeen journalists chosen had to accept censorship at the source and were given a government handbook telling them they would be "expected to help in leading and steadying public opinion in times of national stress or crisis." The Ministry of Defence effectively imposed censorship at the source, and most war information followed a policy of suppression or subtle control of emphasis. After the Falklands War was over, the British press gave a very different picture of the conflict, detailing losses, mishaps, and failures of British forces previously unreported.

For the U.S., the war news issue surfaced again on October 25, 1983, when U.S. forces invaded the tiny island of Grenada. The Defense Department barred all reporters from covering the initial invasion. After two days of rigorous protests from the press, a pool of twelve reporters was finally flown in with a military escort. By the end of one week, with the fighting winding down, 150 reporters were ferried to the island and allowed to stay overnight. The press, however, was not mollified. Walter Cronkite said the Reagan Administration had seriously erred, arguing, "This is our foreign policy and we have a right to know what is happening and there can be no excuse in denying the people that right."[1] But as in the later Gulf war, opinion polls showed that the public supported the ban on press coverage. As a result of the furor, the Defense Department appointed a commission that recommended that a select pool of reporters be allowed to cover the early stages of any surprise military operation and share its information with other press organizations. This seems a fair compromise between the military's need for surprise and the public's need for information. The new guidelines were first tested in December 1989, when U.S. forces invaded Panama. The press arrangements failed miserably. The Pentagon did not get the sixteen-reporter pool into Panama until four hours after fighting began, and reporters were not allowed to file stories until six hours later. Most critics blamed the White House for the mix-up and for insisting that only the military facilitate press coverage. When the first Gulf war loomed, the American generals, Colin Powell and Norman Schwarzkopf, and other Vietnam veterans, were ready to deal with the press.

## The First War with Saddam Hussein

Global television came into its own as CNN and other broadcasters reported a war as it was happening, or as it appeared to be happening—

a "real time" war. After hostilities began early on January 17, 1991, reporters described antiaircraft tracers in the night sky of Baghdad and flashes of bomb explosions on the horizon. On succeeding nights, viewers were provided with live video reports from Tel Aviv and Riyadh of Scud missiles, some apparently intercepted by Patriot missiles, exploding against the night sky, and of television reporters donning gas masks on camera. The press talked of the "CNN effect"— millions anchored hour after hour to their television sets lest they miss the latest dramatic development. Restaurants, movies, hotels, and gaming establishments all suffered business losses: "People are intensely interested in the first real-time war in history and they are just planting themselves in front of their television sets," one expert said. Ratings for CNN soared five to ten times their prewar levels.[2] The first Gulf war was a worldwide media event of astonishing proportions. Global television had never had a larger or more interested audience for such a sustained period of time. Television became the first and principal source of news for most people, as well as a major source of military and political intelligence for both sides. CNN telecasts, including military briefings, were viewed in Baghdad as they were being received in Riyadh or Washington, D.C.—as well as in other non-Western countries.

The combatants, particularly the governments of Iraq and the United States, tried to control and manipulate the media with subtle and not-so-subtle propaganda and misinformation messages. Western journalists chafed at the restraints on news coverage of the war itself and complained that there was much news they were not permitted to report. Most coalition news came from military briefings and from carefully controlled and escorted "pools" of reporters. Some official news presented at the briefings was actually disinformation intended to mislead the enemy, not to inform the public. For example, viewers were led to believe that Patriot missiles were invariably successful in neutralizing Scud missiles, but such was not the case.

Information was tightly controlled; one observer called it "the illusion of news." For its own self-defined security reasons, the military often held back or distorted the news it did release. In the opening days of the war, much was made of the "smart bombs" that hit their targets with about 90 percent accuracy. After the war, the U.S. Air Force admitted that smart bombs made up only 7 percent of all U.S. explosives dropped on Iraq and Kuwait. The Air Force later said that 70 percent of the 88,500 tons of bombs dropped on Kuwait and Iraq missed their targets.[3]

Peter Jennings of ABC News reminded viewers that much of what was revealed in the opening days of war was speculation, mixed with some hard facts and some rumors in the rushing river of information. But whether they were getting hard news or not, many millions of viewers stayed by their television sets. Public opinion polls showed that the overwhelming majority of Americans supported both the war and the military's efforts to control news; further, some thought there should be more controls on press reporting. A *Los Angeles Times* Mirror poll found that half of the respondents considered themselves obsessed with war news, but nearly 80 percent felt that the military was "telling as much as it can." About the same proportion thought that military censorship may be a "good idea."

But after the war, many in the press felt that the traditional right of U.S. reporters to accompany their combat forces and report news of war had been severely circumscribed. Michael Getler of *The Washington Post* wrote, "The Pentagon and U.S. Army Central Command conducted what is probably the most thorough and consistent wartime control of American reporters in modern times—a set of restrictions that in its totality and mind-set seemed to go beyond World War II, Korea, and Vietnam."[4]

President George H.W. Bush and the Pentagon followed a deliberate policy of blocking negative and unflattering news from the U.S. public lest it weaken support for the war. Long after the conflict, the public learned that some Iraqi soldiers had been buried alive in trenches by U.S. plows and earthmovers and that the military had waited months to tell the families of thirty-three dead soldiers that their loved ones had been killed by friendly fire. Not until a year after the war did the public learn that key weapons such as the stealth bomber and the cruise missile had struck only about half of their targets, compared with the 85 to 90 percent rate claimed by the Pentagon at the time.[5] American casualties were reported, but there were few pictures of dead and wounded. Details of tactical failures and mishaps in the bombing campaign were not released, nor was the information that at least twenty-four female soldiers had been raped or sexually assaulted by American servicemen.

But the shooting war itself was quite a media spectacle, which started just as the evening news programs were beginning at 6:30 Eastern Standard Time (January 16 in the United States; January 17 in the

Middle East). The networks and CNN interrupted their prepared news shows to report that aerial bombing had begun in Baghdad. Then followed one of most memorable nights in television history: the opening phases of a major conflict reported in real time by reporters in Iraq, Saudi Arabia, and Washington.

CNN stole the show that night, as three CNN correspondents, John Holliman, Peter Arnett, and Bernard Shaw, gave vivid eyewitness descriptions of the U.S. air attack from the windows of their Baghdad hotel room. As in old-time radio, reporters relied on words, not video, that first night. Other networks reported the fireworks, but CNN with its previously arranged leased lines stayed on the longest after the lines were cut for the other networks. The next day, General Colin Powell jokingly said that the Pentagon was relying on CNN for military information. The second night gave prime-time viewers another long, absorbing evening, when CNN and NBC reporters in Tel Aviv reported live as Scud missiles landed. Reporters, often wearing gas masks, provided raw and unevaluated information. At one point, NBC reported dramatically that nerve gas had been detected in one Scud attack. Tom Brokaw decried the situation for some minutes, but, after the report proved false, NBC apologized. For the first three days, people everywhere stayed glued to television and radio sets, including shortwave receivers. Networks expanded to near twenty-four hour coverage for the first thirty-six hours, and even the daytime soap operas were preempted briefly for war coverage. There was not that much to report at that point, and the same facts, theories, and speculations were repeated again and again. Nevertheless, the mesmerized public stayed tuned.

During this early bombing phase of the war, the Pentagon withheld detailed military information, such as the extent of the bombing and destruction within Iraq. Restrictions were placed on interviews with troops and returning pilots. Reporters could cover field combat only in designated pools, with groups of reporters being accompanied by an escort officer. (One reporter likened a press pool to a group of senior citizens on a conducted tour.) All interviews with soldiers were subject to censorship before they could be released.

If the war had gone badly, the press would have had difficulty reporting the negative aspects. With more than 1,600 reporters in the theater, only about 100 could be accommodated by the pools to report on the American force of 500,000. As the ground war neared, the large press corps became increasingly restive and frustrated at this lack of access.

The response of some reporters was to "freelance"—to avoid the pools and go off on their own. Malcolm Browne reported, "Some reporters were hiding out in U.S. Marine or Army field units, given GI uniforms and gear to look inconspicuous, enjoying the affection (and protection) of the units they're trying to cover—concealed by the officers and troops from the handful of press-hating commanders who strive to keep the battlefield free of wandering journalists."[6] Browne noted that nearly all reporters who tried to reach front-line U.S. troops were arrested at one time or another (including reporters for *The New York Times*, *The Washington Post*, the Associated Press, and Cox papers), sometimes held in field jails for up to twelve hours and threatened with revocation of their press credentials. After the ground war began, these freelancers, particularly John Kifner and Chris Hedges of *The New York Times*, produced some outstanding reportage. Forrest Sawyer of "ABC News," who traveled unofficially with Saudi forces, provided some of the earliest and best reports on the freeing of Kuwait City.

## The Triumph of Twenty-Four Hour Global News

During the American Civil War, in 1861–5, the demand for news was so great that U.S. newspapers for the first time went to seven-day publication. During the 1963 Kennedy assassination, live television emerged as the preeminent medium for reporting breaking news. This story positioned ABC, CBS, and NBC as major news gatherers, but as still reaching essentially U.S. audiences.

During the forty-two day first Gulf war, CNN established the importance of a twenty-four hour news network with true global reach. The concept has certainly changed the international news system, especially during times of international crisis and conflict. The three major U.S. networks were shaken by CNN's success. After CNN's historic scoop on the first night of the war, a number of independent television stations, radio stations, and even several network affiliates relied on CNN in the crisis. Although the three networks had more talented and experienced reporters, they could not compete with CNN either in time on the air or in the vast audiences CNN reached in about 100 countries. The success of CNN encouraged similar services, such as the BBC's World Service Television.

The first Gulf war certainly conditioned viewers everywhere to keep their television sets tuned to CNN (or its later cable imitators) during times of high crisis. Newsrooms from Milwaukee to Cairo to Shanghai routinely keep a television set tuned to CNN or the BBC for the first report of any global crisis. Perhaps the news business today places too much emphasis on immediate and fast-breaking news "as it happens." Video shots of F15s roaring off runways, of "smart bombs" scoring direct hits, of Tomahawk missiles flying through Baghdad, and of tank formations rolling through the desert made memorable viewing. But after the fog of war had cleared, the press and the public found that the war was not quite what they thought it was.

The tragic events in the volatile Middle East also reminded the public that wars and political crises are complex and intricate processes that can still best be reported and explained by the printed word. The best and most complete reporting of the first Gulf war came ultimately from print media, which rounded out the picture and provided the context and perspective necessary for full understanding. During the first several weeks after the cease-fire, it was the print reporters, not television, who dug out and filled in the details of what actually happened during the air campaign and the brief ground war—details that the military on both sides had so effectively screened from public view.

From all indications, the U.S. military as well as the first Bush administration were pleased with the results of their media policy and would do the same thing again. But among American and British journalists, there was a general conclusion that the press had been unduly and even illegally denied access to information about the war.

After the first Gulf war, a report that called military restrictions in the war "real censorship" that confirmed "the worst fears of reporters in a democracy" was delivered to Defense Secretary Dick Cheney. It was signed by seventeen news executives representing the four networks, AP and UPI, and major newspapers and news magazines. The report bitterly complained that the restrictions placed on reporters by the Pentagon were intended to promote a sanitized view of the war. The war was called the first in this century to restrict all official coverage to pools. "By controlling what reporters saw and when they saw it, the military exerted great power to shape and manage the news," the report said. Also criticized were the use of military escorts and "unwarranted delays in transmitting copy."[7] After more than eight months of talks

with news executives, in May 1992 the Pentagon issued a set of principles intended to guarantee that journalists have greater access to future
military operations than they had in the first Gulf war. However, news
media and the government could not agree on whether there should
be any official "security review" of news reports before they are published or broadcast. The statement affirmed that "open and independent
reporting will be the principal means of coverage of U.S. military
operations. The guidelines limited the role of military escorts and said
that "press pools are not to serve as the standard means of covering
operations."[8]

## Marines in Somalia

The incursion of U.S. Marines into Somalia in December 1992 was
intended to provide military protection to the relief organizations trying
to feed starving Somalis caught in the cross-fire of warring clans. Under
these conditions, the Pentagon decided to place no restraints on the
media. Howard Kurtz called what happened the most embarrassing
moment ever in media–military relations: ". . . the infamous night in
December 1992 when Navy SEALS hitting the beach in Somalia were
surrounded by a small army of reporters and photographers who blinded
them with television lights, clamored for interviews, and generally acted
like obnoxious adolescents. That sorry performance, turning a humanitarian mission to aid starving Africans into a Felliniesque photo op,
underscored what the Pentagon had been saying for years: that the press
simply could not discipline itself, that reporters would blithely endanger
the safety of American troops for the sake of journalistic drama."[9] It was
not one of the news media's finer days.

David Hackworth of *Newsweek* wrote, "To lurch from thought control to no control is plain stupid. When the press corps beats the Marine
Corps to the beach, everyone loses."[10] The Pentagon wanted full coverage
of Somalia, so no controls were placed on the press, and what resulted
was a confused circus. There are those, however, who suspected that
the Pentagon deliberately orchestrated the fiasco to make the media
look bad. Somalia raised the question of whether the media, by its
heavy barrage of pictures and stories of starving Somalis, had pushed
President Bush during his last days in office to send troops on their
humanitarian mission. The answer is unclear, but Bush did react by

committing U.S. armed forces to a limited and supposedly feasible assignment of famine relief. When the Somalia assignment expanded in the early Clinton administration to include warlord hunting, it provoked a devastating firefight in the streets of Mogadishu. When eighteen U.S. soldiers were killed and the pictures shown on U.S. television, the American public was unprepared to accept casualties when vital U.S. interests were not at stake. The White House soon announced that the United States was getting out of Somalia.

James Hoge, editor of *Foreign Affairs*, commented, "From its understanding of Vietnam came the military's subsequent emphasis on quick solutions, limited media access and selective release of 'smart' weapons imagery. The public, however, will not remain dazzled when interventions become difficult. As in Vietnam, public attitudes ultimately hinge on questions about the rightness, purpose and costs of policy—not television images."[11]

## NATO's Air War over Yugoslavia

After NATO bombs started falling on Serbia and Kosovo in 1999, military relations with the press deteriorated abruptly. Critics protested that the lack of detailed after-action reports—routinely provided in earlier conflicts—made it impossible to assess NATO's claims that they were steadily dismantling Milosevic's war-making powers. At both the Pentagon and Brussels NATO headquarters, spokespersons stubbornly refused to provide specific information about bombing sorties. These policies were considered even less forthcoming than in the first Gulf war, which the press had considered overly restrictive. Of course, NATO had its reasons: the need to hold the somewhat reluctant alliance together and the need to retain the support of the American public for military action. But most journalists covering the war were highly critical.

Yet the war was reported and, in some basic ways, differently from others. After being forced to watch seventy-eight days of bombing through the lenses of official video cameras, some 2,700 journalists had a chance to see for themselves when NATO troops rolled into Kosovo in June 1999. Even though military censors blocked specific information, satellite communications enabled reporters from Brussels to Kukes, Albania, and other points to triangulate information more easily than in earlier wars. According to editors, the key device for putting together information into coherent stories was the satellite telephone and, more broadly, satellite communications. The satellite uplink was the key information medium for the air war. "Instantaneous communication has changed everything," said Andrew Rosenthal, foreign editor of *The New York Times*. "The ability of a reporter on the Macedonian border to call a reporter on the Albanian border or to call a reporter in Brussels or Washington instantly made a huge difference. Newspapers were able to put together groups of reporters to do joint efforts in a way that was previously impossible," he said.[12]

For television, the same satellite technology allowed a profusion of images to be transmitted at great speed. Whether the vivid video showed the fate of Kosovar refugees or fleeing Serbian troops, the emotional impact of television was great indeed. Some thought such reportage helped to justify the humanitarian aspects of the hostilities and convinced otherwise dubious viewers to support the NATO effort. The expanded role for the Internet and cable television news meant that there were far more outlets for instantaneous reporting and analysis. CNN, MSNBC, and the Fox Cable Channel also offered frequent and compelling debates about the conflict, even though much of it was discounted by critics as lacking in depth and context. For the first time, the Internet was a player in war reporting, providing a plethora of websites (that is, blogs) presenting war issues and other information from diverse viewpoints: Serbian, Albanian, Republican, Democratic; and ranging from the in-depth reporting of the BBC to the erratic sensationalism of Belgrade news outlets. As a result, some observers thought that the sum total of these trends amounted to sharper, speedier coverage. David Halberstam wrote: "Despite all the restrictions and just God-awful limitations and dangers, there were enough different people in different places to give you the dimensions you needed."[13]

Even though CNN had more competition this time—BBC World, MSNBC, and Fox—than in the first Gulf war, the Atlanta cable network emerged from the Yugoslav conflict in a much-enhanced *international* role for its news dissemination as a global twenty-four hour cable news channel. During the first Gulf war, some 10 million households outside the United States had access to CNN. In the Yugoslav war, the number had jumped to 150 million households.

The air war in Yugoslavia demonstrated that the democracies of America and NATO were unwilling to be candid and forthcoming with reliable information to their own peoples while engaged in hostile actions against other states. As in the first Gulf war, the Pentagon gave misleading and exaggerated accounts of the effectiveness of the bombing campaign. Yet despite such deceptions, the events surrounding the air war also showed that today's news organizations can still get much of the news out if they pursue the events with vigor and imagination and make use of their varied tools of communications technology.

## Chasing the Taliban in Afghanistan

The world's press—mainly Americans and Europeans—geared up to cover the war in Afghanistan with essentially the same technologies as well as the limited access to the battlefields that characterized NATO's air war with Yugoslavia two years earlier. But now, global audiences were larger and the news flow, from many more reporters, was much heavier. Unlike earlier wars, individual reporters can now report news from war zones in real time, but often they may have less to tell. Because the military sharply limits access and thus what reporters can know, the war reporter is not in a position to decide what is appropriate and safe to report. Basically, the military today is very uneasy with new media technology. The old battlefield censorship is no longer feasible because reporters carry their means of transmission (that is, satellite phones and videophones) with them. More and more, reporters are kept away from troops and military organizations. As a result, much of what is considered "war coverage" has originated in the Pentagon press briefing room. Today, the global audience is accustomed to getting its news quickly and often. People will check their favorite websites four or five times a day, or tune in to twenty-four hour cable stations for the latest developments.

As mentioned earlier, the Afghanistan war may go down in history as our first "videophone war." From the earliest days of the conflict, the closest views of the fighting were provided in live reports by reporters using videophones, which are literally cameras plugged into satellite phones. The videophone has enabled television news crews to venture out to remote and dangerous areas of Afghanistan, untethered to the more cumbersome satellite uplinks that can weigh over a ton. The videophone can fit into two briefcases, one with one or two satellite phones and the other with the videophone. With that and a car battery, they are ready to roll. The videophone is actually a variation on videoconferencing, which businesses have used for years. The videophones, at about $8,000 each, combine videoconferencing equipment with "store and forward" technology that helps compress very high bandwidth feeds so that they can be transmitted by satellite. The satellite phones also cost about $8,000 each. Early in the war, much of what the public saw and heard on television seemed to come from a correspondent reporting live via a videophone from a remote location in Afghanistan.

The networks also used the "traditional" satellite uplinks in places such as Islamabad, Pakistan, to complement the videophones. Videophone reporting has been criticized for being "too sketchy" or almost "undecipherable." Yet the technology will only improve over time, and it does get the television reporter closer to the battlefield.

But what the press has gained in time and convenience, it has lost in access to the military itself. For families of servicemen and women, this was not considered a good precedent. News about casualties caused by "friendly fire" and other battlefield mishaps tend not to be reported if there are no reporters on the ground. The press has been likened to an uncle representing the family. They go to the front line and say, "Well, how is Johnny doing? What's going on here? Who's running this operation? Are there needless frontal assaults?" Walter Cronkite has said that there is another reason people should care about how the military operates: "We must know what they are doing in our name."[14] The journalists' concerns have not yet aroused similar concern from the public. As noted in a recent survey by the Pew Research Center, half of the respondents said the military should have more control over war news than news media have.

During the opening weeks of the Afghan war, almost all significant information was released from the Pentagon, far from the battlefields, and much of it was considered dated and vague. The extremely restrictive policy toward release of information was set by Defense Secretary Rumsfeld, who said that the nature of the war against terrorism made the constraints necessary. Rumsfeld several times stated that defense officials who leaked information might be in violation of federal criminal law. Because the war reporters could not accompany military units in combat zones, reporters early in the Afghan war had to do what they did decades ago in Cambodia: strike out on their own. For a while, the Afghan situation was one the most dangerous of modern times. Eight correspondents were killed in the first several weeks. As one reporter said, we know less but we are more of a target.

## The Second War against Saddam's Iraq

The invasion of Iraq and the toppling of Saddam Hussein's regime were quickly accomplished by coalition forces—mainly American and some British—in the spring of 2003. Around the world, millions watched the unfolding of this the most heavily televised war in history. As in the 1991 Iraq war, hundreds of journalists and photographers used new and refined communications gadgets—videophones, cellphones, Internet, and e-mail—to flood the world with words and images.

Combat journalism has changed, as has warfare itself. Technology has markedly changed how wars are waged and for how long. Reporters utilize new tools to gather news and send it out faster than ever. In Iraq, the typical television war correspondent found he needed the following essential carry-along gear that weighed about seventy-six pounds: a digital video camera, five pounds; microphones, cables, and batteries, ten pounds; camera tripod, ten pounds; two satellite phones, twenty pounds each; laptop computer, six pounds; and night scope lens, five pounds.

Reporters in Iraq were comfortable with their technology as never before. Television reporters carried hand-held video cameras and print journalists traded their seventy-pound videophones of 1991 for handy models that can be held against an ear. High-speed Internet lines in the desert meant that journalists could make a connection almost anywhere. One reporter said that today's digital devices enable a reporter to provide a more intimate and multi-faceted view of the war than had ever been seen before. The high quality and diverse nature of the reporting reflected this.

The most important policy innovation of the war was the Pentagon's unexpected decision that journalists be "embedded" with the military units fighting their way across Iraq. For the first time since World War II, and on a scale never seen in military history, some 600 reporters, photographers, and television crew members—about 100 of them from foreign and international news organizations, including the Arab satellite news network, Al Jazeera, had access to troops in combat. Embedding was considered the greatest innovation (and improvement) in press–military relations in many years. The results of the experiment were generally positive. The viewing public had a front-row seat during the invasion, with the "embedders" providing a steady stream of news reports, anecdotes, and human interest stories, along with dramatic and vivid video and photos about the military they accompanied.

One observer, Rem Rieder, commented, "Now that the fighting has stopped, it's clear that the great embedding experience was a home run as far as the news media—and the American public—are concerned. Six hundred journalists had a first-hand view of the combat. That's a far cry from the first Gulf war when reporters were at the mercy of government briefers and that misbegotten press pool."[15] But there were negative aspects to embedding. Some critics saw the reporters as tools of the military —only turning out good news. And it was dangerous duty—several correspondents were killed, including David Bloom of NBC News and Michael Kelly of *The Atlantic Monthly*.

Another important dimension was the role of transnational satellite networks in the Arab world. They became important news sources of war news in Arabic, and were in fact challenging the hegemony of the British and U.S. media. Al Jazeera reached about 45 million viewers, and broadcast a very different version of the conflict than CNN or BBC World. The Arab networks were accused of sending inaccurate and biased information. But many millions of Arabs were now receiving news and views in Arabic that differed from those sent out by their own closed national media systems.

How good was the televised reporting of the brief shooting war? At their best, reporters managed to humanize the war without becoming cheerleaders for the military. News organizations went to great expense to provide thorough coverage. But critics questioned how clear and complete the coverage was. One journalist said the war was too big a canvas to capture on the small screen of television. Yet at the same time there was so much television coverage that sometimes viewers became confused. The effectiveness of television was limited by the limitations of the medium itself—the mismatch between words and images. Vivid pictures from one fixed position in a battle of no consequence could overwhelm any context provided by a voice-over correspondent.

Embedded reporters could not report visually a key aspect of the ground war—that incessant bombing attacks had attrited Iraqi ground forces before battles began. And sometimes, reporters were too downbeat about the invasion's early setbacks.

### The Insurgency Phase of the War

After the fall of Baghdad, the war changed into another unexpected phase—a deadly and persistent guerrilla war waged against the occupying forces, and at times the Iraqi public itself. Attacks against U.S. and coalition forces, usually as roadside bombings of cars and trucks or seemingly random suicide bomb attacks in crowded urban areas, took a steady toll of soldiers and civilians during the following two and a half years. The more serious media stayed on and maintained full coverage of the confused and discouraging events in Iraq. By 2005, many journalists had left Iraq—from a total of 2,000 at one time down to 200.

For the reporters, life became much more dangerous. One reporter said it was like being under house arrest and not able to do your job. Just leaving their hotel meant facing the chance of being kidnapped or shot. Increasingly, reporters relied more and more on Iraqi stringers or "fixers" to go out and gather information. Some reporters began to share their bylines with Iraqi colleagues. Every day was a gamble; ten Iraqi fixers were killed; Reuters lost three cameramen; and in all thirty-five Iraqi journalists had been killed. Being pinned down this way, many reporters felt they were getting only part of the story. They said the war looked different on the other side and they were not able to report it.

One of the best, Dexter Filkins of *The New York Times*, said the "business of reporting in Iraq has become a terribly truncated affair, an enterprise clipped and limited by the violence all around. . . . Even in areas of the capital thought to be relatively safe, very few reporters are still brazen enough to get out of a car, walk around and stop people at random. It can be done, but you better move fast."[16] Ironically, it appeared that being embedded with troops at the front was the safest place to be. But not always: Filkins spent two weeks with a U.S. Marine company during the siege of Falluja. In some of the deadliest urban warfare since World War II, 25 percent of the Marines Filkins was with were killed during sixteen hours of continuous conflict. About this experience in Iraq, Filkins said the "list of hits and near misses was long enough to chill the hardiest war correspondent: we have been shot at, kidnapped, blindfolded, held at gunpoint, detained, threatened, beaten, and chased."[17]

An American freelancer, Steven C. Vincent, was abducted and shot dead in the port city of Basra in August 2005. It was believed that Vincent was targeted for writing about the rise of conservative Shiite Islam and the corruption of the Iraqi police in Basra. Vincent was one of nineteen correspondents killed in attacks in which they were the apparent targets. Soon after, on September 29, 2005, an Iraqi journalist and photographer working for *The New York Times* (as did Vincent) in

Basra was found dead after being abducted from his home by a group of armed men. Like Vincent, Fakher Haider had been reporting about the rising violence among Basra's rival Shiite militias, which had apparently infiltrated the police.

Reporting the drawn-out insurgency in Iraq certainly contrasts sharply from riding along with combat troops as they quickly and decisively overwhelmed the army of Saddam Hussein in 2003.

## First Amendment Concerns

From Grenada to Panama to Kosovo and, recently, to Afghanistan and Iraq, the press has been barred from fully covering wars or military incursions that it has historically and traditionally reported. This is important because the U.S. Supreme Court has ruled that the press, in order to inform the public, has a First Amendment right to those places that "historically" and "traditionally" it has had the right to cover, such as trials and town meetings. The Supreme Court has also ruled that the press has a First Amendment right to be present at all "public" events. Certainly, an invasion lasting more than several hours or a full-scale war is a public event.

Perhaps the press's Constitutional rationale for war coverage was best expressed by Justice Hugo Black in the Pentagon Papers case:

> The Government's power to censor the press was abolished so that the press would remain forever free to censure the Government. The press was protected so that it could bare the secrets of government and inform the people. Only a free and unrestrained press can effectively expose deception in government. And paramount among the responsibilities of a free press is the duty to prevent any part of the government from deceiving the people and sending them off to distant lands to die of foreign fevers and foreign shot and shell.[18]

The press has no "right" to report sensitive military information that could aid an enemy, nor would it want to do so; but, we believe, it does have a right to be there, to keep a watchful eye on the military, just as it does on the proceedings of a criminal trial. No modern wars have been fought as quickly and effectively, and with as few casualties, as by the U.S.-led forces in the first Gulf war and the recent war against the Taliban. But when wars go badly, as they often can—with incompetent leadership, confused tactics, and unnecessary casualties—it is essential that the press, as independent representatives of the public and of the forces themselves, be there to report, then or later, what occurred. The peoples of Iraq and Afghanistan had no independent press reporting back to them about the military disasters and political incompetence that led to the battlefield deaths of thousands of their young men—a basic difference between a democracy and a dictatorship.

This view is not shared by Professor Jane Kirtley, who has argued that no First Amendment right of access to military operations exists. She recently wrote, "The message from the court is clear: with no constitutional right to accompany troops the press should be grateful for whatever access the military decides to allow."[19]

Thus, apparently, the Supreme Court of the United States is unlikely to come to the defense of the U.S. press in this matter. Perhaps the best hope of the press is to protest and complain until a significant portion of the public supports their own right to know. In the first Gulf war, it was apparent that the American news media and their owners did not complain loudly and vehemently enough about the pool and censorship restrictions before the bombs started dropping. The more open policy of embedding troops with combat units in the second Gulf war may have been a result of press pressures for more openness. Also, of course, it was very good public relations by the Pentagon to do so.

Few Americans were willing to second-guess the military policy of harsh controls over war news. A sitting president is not likely to modify such restrictions of free expression in wartime until forced to by political pressures. Yet it is imperative for the press to keep pushing for greater access to news relating to our military.

Ironically, the greatly expanded capability of global television and videophones to report instantly on any new information in a modern war provides perhaps the major rationale for governments to control and censor war news. And when American or British journalists are denied access to war news, the rest of the world is denied access as well.

## Notes

1.  "Media Access to Grenada Stirs Controversy," *AP Log*, October 31, 1991, 1.
2.  "Tourism Shaken by CNN Effect," *The New York Times*, January 28, 1992, sec. A, 8.

3.  Tom Wicker, "An Unknown Casualty," *The New York Times*, March 20, 1991, sec. A, 15.

4.  Michael Getler, "The Gulf War 'Good News' Policy is a Dangerous Precedent," *The Washington Post National Weekly Edition*, March 25–31, 1991, 24.

5.  Howard Kurtz, *Media Circus* (New York: Times Books, 1993), 215.

6.  Malcom Browne, "The Military vs. The Press," *The New York Times Magazine*, March 3, 1991, 45.

7.  Jason DeParle, "17 News Executives Criticize U.S. for 'Censorship' of Gulf Coverage," *The New York Times*, July 3, 1991, sec. A, 4.

8.  Robert Pear, "Military Revises Rules to Assure Reporters Access to Battle Areas," *The New York Times*, May 2, 1992, sec. A, 8.

9.  Kurtz, *Media Circus*, 214.

10. David Hackworth, "Learning How to Cover a War," *Newsweek*, December 21, 1992, 32.

11. James F. Hoge, Jr., "Media Pervasiveness," *Foreign Affairs*, July/August 1994, 139–40.

12. Felicity Barringer, "A New War Drew on New Methods to Cover It," *The New York Times*, June 21, 1999, sec. C, 1.

13. Ibid.

14. Kim Campbell, "Today's War Reporting: It's Digital But Dangerous," *Christian Science Monitor*, December 4, 2001, online edition.

15. Rem Rieder, "In the Zone", *American Journalism Review*, May/June 2003, 6.

16. Dexter Filkins, "Get Me Rewrite. Now. Bullets are Falling," *The New York Times*, October 10, 2004, sec. P, 1.

17. Ibid.

18. *New York Times v. United States*, 403 U.S. 713, 717 (1971).

19. Jane Kirtley, "Accompanying the Troops," *American Journalism Review*, April/May 2005, 60.

# Chapter 11

# Public Diplomacy and Propaganda

*When it came to radio waves the iron curtain was helpless. Nothing could stop the news from coming through—neither sputniks nor minefields, high walls, nor barbed wire. The frontiers could be closed, words could not.*

—Lech Walesa

*In wartime, truth is so precious that she should always be guarded by a bodyguard of lies.*

—Winston Churchill

Public diplomacy and propaganda have much in common with the armed forces: in peacetime, they are somewhat ignored and diminished, but during time of war, these activities are mobilized by governments to join the fray and to win the "hearts and minds" of both followers and adversaries.

In modern times, government-sponsored shortwave radio, which reaches many millions almost anywhere on the globe, has been a preferred medium in political warfare—in World War II, the Cold War (including the Korean and Vietnam wars), and other international crises—and now, since 9/11, along with international television it has come to the fore in the war on terrorism. For Western governments, the tools, strategies, and messages of political warfare had been neglected, but were quickly being sharpened for the conflict in Afghanistan and Iraq with the additional tools of satellite television and the Internet.

Commentators have seen the current struggle in large part as an effort to convince world public opinion of the rightness of the antiterrorism cause. The new conflict in Afghanistan was quickly seen in part as a propaganda war between the West and the radical Islamists, as personified by the elusive Osama bin Laden. Western efforts to penetrate the hearts and minds of Arabs, as well as Muslims in general, were fitful and ineffective due in part to the widespread unpopularity at what was seen as President George W. Bush's war against Iraq and the failure to project an effective information (that is, propaganda) campaign via global radio and regional satellite television programming in Arabic. Finally, in mid-2005 the U.S. public diplomacy effort had a new leader, Karen Hughes, a top Bush aide, but the campaign to reach and persuade the Middle East of the rightness of U.S. goals was still sputtering.

Since the end of the Cold War in 1989 and before September 2001, global broadcasting over shortwave radio had not, however, receded in volume but had less impact than global television. On any given evening, an Arab in a café in Algiers, a Peruvian llama herder in a shelter in the Andes, or an African in a Ghanaian village can share a common communication experience. By merely flicking on a shortwave radio receiver and twisting the dials, each will hear the same polyglot cacophony of sounds detailing the news, unfolding diverse feature programs, and playing all sorts of music. The variety of languages spoken is immense, but each listener can, with little difficulty, find a program he or she understands. Nowhere is the prism of international communication more apparent. In shortwave radio broadcasting, one person's "truth" or news is another person's "propaganda," and vice versa. And again, one person's music is another's "noise." Transnational radio (now supplemented by global television, the Internet, and AM radio) is also a major conveyor of what is sometimes called public diplomacy.

For more than forty years, public diplomacy (a government's overt efforts to influence other governments and their publics) and shortwave radio were dominated by the great East–West struggle called the Cold War, which in effect ended in 1990 with the reunification of Germany and the withdrawal of Soviet troops from Central Europe. But public diplomacy and propaganda wars continued on other polemical battlefields: in the Persian Gulf after Iraq invaded Kuwait; in the tragic and protracted struggle among Serbs, Croats, and Bosnian Muslims in the former Yugoslavia; in the Israeli/Palestinian struggle; and in clashes over human rights in China.

With the globalization of the economy, international frictions were for a time more concerned with economic competition and business contentions between nations, rather than with political and ideological differences. Concerns about incipient war in, say, the Korean peninsula, in Kashmir, or in the Middle East were partially replaced by worries about the flagging economies in Indonesia, Japan, or Argentina, and how these trends might undermine more stable economies of the West. For a time, political espionage was replaced by economic espionage and concerns about the global pirating of videos, movies, CDs, and computer software. For example, 90 percent of the software used on China's computers is reported to have been pirated. The privacy issue has been pushed aside by national security concerns raised by international terrorism.

Much of the torrent of messages constantly washing over the globe is not neutral or "disinterested" information (that is, news) but "purposive" communication—words, sounds, and images intended to influence people's perceptions and opinions. A great deal of what refracts through the prism of international radio is purposive and is often called "propaganda"; that is, the systematic use of words or symbols to influence the attitudes or behaviors of others. *Propaganda* is a loaded term, a pejorative epithet subjectively defined as a "persuasive statement I don't like." No one—journalist, broadcaster, writer, or educator—wants to be called a propagandist. Transnational communicators put on their ideological blinkers when they insist, "We deal in information or truth. They deal in propaganda."

International political communication (IPC), a cumbersome term though it is, is a useful and neutral expression encompassing such terms as public diplomacy, overseas information programs, cultural exchanges, and even propaganda activities and political warfare. A useful definition for IPC is as follows: the political effects that newspapers, broadcasting, film, exchanges of persons, cultural exchanges, and other means of international communication can achieve.

However, a distinction should be made between official and private communications and between international communications designed to have a political effect and those that are not. Here, then, are four broad categories of IPC:

1. Official communications intended to influence foreign audiences (that is, public diplomacy), such as those of the Voice of America, Deutsche Welle, Radio France International, and the BBC's World Service. Most international shortwave broadcasting falls into this category, and almost every nation with the capability will sponsor some broadcasting efforts across its borders.

2. Official communications not intended to influence foreign audiences, a small category indeed. One example has been the U.S. Armed Forces Radio and Television Network. At its peak, AFN operated some 200 radio and thirty television transmitters serving American forces overseas and had large eavesdropping audiences.

3. Private communications intended to influence foreign audiences politically, including various organizations and groups working to promote international understanding—for example, peace groups advocating a freeze on nuclear weapons. Terrorist organizations belong here because they are technically nongovernmental. Every terrorist act is an effort to influence opinion.

4. Private communications without a political purpose. Among these would be Western news agencies, advertising agencies, and distributors of motion pictures, television programs, videos, and so forth. Activities of relief organizations, important in poor countries, belong in this classification as well. The vast flood of American mass culture (much of it movies, music videos, pop recordings, and television programs, most of it produced within a five-square-mile area of Hollywood), has both negative and positive effects, but not intentional effects on international political communication.

Without doubt, the overseas impact of private U.S. communications is far greater than that of U.S. public diplomacy, but the actual influence is difficult to assess. As we have seen, Western pop culture has certainly contributed to political change in Eastern Europe in recent years. Unintended effects sometimes can be more profound than those caused intentionally.

The international news media of all nations play a significant role in international political communication. The privately owned media organizations of the West serve their own commercial purposes by distributing and selling news and entertainment around the globe without intentional political aims. Yet at the same time, the news media transmit a good deal of purposive official information—that is, propaganda—because all governments work hard at getting their versions of news and events into the world's news media. Much of the news from official sources in national capitals is intended to serve foreign-policy goals. News and propaganda are not mutually exclusive categories. The media serve the purposes of public diplomacy when they carry a story of President Bush's views of Osama bin Laden, yet what a U.S. President or British Prime Minister says is always "news." A continuing problem for professional journalists is that of separating legitimate news from self-serving official "interpretations" of the news, whatever the source. Nevertheless, the two are often identical.

News media of authoritarian nations, less independent of official controls, often serve as unquestioning conduits of political communication from their own governments. Editors in Beijing or Tehran usually face no professional dilemmas over whether to carry stories supporting their governments' foreign policies. Less-developed nations are mostly on the receiving end of public diplomacy, because most lack the communication capability to compete effectively on a global basis.

## International Radio Broadcasting

In this day of direct-broadcast satellites, global television, and the Internet, the powerful and pervasive medium of international radio broadcasting, long capable of carrying messages around the world almost instantaneously is still important in the poor nations of the South. According to audience surveys, listening on shortwave radio continues to increase. A BBC study found that 143 million people tune in weekly and according to sales figures, there are about 600 million shortwave radios around the globe—half in Asia and Africa. That is indeed mass communication, beamed mainly at the most populous and poorest nations.

In the 1930s, political leaders such as Nazi Germany's Josef Goebbels talked of international radio as a "limitless medium" and saw it as a powerful instrument of international diplomacy, persuasion, and even coercion. For more than half a century, transnational radio has been just that—a key instrument of international political communication as well as many other things. The medium enjoyed a rapid and diverse expansion and by the late 1930s was being used by national governments, religious organizations, commercial advertisers, domestic broadcasters, and educators to carry their messages across national borders.

As the twentieth century was closing, the total number of national broadcasters rose to more than 150, and the number of hours broadcast almost doubled that of the 1960s.[1] Shortwave radio messages are sent from transmitters directly throughout the world to receiving sets, but international radio's growth and diversity continue today with the utilization by national broadcasters of local AM and FM with signals sent down by satellites. The BBC does this with 800 stations around the world, 200 of them in the United States. But most in affluent nations do not listen much to international radio and so are unaware of how pervasive it is: 1,600 shortwave stations, the voice of 160 countries. These stations offer a choice of some sixty or more language services, broadcasting for a total of 100 hours a day or more. The formats are equally diverse: newscasts, talks, interviews, editorial comments, press reviews, documentaries, and a good deal of music. News on the hour, every hour about domestic and foreign events is a common feature, but other informational programs try to reflect the broader cultural, social, and economic aspects of particular nations through dramas, music, sports events, and religious services. Today, international broadcasters often have websites as well to transmit their messages over the Internet.

Here, we are concerned with the largest international broadcasting operators. Currently, in order of numbers of weekly listeners they are Britain, the United States, Germany, and France. The BBC World Service broadcasts in forty-three languages to 149 million listeners weekly. The Voice of America broadcasts fifty-three languages to about 86 millions weekly. Deutsche Welle goes out in thirty-five languages and uses 1,700 journalists. Radio France International uses eighteen languages to reach about 30 millions weekly.[2] The most widely used languages, in descending order of usage, are English, Russian, Mandarin Chinese, Arabic, Spanish, French, Japanese, Indonesian, Portuguese, German, Italian, Persian (Farsi), Swahili, Hindi, Hausa, and Korean.

A significant portion of international political rivalries and frictions are refracted through the prism of international broadcasting: the nationalistic and ethnic animosities in the post Cold War world; the Arab versus Israeli tensions as well as those between moderate and radical Arab regimes; the North–South disputes between rich and poor nations; plus dozens of smaller regional controversies and disagreements between neighboring nations. More recently, increasing concerns about terrorism have dominated. Any major global crisis will be widely reported, analyzed, and commented upon on shortwave radio.

As the Cold War was winding down, Radio Moscow and its related Soviet broadcasters were on the air 2,257 hours weekly during 1988.[3] The United States countered with sixteen hours daily of Russian-language VOA broadcasts into the Soviet Union, while U.S.-backed Radio Free Europe broadcast into Eastern Europe, and Radio Liberty broadcast in non-Russian languages to various parts of the Soviet Union. In 1988, the United States was broadcasting globally 2,360 hours weekly; China, 1,517 hours weekly; the United Kingdom, 756 hours; and India, 444 hours.[4] By June 1994, after the demise of the Cold War, the United States had dropped to 2,000 hours weekly and Russia to 1,400 hours; China was steady at 1,600 hours, the U.K. was up to about 1,800 hours, and India was steady at 500 hours.

Amid the cacophony of sometimes strident and pejorative voices clashing over the international airwaves, it is important to remember that international radio also is a substantial news source for many millions, but nowhere is the truism that one person's news is another person's propaganda more apparent. Listeners can twist the dials to find a version of world events that suits their own needs and world views; this is especially true for people living under autocracies that lack popular support. News on international radio may often be acrimonious and self-serving, but without question it provides a diversity of news and views for untold millions. The importance of shortwave news is demonstrated, for example, when a political crisis or attempted coup occurs in an African nation. At such times, local broadcasters usually go off the air, and local residents habitually tune to the BBC or the VOA to learn what is really happening in their own country.

With so much of what fills the night air (when reception is best) perceived by many as propaganda, the credibility of an international station's news and commentaries is crucial for its reputation among foreign listeners. The international broadcaster that has long enjoyed the best reputation for believability and objectivity is the World Service of the BBC. As a public corporation, the domestic BBC radio is financed by license fees paid by each British household with a radio or television set. The BBC World Service is not funded by license fees; instead, it receives about $160 million annually in parliamentary grants-in-aid. The government, in consultation with the service, has the final decision over which languages are broadcast, but editorial control of the programs rests entirely with the BBC. The World Service broadcasts in English and forty-four other languages and, according to its research, reaches 143 million regular listeners in a week. Of those, 122 million listen directly, whereas about 27 million, with some overlap, listen to rebroadcasts on local stations. Of the total audience, 35 million listen in English. The World Service receives about half a million letters a year; the total in 1996 was 671,002. Languages used in most letters were

English, with 119,897, followed by Hindi, 107,602; Burmese, 103,602; Tamil, 86,102; and Arabic, 38,303.

During Britain's war with Argentina over the Falkland Islands, Prime Minister Margaret Thatcher bitterly criticized the BBC for not sufficiently supporting the British war effort. Some saw this as evidence of the BBC's independence—the independence that draws so many listeners to the BBC during times of crisis.

Shortly after the BBC World Service announced the start of the Gulf War in January 1991, it expanded its Arabic-language radio broadcasts to fourteen hours a day, five hours longer than before the crisis.[5] Today, an estimated 10 million Arabs from North Africa to the Persian Gulf listen in, a far larger number than listen to either the Voice of America or Radio Moscow. Currently, the BBC plans an ambitious news and information expansion for the Arab world. In October 2005, the BBC announced that it would open an Arabic-language television news and information service for the Middle East. The new venture, set to begin in 2007, is to be called the BBC Arabic television service: It will broadcast 12 hours daily and will be free to anyone with a satellite or cable connection. The BBC will become the only tri-media international news provider offering Arabic news and current affairs on television, radio and online.

## U.S. Activities in Public Diplomacy

In the past, U.S. activities in public diplomacy shared many similarities with those of the United Kingdom, but with some important differences. The United States Information Agency (USIA) was one of the key organizations, working closely with but separately from the State Department. The Voice of America began broadcasting in 1942 and was largely under the aegis of the USIA. During the Cold War, the VOA's efforts were supplemented by Radio Free Europe, which broadcast 555 hours weekly in European languages to Eastern Europe, and by Radio Liberty, which broadcast 462 hours weekly in Russian and fourteen other languages (but not English) to the Soviet Union.

The USIA, usually operating with a budget of about $900 million, employed about 12,000 people between Washington and some 275 U.S. Information Service (USIS) posts in 110 countries. Typically, a USIS post worked under a U.S. ambassador and included a public library. USIS personnel cooperated with local media by providing news and related material, holding exhibits, running language courses, giving seminars of various kinds, and arranging visits and cultural exchanges of both Americans and local people. (However, on October 1, 1999, the USIA was abolished.)

The USIA and the VOA have long had an identity crisis: Are they objective news and cultural organizations reflecting the diversity of American life and culture, or are they arms of the State Department, vigorously advocating U.S. foreign policy objectives? (This dispute has risen again during the war against terrorism.) Past managerial participation by such well-known journalists as Edward R. Murrow, Carl Rowan, and John Chancellor suggested the former. At other times, as during the Vietnam War and the Reagan administration, the latter role has been stressed. Under Reagan, the VOA was accused of repeatedly compromising its news integrity by broadcasting misleading and biased reports.[6]

Another policy issue debated within public diplomacy circles is audience targeting, revolving around the question of who we are trying to influence. If it is the ruling elites of the world's nations, then the person-to-person efforts of diplomatic posts and various cultural and educational exchanges seem called for. If the target is the mass public, then expanded and more aggressive radio broadcasting seems appropriate.

After 1981, the agency undertook the development of a government television network called Worldnet, with the potential of linking sixty overseas television systems to the USIA headquarters in Washington. In addition to producing cultural and public affairs programs for local overseas networks, Worldnet employed satellite links for two-way televised news conferences between foreign journalists and American public figures. Part of the programming in its first years included a two-hour program of news and features to Europe, five days a week. During the first Gulf war crisis, President George H.W. Bush used Worldnet to address foreign publics.

Another Reagan project was Radio Marti, a VOA-linked facility patterned after Radio Free Europe to broadcast news and commentary specifically to Cuba. Named for a Cuban independence hero, the radio station went on the air in May 1985, broadcasting news, entertainment, and sports in Spanish for fourteen hours daily from studios in Washington and a 50,000-watt AM transmitter in the Florida Keys. A Television Marti service was later added and has since been more controversial. Opponents had argued that since Cubans regularly listen to nonjammed

U.S. radio and television stations from Miami, the new service was unnecessary.

## Public Diplomacy after the Cold War

The dramatic and unexpected ending of the Cold War during 1989–90 and the accompanying demise of communist regimes in Eastern Europe profoundly altered public diplomacy, because East–West rivalries had so long dominated the propaganda wars. Most agreed that the West had "won" the Cold War. However, there was not the same certitude about many aspects of the victory. Foreign radio broadcasting by the VOA, Radio Free Europe, and Radio Liberty, as well as the BBC and the other Western broadcasters, had proved far more effective than most Western experts had supposed. In 1990, journalist Morton Kondracke commented, "If ever there was an American foreign policy success story, it's in international broadcasting. By the testimony of everyone from Václav Havel (of Czechoslovakia) to Lech Walesa (of Poland) to ordinary people in the streets of Bucharest and Beijing, democracy would not be what (and where) it is today without the two U.S. foreign broadcast networks, the Voice of America and Radio Free Europe/Radio Liberty."[7]

Michael Nelson, in his book *War of the Black Heavens: The Battles of Western Broadcasting in the Cold War,*[8] argues that the Western radio programs presented a compelling message of the good life that under-mined communist regimes and connected listeners with the cultures of Europe and North America. Nelson believes that radio, not diplomacy or the global economy, raised the iron curtain.

Despite their Cold War successes, U.S. planners talked of consolid-ating the U.S. radio services as well as cutting back on their budgets because they no longer seemed needed. But due to the uncertainty of economic reforms and political instability in Russia, unrest in the former Soviet Republics, and unresolved crises in the Balkans, the survival of both Radio Liberty and Radio Free Europe seemed necessary. President Václav Havel of the Czech Republic and the new democratically elected leaders of Poland and Hungary all pleaded that the stations be saved, because they considered those broadcasts irreplaceable. The adminis-tration and Congress agreed to continue funding the stations. So, with pared-down budgets, RFE and RL moved to Prague in 1995 from Munich, where they had been since the CIA established them in 1951.

The success of RFE and RL during the Cold War led to proposals in Congress for a similar broadcaster to beam news and persuasive communications into China, ruled by a communist government and beset with human rights problems. The VOA and the BBC had played a key role during the Tiananmen Square events in 1989, by providing the only Mandarin-language news reports not controlled by China's government that were received throughout the Chinese hinterland, where most Chinese live.

Congress agreed in early 1994 to establish a new radio service, Radio Free Asia, to beam news and other programming to mainland China, Burma, Cambodia, Laos, North Korea, and Vietnam—all essentially authoritarian nations with serious human-rights problems. The station was modeled after RFE and RL, with grants to the new station set at $30 million a year. Radio Free Asia got off to a shaky start in September 1996. Neighboring countries loudly opposed it and it was resented by other international broadcasters. Most Chinese who listen to radio broadcasts are devoted to the BBC, the VOA, and Radio France International, all of which had bolstered their Asian broadcasting in the two previous years.

By early 2001, Tibet and China's western deserts were the scene of a radio battle for the hearts and minds of restive minorities in the region. The VOA was transmitting in two Tibetan dialects, and Radio Free Asia had eight hours daily of Tibetan broadcasting. Other foreign broadcasters represented Muslim separatists and Saudi religious programming. Beijing was fighting back by expanding programming in local languages and extending Chinese radio into remote corners of Tibet and the Muslim region of Xinjiang. Further, the Chinese were building facilities to jam foreign broadcasts. The jamming was called China's new Great Wall and part of the effort to rein in the restive western province, with its threat of Muslim fundamentalism and terrorism.

On April 30, 1993, President Clinton signed the International Broadcasting Act, establishing the International Broadcasting Bureau, which for the first time combined all U.S. government international broadcasting services under a Broadcasting Board of Governors. The board oversees the operation of the VOA, Worldnet television service, and Radio and TV Marti to Cuba, as well as Radio Free Europe/Radio Liberty and Radio Free Asia. These services transmit nearly 2,000 hours a week in sixty languages. No one knows how much money is wasted due to duplication. No one knows how many people are listening. The VOA says surveys show 65 million, but that figure could be 86 million. RFE/ RL may have 20 million "listeners," defined as persons who tune in one or more times a week.[9]

U.S. global broadcasting employs about 3,500 people. Besides the shortwave audience, millions more listen to VOA programs placed on local AM and FM stations around the world. The VOA's original programming, all of it produced in studios in Washington, D.C., totals almost 700 hours a week. Most programs concern news and news-related topics. Music programs, from jazz to rock, classical to country, are popular.

Radio Free Europe/Radio Liberty broadcasts from Prague, including its Czech and Polish affiliates, more than 500 hours weekly in twenty-three languages. Its programs target Central Europe, Russia, and the various republics of the former U.S.S.R., several of them near Afghanistan.

In 1994, the VOA began distributing, via the Internet, its newswire and selected newscasts and program audio files in nineteen languages, along with VOA frequency and satellite information. The VOA launched a web page on the Internet in May 1996. (The BBC World Service offers similar information on the Internet.) Using a network of fourteen relay stations worldwide, the VOA transmits its programs to its global audience via satellite, shortwave, and medium wave. The connection is instantaneous, so listeners may never realize that the signal passes through several different channels before it reaches their receivers.

Since 9/11, there has been concern that since the abolition of the United States Information Agency in 1999, the nation's ability to conduct public diplomacy has been diminished. On a per capita basis, France and many other countries, including Spain, spend more money on public diplomacy than does the United States. Yet public diplomacy is needed by a nation at war.

After the Soviets withdrew from Afghanistan in 1989, the United States began losing interest in Pakistan. After budget cuts, five American cultural centers there were either closed or greatly reduced in scope. Pakistan was only one of many countries where the United States cut its public diplomacy programs in the early and mid-1990s. Across the Arab world, where anti-Western propaganda is a staple, the Voice of America broadcasts are barely audible and reach less than 2 percent of the population in the twenty-two countries targeted. The budget in 2001, which allotted $370 billion for the military, gave $22 billion for all nonmilitary spending abroad, including foreign aid grants, VOA and radio projects, and budgets of the State Department, which has absorbed the USIA functions. Funding for foreign exchanges such as the Fulbright grants, measured in constant dollars, fell by nearly a third from 1993 to 2000. But now policy makers in Washington are listening again to advocates of increased cultural exchange and public diplomacy.[10]

In 1994, when public diplomacy was being dismantled, historian Walter Laqueur warned:

> No specialized expertise is needed to realize that, far from being on the verge of a new order, the world has entered a period of great disorder. This refers to all kinds of regional conflicts as well as to the proliferation of the means of mass destruction, all of which makes nuclear war in the not-too-distant future a distinct possibility. It also refers to a potential second coming of fascism and communism and anti-Western onslaughts by other forces. . . . Cultural diplomacy, in the widest sense, has increased in importance, whereas traditional diplomacy and military power (especially of the high technology variety) are of limited use in coping with most of these dangers.[11]

The "long thin war" against terrorism, the first of its kind, has no end in sight. Without question, public diplomacy and propaganda have important roles to play; and very likely Congress will substantially strengthen various facets of our public efforts—the VOA and more targeted broadcasting, cultural exchanges, and more person-to-person contacts with foreign nationals overseas.

A key question for policy makers at war is whether the Voice of America should be a propaganda tool, pushing hard for American policy objectives or whether the Voice should be a reliable source of accurate, unbiased news. A former VOA director, Sanford Ungar, commented recently that before 9/11, the VOA had evolved into a

> . . . highly effective and credible player in the worldwide flow of information across borders. In many hot spots around the world, its correspondents are among the best and most courageous. Its two-source rule prevents it from making mistakes common to some other international news services. It reflects the daily experience of American democracy, warts and all. . . . Now more than ever, the Voice of America has important work to do. It must be able to interview anyone anywhere at any time, without fear of rebuke or reprisal, in order to provide honest and

full coverage of momentous events. The State Department should keep its hands—and editing pencils—off the news."[12]

## The Propaganda War in the Arab World

As the Pentagon geared up for war in late 2001, the White House began to mobilize its resources for political warfare. Although the 9/11 attacks had evoked sympathetic responses from the Western nations, in much of the Arab world terrorism was applauded and hailed throughout the Arab and Muslim nations. Subsequent television statements by Osama bin Laden made it clear that a war of words had begun, and the U.S. and its allies were at best playing catchup or even losing.

After the U.S. invaded Iraq, against the vocal opposition of most of the United Nations and even such traditional NATO allies as France and Germany, much of world public opinion was overwhelmingly against the war. American popularity was at an all-time low throughout this period. America's long-time support for Israel had been an important contributor to anti-American feelings.

For Americans, there was a broad chasm between the way Americans saw themselves and the way they were seen by other peoples. Traditional cultures have long been troubled by the invasion of their cultures by powerful outside interests which have featured social mobility and cosmopolitan thinking that has undermined the traditional ways of clans, religious elders—and dictators. And, of course, just the presence of over 150,000 Western soldiers in Iraq created animosity in neighboring Arab nations and subsequent problems for U.S. public diplomacy.

These factors represented a great and perhaps insurmountable challenge to the Voice of America and subsequent satellite television efforts. The first efforts to reach Islamic audiences were ineffective. The State Department brought in Charlotte Beers, a former advertising executive, to use her marketing skills to make American values as much a brand as Ivory Soap. She soon quit and was replaced by Margaret Tutwiler, the next undersecretary of state for public diplomacy. She lasted a year.

A major effort was Al Hurra ("the free one" in Arabic), a satellite news station that began broadcasting in northern Virginia, with a $62 million first-year budget, to provide an alternative to pan-Arab news stations such as Al Jazeera and Al Arabia. The purpose, according to President Bush, was to cut through the barriers of hateful propaganda and provide reliable news across the region. But Al Hurra earned little praise from its target audience. Many Arab commentators were quick to condemn the new station. The consensus was that the station was an abysmal failure and it was beset with poor ratings.

The next U.S. entry in the propaganda war was Radio Sawa, an Arab-language pop music and news station, which was touted as a success in reaching out to the Arab world. But a State Department report on the station charged that Radio Sawa was so interested in building its audience for music that it failed to measure whether it was influencing minds. It too had not been a critical success in the war of ideas.

In early 2005, Karen Hughes, a close adviser to President Bush, was appointed to launch a bold new approach to U.S. public diplomacy. But apparently there was no hurry, as Hughes did not assume her post for six months. At the same time, a government report criticized the administration for failing to develop a strategy to improve the image of the U.S. at a time when data showed that anti-Americanism was spreading and deepening around the world.

At her confirmation hearing, Hughes said she wanted to enlist the private sector, including the music, film and travel industries, in a reinvigorated effort to help the Muslim world understand America. She said that the long-term way to prevail in this struggle is through the power of our ideas. Another aspect of Hughes's assignment is to publicize the President's campaign for democracy in the Middle East.

Ms. Hughes's maiden voyage to the Middle East in September 2005 was considered notably unsuccessful. With no diplomatic experience or expert knowledge of the Arabs, she managed to antagonize several Muslim audiences she met with. Her experience seemed to reflect the difficulties of winning over a region that was so deeply hostile to the policies of the U.S. government.

## Notes

1.  "Candor Becoming a Staple of Shortwave," *The New York Times*, March 13, 1989, 18.
2.  Daya Kishan Thussu, *International Communication* (London: Arnold, 2000), 161.
3.  "Candor Becoming a Staple of Shortwave."
4.  Ibid.

5.  Deborah Stead, "BBC is Expanding its Arabic Radio Broadcasts," *The New York Times*, February 18, 1991, 27.
6.  Carolyn Weaver, "When the Voice of America Ignores its Charter," *Columbia Journalism Review*, November/December 1988, 36–43.
7.  Morton Kondracke, "Fine Tuning," *New Republic*, May 28, 1990, 8.
8.  Michael Nelson, *War of the Black Heavens: The Battles of Western Broadcasting in the Cold War* (Syracuse: Syracuse University Press, 1997).
9.  Mark Hopkins, "A Babel of Broadcasts," *Columbia Journalism Review*, July/August 1999, 44.
10. Stephen Kinzer, "Why They Don't Know Us," *The New York Times*, November 11, 2001, sec. A, 5.
11. Walter Laqueur, "Save Public Diplomacy," *Foreign Affairs*, September/October 1994, 19.
12. Sanford J. Ungar, "Afghanistan's Fans of American Radio," *The New York Times*, October 5, 2001, sec. A, 23.

# Chapter 12

# Western Media to World Media

*Western values and assumptions have been internalized to a remarkable degree in almost every other major culture. . . . What the West has done to the rest of the world has been done indelibly. Nothing can be the same again. History has been changed by the West, which has made the world One World. . . . What seems to be clear is that the story of western civilization is now the story of mankind, its influence so diffused that old oppositions and antitheses are now meaningless. "The West" is hardly now a meaningful term, except to historians.*

—J.M. Roberts

Modern mass communications, from newspapers and television sets to communication satellites and computer technology, are among the many devices and cultural artifacts of Western society that have so inexorably spread throughout the world since 1945. Words on paper, electronic impulses, and images on tape, film, and recordings have penetrated the minds and cultures of non-Western peoples with tremendous impact. Along with pop and classical music, Hollywood movies, television programs, and youthful life styles have come ideas and ideology: equality, human rights, democracy, freedom of expression, individual autonomy, and free enterprise. John Locke, Thomas Jefferson, John Stuart Mill, Abraham Lincoln, and Adam Smith were Westerners, as was Karl Marx.

International communication, travel, industrialization, commerce, and trade have all participated in this Westernizing process, an aspect of globalization, which perhaps should be termed the *modernization* of the world because so many non-Western societies now contribute to the process. The practices of Western mass communication have been so widely dispersed and accepted by people everywhere that the adjective

*Western* perhaps should be reserved for historians, as Professor Roberts has suggested.[1] The September 11 events, and later bombings in Madrid and London—as well as the tsunami and hurricane Katrina—showed the crucial role that professional journalism, free of government controls, plays at a time of crisis by supplying reliable and verifiable news to the world. In many nations, the familiar anchors of network television have not only reported the news but have also reassured, steadied, and consoled millions of viewers. When national security is endangered or great natural calamities threaten, people everywhere are reminded how important it is to know and understand the greater world.

## Checklist of Global News Impacts

To summarize the main points of this book, we list some ways that the new global journalism has influenced and, yes, even changed our world, for high-speed, international news communication is something new and different—in matters of degree if not in kind. Some of these effects have been global or geopolitical, others have directly influenced the media themselves, and some effects have been felt mostly by individuals.

- *The triumph of Western journalism.* Since the fall of the communist "second" world, the Western concept of journalism and mass communication has become the dominant model throughout the world and is widely emulated. In journalism, many non-Western nations have adopted not only the equipment and gadgets of the Western press and broadcasting but also its practices, norms, ethical standards, and ideology. Throughout the developing and former communist nations, print and broadcast journalists today increasingly seek editorial autonomy and freedom from government interference. These journalists understand and aspire to the professional values of fairness, objectivity, and responsibility as well as the "checking effect"— the role of the press as a watchdog of government and authority. They want to report the news as they see it—not some government's version of events. But, of course, many autocratic nations still have controlled media.
- *Globalization of media.* The internationalization of mass communication has grown hand in hand with the globalization of the world's economy. In fact, the expanding international business media play a

key role in "servicing" the world economy by supplying rapid, reliable economic and financial news. Globalization has its negative traits and independent news media provide forums for dissent and complaints. The spread has been a dynamic process and has provided more diversity and variety to the global mix, particularly in China and its neighbors.

- *Mass culture accepted.* For better or worse, Western mass media also have conditioned much of the world to use media for entertainment and leisure. (Political indoctrination by media has been rejected by many people. But with the war on terrorism, political persuasion—that is, propaganda—has increased on global media.) Ever-growing audiences accept and enjoy the movies, television, pop music, and even the ever-present commercials. Today, the most traditional of parents find it almost impossible to prevent the influence on their children of that most powerful engine of mass education the West has yet produced, commercial advertising. Parents and others over thirty years old almost everywhere must be offended and repelled by the noisy, brassy music videos of MTV, but there is no doubting their appeal to teenagers literally everywhere. Yet in lands under the sway of religious fundamentalism, opposition to Western mass culture remains strong, and yet even modern and traditional cultures tend to meld and combine.

- *The impact on the Cold War.* Today, many experts agree that news and mass culture from the West contributed to the demise of the U.S.S.R. and the communist regimes in Eastern Europe. Western media provided news not available otherwise and served the "forbidden fruit" of Western movies, rock music, life styles, and the promise of a better life—democracy, market economies, and a higher standard of living.

- *Global audiences growing.* Each year, literally millions more people are being drawn into the global audience, mainly through competing satellite and cable services, computers, and shortwave radio. With satellite dishes and antennas sprouting everywhere, the lands of Asia, particularly China and India, are flocking to join the global village. Recent terrorism events and the tsunami saw a tremendous surge of interest for global television news. Some Asian nations welcome global television, but others see it as a threat to their cultural identity and political stability. Across the former Third World, governments have had only limited success in blocking satellite services. Governments are finding it nearly impossible to prevent people from getting news and entertainment from the skies. Satellite dishes, which are growing smaller, cheaper, and more powerful, are easily put together from imported kits.

- *Vast audiences for global events.* Great events—the terror attack on the World Trade Center and Pentagon, or the quadrennial Olympic Games—can attract significant parts of the global audience. About 3.5 billion people watched some of the 1996 Olympics in Atlanta. The biggest share of that audience was in China, because more than 900 million Chinese had access to television sets, and three channels broadcast events there all day long.

- *History speeded up.* Nations and people today react faster to important events because information moves so quickly and widely. A bomb explodes in an airliner and security measures tighten up in airports everywhere. War breaks out in the Middle East and the price of gas at the pump goes up everywhere. Actions that would have been taken later are now taken sooner, thus accelerating the pace of change.

- *"The whole world is watching."* The reality that many millions can watch on television as tanks rumble across borders, troops storm ashore in a distant land, or police fire on peaceful protesters gives much greater import and consequences to news reports. A camcorder's report of Los Angeles police beating a man named Rodney King set off repercussions lasting for years. Video taken by camcorders in the hands of European tourists and broadcast on television showed the horror of the tsunami. A discarded "home videocassette" showing Osama bin Laden rejoicing over the New York City terror attacks provided what many considered the "smoking gun" that proved his complicity in the attacks.

- *Diplomacy changed.* Foreign relations and the ways that nations react to each other are clearly influenced by public (and world) opinion formed by global communication. Television viewers concerned by watching starving children in Somalia can exert pressures on their government to intervene with military force in a place they later regret going to. Media discussions and debate between diplomats and leaders can clarify policy and influence nations or alliances to act. Nonstop coverage by CNN and the BBC provides the opportunity to monitor news events constantly and disseminate timely diplomatic information. But some politicians are more concerned than elated by global, real-time broadcasting, fearing a loss of control and the absence of quiet time to make deliberate choices, reach private agreements, and mold the public's understanding of events.

- *Autocrats' loss of control.* Authoritarian regimes can no longer maintain a monopoly over news and censor what their people know. They cannot stop news from coming into their nation or getting out. Shortwave radio, fax, the Internet, cellphones and videophones, and communication satellites have changed all that and blunted the power of state censorship. During times of crisis, dictators can no longer seal their borders and control information. The news will get out.

- *"Revolution" by personalized media.* Internet blogging, desktop publishing, camcorders, and cellphones have turned individuals into communicators who can reach out to their own audiences. Even photocopiers and audiocassettes have been shown to facilitate political upheavals or revolution.

- *Surrogate media for fettered people.* Independent media from outside now provide news and information for people who are captives of their own governments. By publicizing human-rights violations, torture, and political imprisonment, independent media help those victims to survive. It has been argued that a famine never occurs in a nation with a free press because the press, by reporting incipient food shortages, will bring pressures on its government to act before people begin dying. Western reporting of the harsh and brutal life of Afghans living under the Taliban augmented the argument for U.S. intervention.

- *Reporting pariah states.* The foreign press's persistent reporting about pariah states, such as South Africa under apartheid or the Philippines under Marcos, can apparently help to facilitate political change by forming world public opinion, which in turn can lead to actions by governments. Persistent American and European press reporting of the civil war in Bosnia and growing evidence of genocide by Bosnian Serbs undoubtedly pushed the Clinton administration and NATO to intervene and impose a cease-fire.

- *The "copycat" effect.* With global news so pervasive and widely available, sometimes imitative acts occur that have unexpected consequences. A terrorist's car bombing in one country, widely shown on television, is replicated 3,000 miles away. Somali clansmen defy U.S. soldiers in Mogadishu, and a few days later, Haitian thugs are encouraged to stage a near-riot as U.S. troops try to land at Port au Prince, causing the U.S. forces to withdraw.

- *Profit-driven media.* The international communication system has grown and expanded so rapidly because there was money to be made by globalization of the world economy. The profit motive is, of course, a powerful force for technological change. The INTELSAT system, a crucial early component in expanding the reach of global news, expanded so rapidly and effectively because there were real profits from a more efficient and cost-effective way to make international telephone calls. Other innovations in media technology, such as interactive television, have failed so far to become widely adopted because they are not (yet) profitable.

  Whatever their faults, the "media barons"—Rupert Murdoch and Ted Turner, among others—are entrepreneurs who will take risks and are willing to innovate. When Turner proposed a twenty-four hour global news channel, many thought he was crazy.

  Now a kind word for the much-criticized media conglomerates. Commenting on the global activities of News Corporation, Time Warner, the Walt Disney Company, Bertelsmann A.G., Sony, and CNN, John Keane commented, "These global media linkages have helped to achieve something much more persuasively than the maps of Geradus Mercator ever did: to deepen the visceral feelings among millions of people (somewhere between 5 and 25 percent of the world's population) that our world is 'one world' and that this worldly interdependence requires humans to share some responsibility for its fate."[2]

- *Globalization of advertising and public relations.* The two persuasive arms of Western mass communications, advertising and public relations, have become globalized as well. Here again, the Anglo-American model, speaking English, is the world standard. Though often criticized, advertising and public relations are necessary and inevitable components of market economies and open societies. Moreover, advertising and public relations often make news and are, in fact, an aspect of news.

## The Downside of Global Media Effects

Rapid change causes dislocations and inequities, and global communication certainly has its negative impacts as well.

- *The fragility of democracy and open societies.* The worldwide surge of the late 1980s toward democracy and market economies—from Eastern Europe to Tropical Africa and South Asia—provided the promise and possibility of press freedom and independent media in nations long under one-party or military rule. Recently, more than half, or 99 out of 191, countries held competitive elections with varying but promising guarantees of political and individual rights. Yet most efforts to move from authoritarianism to democracy have failed more often than not after most revolutions, according to Seymour Martin Lipset. He wrote that cultural factors appear more important than economic ones. Some of the factors that have promoted democracy in the past are capitalism, economic growth, a moderate opposition, British influences, and Protestantism.[3] As a result of ethnic and nationalistic clashes, the democratic outlook for some nations in Eastern Europe, the Middle East, and Africa today is not promising. The "failed states" of the Arab world, which have been unable to modernize economically or to acquire democratic rule, have been a major breeding ground for terrorists.

The failure to relieve economic misery in the newly democratic governments in Africa has led to discouragement with democracy, and this may lead to new military or civilian dictators. L. Gray Cowan said, "In most of the African countries where they have had elected democratic governments, the fundamental problem is that they are left with precisely the same economic and social problems they had before."[4]

The rise of democracy and a free press has been associated with market economies, but market economies do not guarantee democratic societies. Currently, the capitalist nations of Indonesia, Thailand, and Malaysia have modern media systems and rising standards of living, but are not yet fully democratic and are facing financial difficulties as well.

Even the robust and successful Western nations have proved vulnerable to sneak terrorist attacks. The chief characteristics of globalization—open borders, lenient immigration policies, individual freedoms including privacy protection, and ample free trade—has made the United States and Europe particularly vulnerable to terrorist attacks. Terrorism has been rightly called the dark side of globalization. And when thousands of civilians are killed or endangered, national security becomes a dominant imperative and government controls are tightened.

- *Poor nations lag in the information age.* Optimism about the trends in global communication is based mainly on what is happening in the prosperous societies of the United States, Europe, and Japan, and in the modernized sectors of China and India. Among the poorer nations of the Southern Hemisphere, especially in Africa, development and growth of media and their audiences have been painfully slow in large part because the stubborn problems of poverty, overpopulation, poor health, illiteracy, and economic underdevelopment still defy solution. African countries and some other nations are not acquiring the technology and infrastructure needed to travel on the information superhighway. In absolute terms, the poorer nations are falling further behind and becoming further marginalized. In addition, the onrush of rapid technological change is further widening the gap between rich and poor nations. The lack of skilled workers, an industrial base (including investment capital), and a literate and educated middle class precludes the poor nations from participating fully in the information revolution, particularly the Internet. When most of a country's population still lives as illiterate peasants on subsistence agriculture, as in much of Africa, Asia, and parts of Latin America, terms such as "transnational data flows," "free flow of information," or "logging on" have little practical meaning. Further, deep political and cultural differences still contribute to hatred, envy, and animosities among many millions toward affluent Westerners. The communication revolution has been coming about through education, communications, technology, and dynamic free-market economies— regrettably all in short supply in too many developing countries.
- *Trends toward media monopoly.* The financial activities of the big players in international communication—Murdoch, NBC, Time Warner, Disney/ABC, the BBC, Sony, Viacom/CBS, and Bertelsmann— seem to be moving in one direction: toward consolidation and monopoly of the main structures of international communication. (But some media giants, like Vivendi, do fail.) Bigger conglomerates and fewer competitors mean greater profits but less variety and diversity. Problems of regulating these transnational entities are already proving formidable, especially in light of recent megamergers among U.S. media giants. (The U.S. government today has been backing off from antitrust regulation of media giants.) Primarily involved with profitable entertainment enterprises, these conglomerates show slight concern with quality news dissemination. Critics fear that

consolidation means a loss of diverse opinions and less competition among competing news media.

- *Declining standards.* Some critics ask, where in this commercial scramble for profits and power is the concern for serious journalism and quality entertainment? Europeans, for example, lament the decline of public service broadcasting and of quality drama and entertainment. Serious international news is often pushed aside for stories that are more sensational and celebrity oriented. Entertainment values are degrading news values.

- *Shortcomings of audiences.* In the affluent West, the majority of people attending to mass media have only a superficial interest and knowledge of world affairs. They may know that Russia is having economic problems, but they do not understand the reasons. Most Americans were deeply shocked by the 9/11 attacks, in part because the news media, as well as the government, had paid scant attention earlier to the possibilities of surprise terror attacks on America. In less affluent nations, most people lack the education and standard of living to pay attention to world events. In many cases, their own inadequate media are incapable of providing significant foreign news.

## Indications of Improvement

The expanding capacity to communicate information rapidly around a world that has become ever more interdependent has begun to erase some differences and perhaps improve understanding among diverse societies. The better educated and more affluent people of most nations—the media users—know more about the outside world and have access to more information than ever before. The educated elites of the developing nations, though small in number, travel more and are more conversant with world affairs than were their predecessors under colonialism. However, the euphoric reaction of some in the Islamic world to the 9/11 attacks was a sobering reminder to Westerners of the widespread hatred and anti-Americanism and anti-Westernism found abroad. Americans, who like to be liked, were shocked that so many do not like them.

The international news system, despite its inadequacies, moves a great deal of information, data, and pictures much faster than ever before, and there is every indication that this flow will expand in the years ahead. Walter Goodman, a frequent critic of television, had some good things to say recently about the little box: "Television, that product of the West, is by its nature on the West's side when it comes to freedom of information. Censors may hedge it in and manipulate it, but they cannot contain it; the content flows across boundaries and over the globe. When Communism fell, television, which every East bloc country boss thought was his to run for purposes of celebrating himself and suppressing his critics, was among the forces that gave it a shove. . . . Television's natural impulse is to reveal, not conceal."[5]

These are some of the reasons why the West's version of world news and events, largely gathered and disseminated by American and West European journalists, often antagonizes and annoys non-Western governments and peoples, despite their reliance on these sources of information.

To assist governments in dealing with their formidable problems of poverty, massive debt, environmental degradation, disease, and sometimes famine, some leaders would harness mass communications—a clear invocation of the Developmental concept of the press. But under the Western concept, the press must be free of government to maintain liberty, to make democracy possible, and to provide reliable and objective news. Liberty is not the same as social justice or economic equality. History shows that when press freedom is sacrificed for some "greater good," political liberty and human rights usually disappear.

To the Western journalist, the press must be independent of authority, not an instrument of government, so that it can report the news and expose the abuses of governments at home and abroad. Now more than ever, because of their global reach, governments (and corporations) need watching. But whether democratic or authoritarian, only governments—not multinational corporations or media conglomerates—have the power to start wars, nuclear or conventional; to conscript soldiers and send them off to dubious wars; to punish dissidents; to establish gulags; to "ethnically cleanse" people with a different religion—or to deal with terrorists. Media in both North and South must contend with governments that try to control, manipulate, and suppress what the news media wish to report—and often succeed. Democratic government and private ownership give the press a better chance of resisting government control and serving the public interest, but they are no guarantee of independence. (But also it should be remembered that when national security is threatened, as after 9/11, people quickly turn to government for help to counter subversive terrorism.)

Modern history is replete with regimes marred by incompetence, venality, corruption, and brutality. Some journalists believe that the world's free press has done far too little, rather than too much, critical reporting about economic failures and political abuses, especially among developing nations. This basic impasse over the proper purpose of international news communication and the relations between the press and government will continue. But the greater the threat from abroad, the greater will be the interest and need for foreign news.

## What Can Be Done

Improvements in international news communication must come from several quarters. Western journalists and mass communicators can do much to improve their own effectiveness. And governments and journalists of the communications-poor developing nations can do more to involve themselves in transnational news, both as senders and receivers. Much can be accomplished as well by nations and journalists working together through international organizations to arrive at some consensus on policy questions and proposals for improved news communication. But it should be remembered that most journalism is essentially local and parochial—it serves the interests and needs of its own audiences. Therefore, the front pages of the leading papers in Japan, Turkey, Norway, and Nigeria will always feature quite different stories. And yet, high-quality foreign news is still essential and does bring diverse peoples closer together.

## Western Initiatives

Western media, with their greater resources, should gather and report more news of the non-Western world and do it with more understanding of the problems and concerns of those nations. The coups, the economic disasters, the civil wars, the famines, and other disasters must be reported, of course, but the press also should provide more sustained, comprehensive coverage of social and cultural aspects in a historical perspective. The public requires more general knowledge of the greater world so that if, say, Algeria or Pakistan suddenly dominates the news, readers can react more knowledgeably.

Even in noncrisis times, television news needs to expand its foreign coverage and, furthermore, do more than provide blanket coverage of a single running story, such as a notorious celebrity trial, while virtually ignoring other important stories elsewhere. CNN's round-the-clock coverage of the first Iraq War revealed the inadequacies of the major networks' formats. Commercial networks should revive the hour-long news documentary, which has almost disappeared from television screens, and not leave it entirely to public television. News media in general need to show more responsibility and sense of public service—and to cover foreign news even when no crisis looms.

More Western media should invest more money and human resources in covering foreign news and not leave the immense task to the few media groups that do maintain correspondents abroad. And newspapers and broadcasters without their own reporters abroad should do a better job of using the considerable amount of foreign news available from news services and syndicates.

Foreign-news editors could make much more use, as well, of academic sources. Hundreds of area specialists who have current and reliable information about every corner of the world are to be found throughout American universities.

Programs to train journalists from abroad should be continued and expanded. Western news organizations have helped to establish national news agencies and trained personnel to run them. For years, a steady stream of journalists and broadcasters has come to Europe and America for training and internships, but training journalists in their home countries or regions still has merit and perhaps priority.

Western media organizations might also consider selectively establishing newspapers in non-Western countries. Although fraught with political risks, some previous ventures have markedly raised the level of journalism in those countries. Two of the best newspapers in black Africa, the *Daily Times* of Nigeria and the *Daily Nation* of Kenya (now both African owned) were started by foreign publishers as commercial ventures. India has a number of vigorous newspapers today because British interests started newspapers there during colonial rule. Since independence, these papers have been managed completely by Indians and have served that nation well.

Closer Western ties can be established between journalists of different nationalities through professional groups such as the Journalists Without Borders and Inter-American Press Association. This can lead to better understanding and cooperation. These organizations and others, such as Amnesty International and the Committee to Protect Journalists, often come to the aid of journalists who have become victims of political repression and violence. Journalists of various nations working together in professional organizations can assist developing nations in such practical matters as subsidies for expensive newsprint, which is almost entirely produced in northern nations, obtaining media equipment such as used presses and broadcast electronics from Western media, and helping to obtain cheaper preferential rates for news transmissions via Comsats and cable.

## Non-Western Initiatives

To balance the flow of information better, the news media in developing nations must be improved and expanded, but this will not be easy, because any nation's mass media grow and expand along with general economic and social development and the modernization of individuals. Educated and informed individuals are required for media jobs as well as for media audiences. Although training and technical assistance from outside can be helpful, the impetus for media improvement must come from within.

A few Western news agencies and other media ideally should not dominate global news gathering as they do now, but they themselves are incapable of correcting the inequities of the system—nor should it be expected they can. Newspapers and broadcasters in Africa or South Asia should not have to rely upon a news agency based in London or New York City to find out what is happening in their own region. A much greater diversity of news sources is needed for the world's media to draw upon. For that reason alone, the persistent efforts in Asia, Africa, and Latin America to establish regional news agencies and broadcasting exchange agreements should be encouraged, despite the difficulties involved. Happily, some regions are producing more and more of their own movies, television programs, and popular music. The rise of the Al Jazeera satellite television news service in Qatar, heard in Arabic all over the Middle East, was an important addition to news diversity in a region of government-controlled news.

How soon and how effectively developing nations can improve their news media may well depend on how their governments respond to the following policy questions.

1.  Will non-Western nations cooperate effectively in developing regional and continental telecommunications and news exchange?

    In Africa, for example, long-distance telecommunications can have a revolutionary potential for the sub-Saharan region by providing a truly continental system of telecommunications where none has previously existed. An integrated system of regional satellites, Internet connections, cable systems, ground stations, improved AM and FM broadcasting, and microwave relays can have important implications for intra-African exchanges of news, educational broadcasting, telephone service, television programming, and high-speed data transfers. Recently there have been hopeful signs out of Africa that these kinds of communications improvements are being made.

2.  Will non-Western governments show more concern both for their own peoples' right to know and for an unimpeded flow of information throughout the world?

    Too much of the world news controversy has involved the claims of professional journalists versus the claims of governments over regulation of news and information. In today's world, any person, whether born in Pakistan, Norway, Peru, or Tanzania, has the right, at least in theory, to acquire information that affects his or her own welfare and future. And the government under which that person lives should respect that right—a hopeless ideal, some will say, since so many of the world's poor peoples live under authoritarianism and are far removed from information sources. Nevertheless, that is the direction in which the world has been moving.

    To participate in global news flow requires that information, news, technical data, and cultural fare be permitted to move unimpeded across borders. It also requires that journalists be protected by law from government intrusion in their activities.

3.  Will non-Western nations encourage more diversity and freedom in news and information?

    Regional and alternative news agencies can be helpful and should be actively fostered. A key question is whether the governments will provide their own journalists and broadcasters with greater autonomy and independence. Journalism flourishes best in an atmosphere of freedom from authority and corporate interference, but few journalists in non-Western nations enjoy such latitude. Too many, unfortunately, either work for autocratic governments or are at the mercy of arbitrary political interference. Too few governments in the world today permit their own journalists the freedom to probe serious internal problems, much less allow them to criticize even mildly the performance of those in authority. In general, these nations will continue to lag behind the information societies of the West until they evolve into constitutional, democratic societies with market economies. That will take time, and some nations obviously will not opt for that path to development. But to date, few one-party nations have shown the flexibility and dynamism to join the information societies.

In conclusion, what has happened to international news communication in the past quarter-century is, of course, only one aspect of the broad trend of the revolution in information processing and diffusion that has been transforming the modern world and its economy. The frictions we have seen between various concepts of journalism—Western, Developmental, Revolutionary, Authoritarian, and Communist—are just aspects of broader issues of international relations.

For the foreseeable future, the current system of international communication will probably retain its present basic structure, with the flow of information and news steadily expanding and audiences steadily increasing. Modifications will come mainly from the adoption of more technological and economic innovations in the media themselves. In recent decades, communication technology and economic forces have proved powerful forces for change. The future of global journalism is tied to the future of political democracies where a free press can flourish. More open societies mean greater flow and exchange of news across borders, whereas autocracies try to block or distort the flow of news.

But more than that, a reliable flow of global news and other essential information is an absolute necessity for our interdependent world, and the "closed" nations that try to block out that flow will find themselves unable to compete and prosper. Global politics and wars influence and shape international communication, and in this uncertain and danger-fraught era, the world's news media will play a central role in helping people everywhere understand the world beyond their borders.

## Notes

1. John M. Roberts, *The Triumph of the West* (Boston: Little, Brown, 1985), 290–5.
2. John Keane, "Journalism and Democracy Across Borders" in *The Press*, G. Overholzer and K.H. Jamieson, eds. (New York: Oxford University Press, 2005), 94.
3. "New Democracies Face Long Odds for Survival," *Stanford Alumni Review*, September 1993, 5.
4. Howard French, "African Democracies Fear Aid Will Dry Up," *The New York Times*, March 19, 1995, sec. A, 1.
5. Walter Goodman, "Even If Used as a Weapon, Television is True to its Nature," *The New York Times*, January 20, 1998, sec. B, 3.

# Selected Bibliography

(Related books published since 1990.)

Alleyne, Mark D. *News Revolution: Political and Economic Decisions About Global Information*. New York: St. Martin's Press, 1997.

Anokwa, Kwadro, Carolyn Lin and Michael Salwen (eds.). *International Communication: Concepts and Cases*. Belmont, CA: Wadsworth, 2003.

Blumler, Jay (ed.). *Television and the Public Interest*. Newbury Park, CA: Sage, 1992.

Boyd, Douglas A. *Broadcasting in the Arab World*. 2nd edn. Ames: Iowa State University Press, 1993.

Boyd-Barrett, Oliver, and Daya Kishan Thussu. *Contra-Flow in Global News*. London: John Libbey, 1992.

Couldry, Nick and James Curran (eds.). *Contesting Media Power*. New York: Rowman & Littlefield, 2003.

Demers, David. *Global Media: Menace or Messiah?* Cresshill, NJ: Hampton Press, 1999.

Dizard, Wilson P. *Meganet: How the Global Communications Network Will Connect Everyone on Earth*. Boulder, CO: Westview, 1997.

———. *Old Media New Media*. New York: Longman, 1994.

Fenton, Tom. *Bad News: The Decline of Reporting, the Business of News and the Danger to Us All*. New York: HarperCollins, 2005.

Flournoy, Don and Robert K. Stewart. *Making News in the Global Market*. Luton, U.K.: University of Luton, 1997.

Fortner, Robert S. *International Communication*. Belmont, CA: Wadsworth, 1992.

Friedland, Lewis A. *Covering the World: International Television News Services*. New York: Twentieth Century Fund, 1992.

Friedman, Thomas L. *The Lexus and the Olive Tree: Understanding Globalization*. New York: Anchor Books, 2000.

————. *The World is Flat: A Brief History of the 21st Century*. New York: Farrar, Straus & Giroux, 2005.

Geyer, Georgie Anne. *Buying the Night Flight*. Washington, D.C.: Brassey's, 1996.

Gwertzman, Bernard, and Michael T. Kaufman (eds.). *The Collapse of Communism*. New York: St. Martin's Press, 1990.

Hachten, William A. *Growth of Media in the Third World: African Failures, Asian Successes*. Ames: Iowa State University Press, 1991.

————. *The Troubles of Journalism: A Critical Look at What's Right and Wrong with the Press*. 3rd edn. Mahwah, NJ: Lawrence Erlbaum, 2005.

Hallin, Daniel C. and Paolo Mancini. *Comparing Media Systems: Three Modes of Media and Politics*. New York: Cambridge University Press, 2004.

Harasim, Linda. *Global Networks: Computers and International Communication*. Cambridge, MA: MIT Press, 1993.

Hawk, Beverly G. *Africa's Media Image*. New York: Praeger, 1992.

Heisey, D. Ray and Wenxiang Gong (eds.). *Communication and Culture: China and the World Entering the 21st Century*. Amsterdam: Editions Rodopi, 1994.

Herman, Edward S., and Robert W. McChesney. *The Global Media: The New Missionaries of Corporate Capitalism*. London: Cassell, 1997.

Hess, Stephen. *International News & Foreign Correspondents*. Washington, D.C.: Brookings Institution, 1996.

Kaplan, Robert D. *The Ends of the Earth*. New York: Vintage, 1996.

McPhail, Thomas L. *Global Communication: Theories, Stakeholders, and Trends*. Boston: Blackwell, 2006.

McQuail, Denis. *Mass Communication Theory*. 3rd edn. Newbury Park, CA: Sage, 1994.

Merrill, John C. *Global Journalism: Survey of International Communication*. 3rd edn. New York: Longman, 1995.

Mickiewicz, Ellen. *Changing Channels: Television and the Struggle for Power in Russia*. New York: Oxford University Press, 1997.

Mueller, Barbara. *International Advertising: Communicating Across Cultures*. Belmont, CA: Wadsworth, 1996.

Mytton, Graham. *Global Audiences: Research for World Broadcasting, 1993*. London: BBC World Service/John Libbey, 1993.

Nacos, Brigitte L. *Mass-Mediated Terrorism: Central Role of the Media in Terrorism and Counter Terrorism*. New York: Rowman & Littlefield, 2002.

Naisbitt, John, and Patricia Aburdene. *Megatrends 2000*. New York: Avon, 1990.

Nelson, Michael. *War of the Black Heavens: The Battle of Western Broadcasting in the Cold War*. Syracuse: Syracuse University Press, 1997.

Overholzer, Geneva and Kathleen Hall Jamieson (eds.). *The Press*. New York: Oxford University Press, 2005.

Parks, Lisa and Shanti Kumar (eds.). *Planet TV: A Global Television Reader*. New York: New York University Press, 2003.

Paterson, Chris and Annabelle Sreberny (eds.). *International News in the 21st Century*. Eastleigh, U.K.: John Libbey/Luton Press, 2004.

Pavlik, John V. *Journalism and New Media*. New York: Columbia University Press, 2000.

Rosenblum, Mort. *Who Stole the News?* New York: John Wiley, 1993.

Seib, Philip. *Headline Diplomacy: How News Coverage Affects Foreign Policy*. Westport, CT: Praeger, 1997.

Semati, Mehdi (ed.). *New Frontiers in International Communication Theory*. Lanham, MD: Rowan and Littlefield, 2004.

Shenk, David. *Data Smog: Surviving the Information Glut*. New York: Harper Edge/HarperCollins, 1997.

Silvia, Tony. *Global News: Perspectives on the Information Age*. Ames: Iowa State University Press, 2001.

Smith, Anthony. *The Age of Behemoths: The Globalization of Mass Media Firms*. New York: Priority, 1991.

Stevenson, Robert L. *Global Communication in the Twenty-first Century*. New York: Longman, 1994.

Strobel, Warren. *Late-Breaking Foreign Policy: The News Media's Influence on Peace Operations*. Washington, D.C.: U.S. Institute of Peace Press, 1997.

Thussu, Daya Kishan. *International Communication: Continuity and Change*. London: University of North London, 2000.

Toffler, Alvin. *PowerShift*. New York: Bantam, 1990.

Tumber, Howard and Jerry Palmer. *Media at War: The Iraq Crisis*. Newbury Park, CA: Sage, 2004.

Van Ginneken, Jaap. *Understanding Global News*. Thousand Oaks, CA: Sage, 1998.

Walker, Andrew. *A Skyful of Freedom: Sixty Years of the BBC World Service*. London: Broadside, 1992.

Weaver, David H. (ed.). *The Global Journalist*. Cresskill, NJ: Hampton Press, 1998.

Wilhelm, Donald. *Global Communication and Political Power*. New Brunswick, NJ: Transaction, 1990.

Wolfsfeld, Gadi. *Media and Political Conflict: News from the Middle East*. New York: Cambridge University Press, 1997.

Zhou, He, and Jian Hua Zhu. *The "Voice of America" and China*. Journalism Monographs, no. 143, February 1994.

# Index